Vorwort

W0417393

Konzeption

Grammar in Profile ist ein grammatisches Übungsbuch für die Sekundarstufe II. Es ist in zwei Schwierigkeitsstufen gegliedert: Die Abschnitte *Check-up* und *Basic Rules and Exercises* können ab Klasse 11 eingesetzt werden, in leistungsstarken Gruppen auch früher. Die *Advanced Exercises* wenden sich vor allem an Grund- und Leistungskurse.
Das Übungsangebot hat die Förderung der mündlichen und schriftlichen Ausdrucksfähigkeit zum Ziel. Darüber hinaus wird die Kenntnis und der sichere Gebrauch der wichtigsten Strukturen der englischen Sprache gefestigt. Die Darstellung der strukturellen Phänomene und die entsprechenden Übungen zielen nicht auf eine vollständige Abdeckung aller grammatischen Gebiete ab, sondern konzentrieren sich auf besonders fehlerträchtige Bereiche der englischen Grammatik.
Die einzelnen Kapitel sind in sich abgeschlossen und brauchen daher nicht in der vorgegebenen Reihenfolge behandelt zu werden. Je nach den grammatischen Defiziten einer Lerngruppe können einzelne Kapitel oder Teile davon gezielt im Unterricht eingesetzt werden. Neben dem Einsatz im Klassenunterricht eignen sich die *Check-ups* in Verbindung mit den *Basic Rules* in besonderen Maße auch für das Selbststudium.
Ergänzend zu *Grammar in Profile* kann und sollte eine systematische Schulgrammatik verwendet werden, z. B. *Learning English – Grundgrammatik – Ausgabe für Gymnasien* (= GG, Klettbuch 51151) oder die *Grammatik des heutigen Englisch* (= GhE, Klettbuch 205057) bzw. die einsprachige Parallelausgabe *A Grammar of Present-Day English* (Klettbuch 5058). Exakte Verweise auf diese Grammatiken ermöglichen einen schnellen Zugang zu detaillierten Informationen und sollen zum Nachschlagen anregen.
Grammar in Profile setzt einen im Verlauf der Unter- und Mittelstufe erworbenen Grundwortschatz voraus. Seltenere und nicht ohne weiteres erschließbare Vokabeln werden in der Regel einsprachig erklärt.

Aufbau

Die 22 Kapitel gliedern sich jeweils in die drei Teile *Check-up, Basic Rules and Exercises* und *Advanced Exercises.*

Check-up
Jedes Kapitel wird durch eine Seite mit *Check-up*-Übungen eingeleitet. Hierbei handelt es sich um relativ einfache Übungen mit eindeutigen Lösungen. Sie dienen zur Beurteilung des Kenntnisstandes. Die Lösungen der *Check-up*-Übungen sind am Ende des Buches abgedruckt. Dadurch ist eine umgehende Selbstkontrolle möglich.

Basic Rules and Exercises
Die ***Basic Rules*** zu Beginn dieses Teils sind eine Zusammenfassung der wichtigsten Strukturen des Kapitels. Grammatische Regeln werden hier in leicht verständlichem Englisch gegeben, einprägsame Beispielsätze verdeutlichen das jeweilige grammatische Phänomen. Dadurch ermöglichen die *Basic Rules* eine schnelle Wiederbewußtmachung von Grammatikregeln. Gleichzeitig bieten sie Hilfestellung bei der Bearbeitung der auf sie folgenden *Basic Exercises.*
Die ***Basic Exercises*** werden meistens durch einen authentischen Belegtext eingeleitet, der zur Demonstration des strukturellen Phänomens dient und in Verbindung mit den *Basic Rules* zu einer kognitiven Analyse der Verwendungsweise der jeweiligen Strukturen auffordert. Außerdem werden auch inhaltliche Fragen zum Text gestellt, bei deren Beantwortung die betreffenden Strukturen verwendet und geübt werden.
Es folgt ein breites Angebot unterschiedlicher Übungstypen.
Sowohl die *Basic Exercises* als auch die *Advanced Exercises* enthalten Übersetzungsübungen. Diese sollen Unterschiede zwischen dem englischen und dem deutschen Sprachgebrauch bewußt machen und dadurch Interferenzgefahren vorbeugen.
Die Übungen sind mit vielfältigen, interessanten Inhalten gefüllt und vermitteln viel Landeskunde. Vom Prinzip der eindeutigen situativen Einbettung und der völligen Kontextualisierung wird nur in einigen wenigen Fällen abgewichen, um gezielt bestimmte wichtige Besonderheiten darzustellen und zu üben.

Advanced Exercises

Die *Advanced Exercises* umfassen ein Angebot anspruchsvollerer Übungen, die für Grund- und Leistungskurse erhöhte sprachliche Anforderungen stellen. Bei umfangreicheren Grammatikkapiteln (z. B. *Conditional Sentences*) enthalten sie grammatische Regeln, die über die *Basic Rules* hinausgehen. In anderen Kapiteln (z. B. *The Infinitive*) fehlt diese Regelerweiterung, die *Advanced Exercises* unterscheiden sich nur im Schwierigkeitsgrad von den *Basic Exercises*.

Textsorten

Grammar in Profile bemüht sich, Grammatik nicht isoliert, als Selbstzweck zu behandeln, sondern die enge Verbindung von Text und Struktur, von Stil und Grammatik und die Einheit von Grammatik und Sprache sichtbar zu machen. Die Übungstexte sind deshalb weitgehend authentisch und führen somit die reale Verwendung der englischen Sprache vor Augen.
Über die rein sprachpraktische Übungsfunktion von *Grammar in Profile* hinaus versucht das Buch, zur Lektüre englischsprachiger Originaltexte anzuregen.

Sachtexte

Die authentischen Übungstexte umfassen landeskundlich informative Auszüge aus Sach- und Geschichtsbüchern, Artikel aus der britischen und amerikanischen Presse, Anzeigen, Reklame und Broschüren.

Cartoons

Neben Cartoons, die für bildgesteuerte Übungen verwendet werden, enthält das Buch eine große Anzahl von Cartoons, an die sich keine Übungen anschließen. Diese stellen auflockernde Elemente dar, dienen jedoch gleichzeitig als authentische Belege für die Verwendung bestimmter Strukturen. Alle Cartoons bieten vielfältige Sprachanlässe im Rahmen des zu behandelnden Grammatikpensums.

Literatur

Bei der Auswahl der vielfältigen literarischen Übungstexte wurden neben den strukturellen Gesichtspunkten vor allem auch motivationale Aspekte berücksichtigt. Die Textauswahl umfaßt Auszüge aus Romanen, Kurzgeschichten und Dramen sowie Gedichte, darunter einige Limericks, die vorwiegend zur Auflockerung dienen. Bewährte „Schulklassiker“ wie Hemingway, Huxley und Orwell fanden ebenso Beachtung wie modernere Autoren, die in der Schule vielleicht noch nicht so bekannt sind (Alan Ayckbourn, John Irving, Alan Sillitoe, etc.). Neben bekannten britischen Autoren kommen auch zahlreiche Vertreter der amerikanischen Literatur zu Wort. Auch auf eine repräsentative Auswahl weiblicher Autoren wurde Wert gelegt (Patricia Highsmith, Anne Tyler, Sylvia Plath, etc.).

Die Textsortenvielfalt in *Grammar in Profile* soll die mannigfaltigen Verwendungsmöglichkeiten struktureller Elemente verdeutlichen. Die sorgfältig abgestuften Übungen haben zum Ziel, die Schülerinnen und Schüler zum sicheren, stilistisch richtigen Gebrauch der englischen Sprache hinzuführen.

Contents

Abkürzungen und Symbole

AE	American English
GG 56	Verweis auf § 56 von *Learning English – Grundgrammatik – Ausgabe für Gymnasien* (Klettbuch 51151)
GhE 186	Verweis auf Randziffer 186 der *Grammatik des heutigen Englisch* (Klettbuch 5057) bzw. der Parallelausgabe *A Grammar of Present-Day English* (Klettbuch 5058)
s.o.	someone
s.th.	something
[]	Wörter in eckigen Klammern sind bei der Übersetzung nicht zu berücksichtigen.

Check-up

1 Good TV?

Fill in the verbs in the present tense – simple or progressive form.

come take go
watch

sit
just watch start
come always find
not mind
not think qualify
like not mean feel
often remember forget
love play

persuade
not need catch
get fall
look
not influence go
only buy wear

come

After a long day at the office, Judy's father … home, … off his coat, and … into the sitting-room. Judy is there. She … TV.

Judy: Hi, Dad!
Father: Hello. Don't say you … in front of the TV again!
Judy: I … the adverts before the six o'clock news … .
Father: Adverts?! You're crazy, Judy. Whenever I … home from work, I … you in front of that box. I … if it's a good programme, but those adverts, well, I … they exactly … as good TV.
Judy: Well, I … watching them. They're fun. I … I … persuaded to buy the things. In fact, I … the advert and … the name of the product! Oh, look, Dad! I … this one with the kittens. See? They … with a ball of wool. Aren't they sweet?
Father: Maybe they are. But the fact is, adverts … people to buy things they … . Just think of all the creams and shampoos that … the dust on our bathroom shelf at the moment. That shelf … so full now that things … off if you so much as … at them!
Judy: O.K., but you needn't pretend that adverts … **you.** Whenever you … shopping, you … well-known makes. That pullover you … now, for example. 'Pure new wool', naturally made by – !
Father: Quiet, Judy, please! The news … on now.

11 **kitten** young cat – 15 **shelf** *Regal*

2 The new postman

Fill in the correct present tense forms.

come
walk
bark

say
just make always do
come
know
never bite
say know
know
know

One day, a new postman … to a house and … in through the gate. To his horror, a big, angry-looking dog … on the front doorstep.

'Don't worry,' … the lady of the house. 'He … a noise. He … that when anyone … to the door. And anyway, you … the old proverb: "A barking dog … ." '

'Yes,' … the postman. 'I … the old proverb, and you … the old proverb. The only trouble is: … the dog … the old proverb?'

'Don't worry, he doesn't bite!'

1 Basic Rules and Exercises

Simple present

It **rains** a lot in Ireland. Fresh air and sunshine **do** you good.	1 to express **facts**/what is generally accepted as **true**
We usually **go** to Spain in the summer.	2 to describe **habits** (what always, often, sometimes, never happens)
It's the usual story: the girl **goes** on holiday, **meets** the boy of her dreams, and they **fall** in love at first sight …	3 for a **series of happenings** (e.g. in a story or summary)
Frank **doesn't like** coach tours.	4 to express **attitudes/feelings**, and **states** that do not change (see list of verbs below)

Present progressive

I'm writing this card on the beach. Right now the sun **is shining**, and it's **getting** really hot.	1 to describe activities/happenings that **are going on at the moment**, and **gradual developments**
You**'re doing** a lot of swimming these holidays!	2 for happenings going on **over a longer period of time** (not necessarily just now), but seen as **temporary**

Common verbs which are normally used only in the simple form:

know	like	see	be	have (= own)
think	love	hear	sound	contain
believe	hate	feel	look	belong to
remember	want	notice	seem	consist of
forget	wish	realize	mean	cost

'I never can remember whether we lose or gain five hours on this trip.'

'You'd better make a decision soon. The continents are starting to drift apart.'

1 What's the moral? GG 56–57; GhE 186–188

1 *Describe each situation in detail. Use the progressive form as often as you can.*

2 *Complete the proverbs below with the correct verbs. (Which form do you need, and why?) Then decide which proverb fits which picture.*

make (2x) get think catch want kill

It's not work that ..., but worry.
Many hands ... light work.
The early bird ... the worm.
Great minds ... alike. (**alike** in the same way)
The more you ..., the more you ... .
It's love that ... the world go round.

3 *Now look at the following proverbs, and explain what you think they mean. Try to think of situations that would fit them. (Do you know German equivalents for any of them?) Can you think of any other English proverbs?*

a It takes two to make a quarrel.
b A watched pot never boils.
c Too many cooks spoil the broth. (**broth** soup)
d When the going gets tough, the tough get going.
e God helps them that help themselves.
f When poverty comes in at the door, love flies out of the window.
g The apple never falls far from the tree.
h He who fights and runs away, lives to fight another day.

2 New at university GG 56–57; GhE 186–188

Fill in the correct present tense forms.

Caroline St John-Brooks, a reporter for *The Sunday Times*, visits Manchester to see how new students settle down to university life.

slowly make / now start / just unpack / contain / realize get / stay say / still look

First day: The students are back. The pavements of Manchester are crowded with figures in jeans who … their way from library to lecture theatre to coffee bar to hall of residence.

Emma and Pippa, both 18, are friends already. They are among 96,000 new undergraduates who … their new life at Britain's 47 universities. The two girls … their things in their rooms at Ashbourne hall of residence. Each of the girls has got a 'campus survival kit' (given by a British tea company, together with the students' union); the kit … coffee, tea, packet soup, and a pen. They both … how lucky they are; not everyone … a place in a hall of residence.

'One of my old schoolfriends … in a bed-and-breakfast hotel,' … Pippa. 'He … for something permanent.'

eat get / feel say / want

First evening: It is 7.30. The girls at Ashbourne … their supper. Outside, it … dark. 'This is the sort of time when people … homesick,' … Pippa. 'But nobody … to show it, of course.'

register meet / collect go / wait decide / study put / rush / consist not like explain / get cost / do leave set

Tuesday: First the girls … with their departments, then they … their tutors and … their timetables. Next they … to the freshers' fair, where more than 150 clubs and societies … to 'catch' new members. Both girls … to join the film society, and Pippa, who … French and German, … her name down for the German society and the art society. Then they … to the coffee bar for lunch, which for Emma … of an apple. 'I … spending much on lunch,' she …. 'We … a good breakfast and supper in hall. Everything else … extra.'

After lunch Emma, who … a nursing degree, … Pippa and … off to collect her new uniform.

stand / wait not know / not / have manage / say spend

Wednesday morning: At 10 o'clock Emma … in the queue at the finance office. She … for news of her grant. She … yet whether she will get one at all. Her sister, in her third year at Birmingham university, …. The average student … only about £3 a day left after paying hall fees. 'At the moment I … all right,' … Emma. 'But I'll have to get a bike. Right now I … half my money on bus fares!'

Adapted from *The Sunday Times*, October 8, 1989

2 **lecture theatre** ['lektʃə] large room in which students listen to their professors, etc. (**lecture** = *Vorlesung*) – 3 **hall of residence** building in which students live – 5 **undergraduate** [ˌʌndə'grædʒʊət] student (who has not yet taken a degree) – 16 **tutor** ['tju:tə] 'personal' teacher (of small groups of students) – 17 **freshers' fair** special 'show' especially for informing new students (**freshers**) – 25 **queue** [kju:] line of people waiting – 26 **grant** [ɑ:] money from the state (e.g. to cover a student's fees, etc.)

What do you find out from the text about university life in Britain? (Think especially of the age young people start university; where they live; organized free-time activities; the financial side.)

3 What's wrong with fastening your seatbelt? GG 56–57; GhE 186–188

Anne Tyler's bestselling novel 'The Accidental Tourist' tells the story of how Macon Leary tries to adapt to life when his wife, Sarah, leaves him. In this scene, Macon and Sarah have met in the Old Bay Restaurant to discuss the situation.

'Sarah,' he said. 'It's been awful living apart. I think you ought to come home … Sarah?'

'It's not possible,' she told him. Her eyes were very steady. He knew that look. She'd never change her mind. 'I'm sorry,' she said more gently. 'But it would never work.'

'All I'm saying is, I think we ought to start over.'

'I am starting over,' she said. 'I'm doing everything I can to start over, but that doesn't mean I want to live the same life twice. I'm trying to branch off in new directions. I'm taking some courses. I'm even dating a little.'

'Dating?'

'I've been going out with this physician.'

There was a pause. Macon said, 'Why not just call him a doctor.'

Sarah briefly closed her eyes. 'Look,' she said, 'I know this is hard for you. It's hard for both of us. But we really didn't have much left, don't you see? Look who you turned to when you broke your leg: your sister Rose! You didn't even let me know, and you do have my telephone number. But no, you called on your family. You're closer to them than you ever were to me.'

'That's not true,' Macon said. 'Or rather, it's true, but it's not the point. I mean, in one sense of course we're closer; we're blood relations.'

'Playing that ridiculous card game no one else can fathom,' Sarah said. 'Picking apart people's English. Quibbling over **method**. The kind of family that always fastens their seatbelts.'

'For God's sake, Sarah, what's wrong with fastening your seatbelt?'

'They always go to one restaurant, the one their grandparents went to before them, and even there they have to rearrange the silver and set things up so they're sitting around the table the same way they sit at home. They have to have their six glasses of water every day. Their precious baked potatoes every night. They don't believe in ballpoint pens or electric typewriters. They don't believe in hello and goodbye.'

'Hello? Goodbye?' Macon said.

'Just watch yourself some time. You don't admit to comings and goings. The best house in the world might come on the market, but you can't buy it because you've ordered these address labels for the old house, a thousand five hundred gummed labels, and you have to use them up before you move.'

'That wasn't me, it was Charles,' Macon said.

'Yes, but it could have been you. And his wife divorced him for it, and I don't blame her.'

'And now you're about to do the same damn thing,' Macon said. 'Ruin twenty years of marriage over whether I fasten my seatbelt.'

'They were ruined long ago, believe me,' Sarah said. Macon laid down his spoon. He forced himself to take a deep breath.

'Sarah,' he said. 'We're getting away from the point.'

After a silence, Sarah said, 'Yes, I guess we are.'

From *The Accidental Tourist* by Anne Tyler

5 **gentle** soft, kind – 7 **to start over** (AE) to start again – 14 **physician** [fɪˈzɪʃn] doctor (formal use) – 17 **briefly** for a short time – 26 **the point** *here:* the important thing – 29 **to fathom** [ˈfæðəm] to understand (s.th. very difficult) – 30 **to quibble** to argue (about s.th. unimportant) – 39 **precious** [ˈpreʃəs] *here:* well-loved – 44 **to admit (to)** *here:* to allow or agree to – 47/48 **(gummed) label** small piece of paper for sticking (e.g. on envelopes) – 50 **Charles** Macon's elder brother – 53 **to be about to** to be just going to

1. *What does this scene tell you about Sarah's new life without Macon?*
2. *Sarah dislikes some of Macon's habits and 'family characteristics'. What are they?*
3. *Now explain the reason for the use of the different present tense forms in ll. 7-12 and ll. 31-42.*
4. *What do you think of Sarah's attitude? Which character do you sympathize with more – Sarah or Macon? Try to explain why.*
5. *What kind of people do* **you** *find fault with? (I can't stand/don't like/hate people who …)*

1 4 A British invasion?

Translate this extract from a German newspaper article. Be especially careful with the present tense forms. These words and expressions may be useful:

terrace(l. 5) – advertisements for property (20) – position (23) – to be up for sale (24-25) – to cast a shadow (31-32) – not to be all of the same opinion (39-41) – valuable (43) – holiday camp (46)

'Come, come, lad ... surely they teach you a little English à l'école.'

Heute ist ein wunderschöner Herbsttag. Die Sonne scheint, und der Besitzer des ‚Café des Pêcheurs' in Honfleur steht draußen auf der Terrasse, wo er bei schönem Wetter jeden Morgen um 10 Uhr Stühle und Tische für seine Gäste aufstellt. An einem der Tische sitzen zwei Gäste und trinken Tee. Sie reden miteinander – auf Englisch. Obwohl man von hier aus einen herrlichen Blick auf den alten normannischen Hafen von Honfleur hat, scheinen sich die beiden Briten nicht besonders für die Aussicht zu interessieren. Der Mann hat eine Regionalzeitung vor sich und studiert die Immobilienanzeigen; gleichzeitig markiert seine Frau auf einem Stadtplan von Honfleur die Lage von Häusern und Appartements, die zum Verkauf stehen. Jedes Wochenende suchen auf diese Weise zehn oder zwölf Briten methodisch nach ihrem zukünftigen Ferienhäuschen.

Der Tunnel unter dem Ärmelkanal wirft jetzt schon seine Schatten voraus. Immobilien in der Normandie kosten zur Zeit nur etwa halb so viel wie im Süden von England, aber da die Briten die Normandie nun mehr denn je lieben, steigen die Preise allmählich. Über diese Entwicklung sind die Bürger von Honfleur geteilter Meinung. Manche von ihnen freuen sich, daß ihre Grundstücke und Häuser wertvoller werden, andere aber sehen die Gefahr, daß ihre Stadt zu einer Art englischer Ferienkolonie werden könnte – und das wollen sie natürlich nicht.

Adapted from *SÜDWEST PRESSE* Ulm, 26.10.89

'So you're writing a book. What a coincidence, I'm reading one.'

'Who's for a quick game of Monopoly while Clive is carving the turkey?'

Present progressive *compared with*	simple present *(further differences)*
Fred **is always borrowing** my books and **forgetting** to give them back. (I'm sick of it!)	Fred always **borrows** my books. (I don't mind.)
to express the speaker's **feelings**, usually of **annoyance**, about someone's habits	for **neutral statements**
I'**m thinking** of joining the library. (Ich überlege, ob …) I usually read the paper while I'**m having** breakfast. (… während ich frühstücke.) My uncle can't read or write. – **Are** you **being** funny? (Machst du Witze?)	I **think** I've read this book before. (Ich glaube …) This dictionary **has** over 1,000 pages. (… hat/umfaßt …) The cartoons in 'Punch' **are** very funny. (… sind sehr lustig.)

Some verbs which normally express a state ('stative verbs', e.g. *think, have, be*) can be used in the progressive form, but with a different ('dynamic') meaning.

Living as 'green' as they can? GG 56 A2, 57.3 A; GhE 185, 188

Compare these sentences, and explain why the different present tense forms are used.

1 a People are always talking about saving energy, but not many want to change their lifestyle.
  b Barry and Helen Davies often talk about how to fight against pollution.
2 a They live in a five-bedroom house in an attractive part of Epsom.
  b 'We're environmentally conscious, and we're living as "green" as we can,' says Helen.
3 a 'Well, it's easier said than done,' says Barry. 'We always take our bottles to be recycled, but on the other hand, we're not thinking of giving up either of our cars yet …'
  b 'Helen is always taking clothes to be dry-cleaned, which I think is a bad habit,' he continues. 'The CFCs in the dry-cleaning process damage the ozone layer.'
4 a 'Barry's being rather unfair!' replies Helen. 'After all, he's always using the car for unnecessary journeys – although I admit I do the same sometimes …'
  b 'Of course, compared with other people, we don't use much energy for heating, because our house really is well-insulated, and it has new double-glazing *(doppelt verglaste Fenster).* So we're doing something useful in that direction at least,' says Barry.
5 a 'We're trying hard to reduce the amount of waste we produce,' says Helen.
  b 'When we go shopping we try to avoid taking home unnecessary packets and plastic bags.'
6 a The Davies have two young children, and they are using up to 12 disposable nappies *(Papierwindeln)* a day. This is producing piles of extra waste – but of course, it is very convenient *(bequem).*
  b 'We're always having arguments about it,' Helen explains. 'Barry thinks we should go back to old-fashioned nappies. But nobody uses those now that they produce such good disposable ones. Honestly, it's a question of convenience. Perhaps I'm just being lazy. I don't know.'

Adapted from *The Sunday Times,* September 24, 1989

How about you?
What do you do (regularly!) to help the environment? How are you trying to improve? What are you always intending to do? (… but never manage to do?) And what about others you know? What part of your lifestyle do you find most difficult to change? Collect all your ideas first, and then organize them in writing. Compare your 'results' with other people's. Who is doing the most to help the environment?

2 Past Tense – Simple and Progressive

Check-up

The Hollerday Hill fire

Complete the text with past tense forms. Use the past progressive wherever suitable.

have live
use
enjoy

About 18 months ago, I … a most unusual experience. At the time, I … in a house on the cliffs between the two Devon villages of Lynton and Lynmouth. I … the railway station at Taunton quite regularly to go to London, and I always … the drive back across Exmoor and along the coast to Lynton.

return
drive see
be be
know come
increase drive
try lose
twist turn seem
spread

At about nine o'clock one winter evening, while I … from Taunton in my car, I … round a bend in the road and suddenly … that the whole of the sky above the hill in front of me … bright orange and red with flames. I … about five miles from Lynton, and I … that must be where the flames … from. Wanting to get home as soon as possible, I … my speed and, while I …, I … to keep my eye on the flames. Sometimes I … sight of them when the road … and …. But even from several miles away, it … clear that a major fire … rapidly through the village.

drive take
reach expect
see be
burn look

Even though I … quickly now, it … me several minutes to cross the moors to the top of Countisbury Hill, where there is a good view down to the two villages. When I … the top of the hill, I … to see at least ten or twenty houses on fire. Strangely, from this position I … nothing at all. There … no fire to be seen, and none of the houses below …. Everything … just as quiet and peaceful as ever.

go ask
tell

Next morning, when I … into the village to collect my newspaper, I … the newsagent about it, and he … me there had been no fire in the village at all the previous night.

see ask
seem
say nod
burn
think say
notice look
explain happen

'Where you … the flames?' he ….

'They … to be coming from some houses on the hill behind the village.'

'Ah. Hollerday Hill,' he …, and … wisely. 'The big house on Hollerday Hill. It … right down to the ground.'

'But I … you … there hadn't been any fire last night!'

Suddenly I … that the old man … at me rather strangely. 'You misunderstand me,' he …. 'The Hollerday Hill fire … over fifty years ago.'

Adapted from *Mind over Body* by Vernon Coleman

Simple past

In 1434 the River Thames **froze** over, and the frost in London **lasted** from November till February. The London train **came** in two hours late yesterday because of the snow.	1 for completed activities, events or states in the past, often with adverbials of past time (*yesterday, last January, 20 years ago, in 1434,* etc.)
It **snowed** all night. Next morning after breakfast Jonathan **ran** outside and **joined** his friends. He **picked** up a handful of snow and **began** to make it into a snowball …	2 for a series of actions or happenings in the past (in stories, reports, etc.)

Past progressive

It **was snowing** when I walked home last night. While I **was passing** the church, Mr Bell stopped and offered me a lift in his car.	1 to describe the 'background' to past events, or the 'accompanying circumstances' (what **was happening** at that time)
Everyone was busy. Marion **was clearing** the snow in front of the garage, David **was sweeping** the path, and little Tommy **was helping** with his toy snow plough. It was just five o'clock, but it **was** already **beginning** to get dark.	2 for several activities or happenings all going on at the same time, and for gradual developments

1

Note
Certain verbs are normally used only in the simple form. *See list on page 10.*

2

3

4

2

1 The Heffalump GG 60; GhE 189–190

A. A. Milne is world-famous for his children's books about Christopher Robin, the little boy whose teddybear (Winnie-the-Pooh) and other toy animals share adventures full of everyday hopes and fears, mistakes and misunderstandings.

One day, when Christopher Robin and Winnie-the-Pooh and Piglet were all talking together, Christopher Robin finished the mouthful he was eating and said carelessly: 'I saw a Heffalump today, Piglet.'

'What was it doing?' asked Piglet.

'Just lumping along,' said Christopher Robin. 'I don't think it saw *me.*'

'I saw one once,' said Piglet. 'At least, I think I did,' he said. 'Only perhaps it wasn't.'

'So did I,' said Pooh, wondering what a Heffalump was like.

'You don't often see them,' said Christopher Robin carelessly.

'Not now,' said Piglet.

'Not at this time of year,' said Pooh.

Then they all talked about something else, until it was time for Pooh and Piglet to go home together. At first as they stumped along the path which edged the Hundred Acre Wood, they didn't say much to each other; but when they came to the stream, and had helped each other across the stepping stones, and were able to walk side by side again over the heather, they began to talk in a friendly way about this and that, and Piglet said, 'If you see what I mean, Pooh,' and Pooh said, 'It's just what I think myself, Piglet,' and Piglet said, 'But on the other hand, Pooh, we must remember,' and Pooh said, 'Quite true, Piglet, although I had forgotten it for the moment.' And then, just as they came to the Six

Pine Trees, Pooh looked round to see that nobody else was listening, and said in a very solemn voice:

'Piglet, I have decided something.'

'What have you decided, Pooh?'

'I have decided to catch a Heffalump.'

Pooh nodded his head several times as he said this, and waited for Piglet to say 'How?' or 'Pooh, you couldn't!' or something helpful of that sort, but Piglet said nothing. The fact was Piglet was wishing that *he* had thought about it first.

From *Winnie-the-Pooh* by A. A. Milne

6 **to lump along** to move along slowly and heavily – 18 **to stump** to walk stiffly – **to edge s.th.** to form the border of s.th. – 19 **acre** an area of land *(Morgen)* – 23 **heather** ['heðə] *Heide* – 30 **pine tree** Kiefer – 31 **solemn** ['sɒləm] serious

1 *Pick out all the past tense forms in the text and, referring to the Basic Rules, explain the author's use of simple and progressive forms.*
2 *Why do you think Christopher Robin's remark about the Heffalump made such an impression on Pooh and Piglet? What sort of animal do you think they were imagining?*

2 The clever cat GG 60; GhE 189–190

Look at the situation in the cartoon, and make up a story around it. Use simple and progressive forms as effectively as you can.
You could start this way:

One evening when Mr Stevens got home from work, he lit a big fire in the sitting-room. When the fire was burning well, …
Go on.

3 A walk in the park GG 60; GhE 189–190

1 *Tell the story in the past tense, with the help of the notes below.*
Start like this: One morning, while Mr Brown …

a one morning – Mr Brown – walk – park – suddenly hear – strange noise – look round – see – UFO – sky – UFO – just – prepare to land
b a few moments later – look again – two strange creatures – leave – UFO – walk – through –park – other direction
c Mr Brown – cannot – believe his eyes – walk on – suddenly – idea – begin – walk faster
d when – get – town – walk – optician's shop – go in – eye-test
e shortly afterwards – run – street – feel – very excited – now
f go – straight – office – local newspaper – rush inside – report – latest news

2 *Which forms did you use more often – simple or progressive forms? Explain why.*

4 At the station GG 60; GhE 189–190

Translate the text, paying particular attention to simple and progressive forms.
These words will be useful:
platform ticket (l. 3) – steps (leading to the platform) (4–5) – to light (a cigarette) (12) – railing (14)

Ich kam ein paar Minuten zu spät zum Bahnhof, und während ich den Groschen in den Automaten für die Bahnsteigkarte warf, versuchte ich, mich an das Mädchen zu erinnern. Ich stellte mich an die Treppe zum Bahnsteig und dachte: blond, zwanzig Jahre, kommt in die Stadt, um Lehrerin zu werden; als ich die Leute, die an mir vorübergingen, musterte, schien es mir, als sei die Welt voller blonder zwanzigjähriger Mädchen – so viele kamen von diesem Zug her, und sie hatten alle Koffer in der Hand und sahen aus, als kämen sie in die Stadt, um Lehrerin zu werden. Ich steckte eine Zigarette an und ging auf die andere Seite des Aufgangs, und ich sah, daß hinter dem Geländer ein Mädchen auf einem Koffer hockte …

From *Das Brot der frühen Jahre* by Heinrich Böll

2

5 Alice in the Duchess's kitchen

GG 60; GhE 189–190

Alice opened the door and went in.

The door led right into a large kitchen, which was full of smoke from one end to the other: the Duchess was sitting on a three-legged stool in the middle, nursing a baby; the cook was leaning over the fire, stirring a large cauldron which seemed to be full of soup.

'There's certainly too much pepper in that soup!' Alice said to herself, as well as she could for sneezing.

There was certainly too much of it in the air. Even the Duchess sneezed occasionally; and the baby was sneezing and howling alternately without a moment's pause. The only things in the kitchen that did not sneeze, were the cook, and a large cat which was sitting on the hearth and grinning from ear to ear.

'Please would you tell me,' said Alice a little timidly, for she was not quite sure whether it was good manners for her to speak first, 'why your cat grins like that?'

'It's a Cheshire cat,' said the Duchess, 'and that's why. Pig!'

She said the last word with such sudden violence that Alice quite jumped; but she saw in another moment that it was addressed to the baby, and not to her, so she took courage, and went on again:

'I didn't know that Cheshire cats always grinned; in fact, I didn't know that cats *could* grin.'

'They all can,' said the Duchess, 'and most of 'em do.'

'I don't know of any that do,' Alice said very politely, feeling quite pleased to have got into a conversation.

'You don't know much,' said the Duchess, 'and that's a fact.'

Alice did not at all like the tone of this remark, and thought it would be as well to introduce some other subject of conversation. While she was trying to fix on one, the cook took the cauldron of soup off the fire, and at once set to work throwing everything within her reach at the Duchess and the baby – the fire-irons came first; then followed a shower of saucepans, plates and dishes. The Duchess took no notice of them even when they hit her; and the baby was howling so much already, that it was quite impossible to say whether the blows hurt it or not.

From *Alice's Adventures in Wonderland* by Lewis Carroll

6 **cauldron** [ˈkɔːldrən] large open cooking pot – 10 **to sneeze** *niesen* – 13 **to howl** [haʊl] to cry loudly – **alternately** [ɔːlˈtɜːnətlɪ] in turns – 16 **hearth** [hɑːθ] the place in front of an open fire – 18 **timid** shy – 44 **saucepan** [ˈsɔːspən] cooking pot (with a lid) – 47 **blow** [bləʊ] *Schlag*

1 *Pick out all the sentences (or parts of sentences) that describe the scene in the kitchen as it is shown in the illustration. Which past tense form does the author prefer for this description? Why.*
2 *Describe the action in the kitchen after Alice's conversation with the Duchess. Explain the use of the past tense forms here.*
3 *At the end of the book, Lewis Carroll writes: '"Oh, I've had such a curious dream!" said Alice, and she told her sister, as well as she could remember them, all of these strange adventures of hers that you have just been reading about ...'*
Imagine that you are Alice, and retell what happened in this part of the dream, picking out what you feel are the most important details. (Close your book for this if possible.)

Advanced Exercises

1 Different form – different meaning GG 60; GhE 189–190

Compare the use of the simple and progressive forms in these two sentences:

Ben **stood** up when I came into the room.	Ben **was standing up** when I came into the room.	*Now explain the difference in meaning.*

Bearing this difference in mind, complete the following sentences with whichever form you find more suitable. Explain your choice, and say whether the other form would make sense or not.

run	1 The boys … off in the opposite direction when they saw us coming.
rise	2 When we set off that morning, the sun … .
wake	3 I … up when the alarm went off.
not speak	4 We asked the girl to translate the menu for us, but unfortunately she … English.
make	5 She … a big pot of coffee when the visitors arrived.
go	6 They … out of the house when the telephone rang.
hide	7 Whenever there was a thunderstorm, the dog … under the kitchen table.
sit	8 On the way home in the car last night, my brother … on the box of eggs we had bought at the farm.
do	9 Please say exactly where you were and what you … when the murder took place.
get	10 It was a long climb up Ben Nevis, and we … very tired.

2 Richard Cory

Whenever Richard Cory went down town,
We people on the pavement looked at him:
He was a gentleman from sole to crown,
Clean favored, and imperially slim.

And he was always quietly arrayed,
And he was always human when he talked;
But still he fluttered pulses when he said,
'Good morning,' and he glittered when he walked.

And he was rich – yes, richer than a king –
And admirably schooled in every grace:
In fine, we thought that he was everything
To make us wish that we were in his place.

So on we worked, and waited for the light,
And went without the meat, and cursed the bread;
And Richard Cory, one calm summer night,
Went home and put a bullet through his head.

Edwin Arlington Robinson (1869–1935)

3 **crown** *here:* the top of the head – 4 **clean favored** *(not in modern use) glatt rasiert* – 5 **to array** *here:* to dress – 11 **in fine** *(not in modern use)* in a word

1 *Use your dictionary to check any words you are not sure about. Then explain what you understand by:*
   a he fluttered pulses (l. 7);
   b he glittered when he walked (l. 8);
   c he was … admirably schooled in every grace (l. 10).

2 *Use the past tense to answer these questions:*
   a *What sort of a person was Richard Cory?*
   b *How did other people feel about him? Why?*
   c *What couldn't they know about him?*
   d *Why do you think he committed suicide?*

3 *Generally speaking, the simple past is used much more frequently than the past progressive. This poem is an example of a text written in the past, in which the progressive form does not occur at all. Try to explain why the poet uses only the simple form.*

3 Present Perfect – Simple and Progressive

Check-up

1 Problems

Decide which fits: present perfect simple or progressive?

start become be have to consist collect be done work go talk act come

1 I just don't know what to do about my mother. Everything used to be fine, but now that she … working, our home life … simply chaotic. This week … especially bad – my brother and I … make our own breakfast four times, and for days now our evening meals … mainly of 'boil-in-the-bag' food. Apart from this, an enormous pile of washing …, and none of the ironing … yet. My mother … for three weeks now, and to be honest, things … from bad to worse all the time. I … to her about it, but all she says is that she … like a slave in the house for too long, and that the time … for a change. Can you give me some advice? *Worried*

sit neglect stop

not be hear mention not show stop

2 Help! Ever since our son, aged 13, got his new computer, he … up in his room, playing computer games, and – not surprisingly – he … his homework. What worries me most, though, is that he … going to basketball practice *and* to the swimming club. In fact, apart from going to school, he … outside the house for days.
I … that there are courses to teach people how to use their home computers sensibly, and I … the possibility to our son several times, but so far he … any interest.
The only positive aspect of all this is that he … watching TV.
Unhappy parent

never like be try think work meet react blame

3 My problem is my two best friends. They … each other, and recently the situation … worse than ever. Whenever the three of us do things together, they start arguing and shouting at each other. For months now I … to think of a way of solving the problem, but nothing I … of so far …. Since their last big quarrel, I … them separately, which I thought might be the best solution, but they both … to this badly – each of them … me all the time for liking the other one better.
What should I do? *Pig-in-the-middle*

2 At Reading station

Use the present perfect – simple or progressive – to explain the situation.
Example:
A young man rushes onto Platform 3. The train is just leaving the station. (miss)
▶ He **has missed** the train.

1 A woman with a young child is sitting on a platform bench. She sat down there 20 minutes ago. (wait)
2 Two girls are in the station snackbar. Both had hamburgers on their plates, but now their plates are empty. (eat)
3 A young boy travelling alone is looking in all his pockets. He is very worried indeed. (lose)
4 The train at Platform 5 came in at 3.55. It is now 4.10, and it is still there. (stand)
5 A young woman is walking away from the bookstall. The magazine she wanted is sold out. (not buy)
6 Two old ladies are waiting in the waiting-room. They went in there quite a while ago. (be)

Simple present perfect

The post **has come.** There are two letters for you. I'm afraid the post office **has** *just* **closed.**	1 to stress the **result of a past activity on the present** and for activities **only just completed** (together with *just, this very moment*)
Has my parcel **arrived** *yet?* – No, it **hasn't been delivered** *yet/so far.* Please write that letter now – **I've reminded** you *a hundred times!*	2 in questions and statements about whether something has **ever, yet, so far** taken place, especially with expressions of **frequency** *(five times, often, always, never)*
When are you going to post these cards? They**'ve been** on the hall table *for days/since the day before yesterday/all week.* **I've had** a lot to do *since I last wrote.*	3 to describe **states** that **began in the past** and have continued **into the present,** together with *for ...* or *since ..., all week,* etc. and together with clauses of time introduced by *since*

Present perfect progressive

Is Dad still on the phone? He**'s been talking** *for ages.* (Will he never stop?)	1 for **activities** that **began in the past** and have continued **into the present** (and may still continue), together with *for ..., since ...,* etc.
Barbara seems to be away. I**'ve been trying** to get in touch with her *since the weekend/since I got her letter,* but no one answers the phone.	2 for activities that have been going on **at intervals,** also together with *for ..., since ...,* etc., but never with expressions of frequency

Note
For verbs normally used only in the simple form, *see list on p. 10*

'I've been coming to this pub for ten years – and I've never been served yet.'

3 1 Junior doctors' long hours GG 58; GhE 191–193

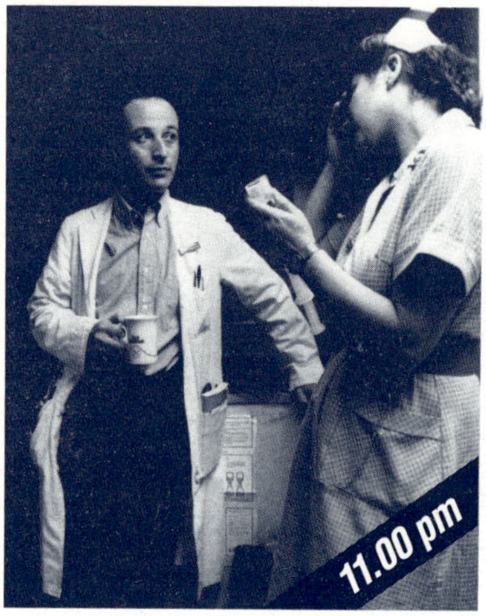

Duty calls: Keith Altman pauses after 14 hours on the ward, before being called to a cardiac arrest

Junior doctors' hours are increasing. A government report shows that over the past two years they have been doing up to five extra hours of work each week. Plans to appoint more consultants to take a greater share of the work have so far been slow. The hours junior doctors work – an average of 67 hours a week on call, and sometimes up to 120 hours – are causing serious concern for the doctors' own health and for the safety of patients.

Studies have shown that after two or three days' continuous duty, doctors' ability to do simple mental arithmetic is seriously impaired. They could make lethal mistakes calculating drug doses.

Apart from the time junior doctors spend 'on their feet', treating patients – which has increased by several hours a week – they spend hours on routine work, booking patients into wards and writing up notes. The doctors have asked for more clerical staff to do this.

The British Medical Association has suggested that hours should be restricted to a maximum working week of 72 hours, with no continuous period of duty longer than 24 hours. Although this has been accepted in principle by the government, health authorities say it is impossible to meet the target without employing more staff.

Keith Altman, junior house officer at a hospital in Stevenage, said at 7 pm last Thursday: 'I've been working for seven days and four nights, and I feel absolutely knackered. Since last Friday I've been on call for 122 hours out of a possible 152. After a week-end on duty, you feel as if you've just crossed the Atlantic – it's like being jet-lagged. It's not a sensible system for us or for the patients. Imagine flying in a plane on a Monday morning, knowing that the pilot has been working since Friday – you wouldn't do it, would you? Well, that's the sort of situation.'

Adapted from *The Sunday Times*, October 22, 1989

cardiac arrest stopping of the heartbeat – 4 **consultant** person giving expert advice; *here:* senior doctor – 7 **on call** ready to treat patients when needed – 8 **concern** worry – 12 **to impair** to damage or weaken – 13 **lethal** ['li:θl] deadly, causing death – 17 **ward** section of a hospital, often with a large number of beds – 18 **clerical staff** clerks, people dealing with paper work – 21 **to restrict** to limit – 25 **health authorities** group of people in charge of (local) health system – **to meet a target** ['tɑ:gɪt] to achieve what one is aiming at – 30 **knackered** *(informal)* exhausted – 33 **jet-lag** the feeling of tiredness travellers can get after long flights into countries with very different time-zones

1 *Find all the examples of the present perfect in the text and, referring to the Basic Rules, explain the use of simple and progressive forms.*
2 *Write a summary of the report, using present perfect forms wherever suitable. Mention*
   a *the main problem facing junior doctors over the past few years;*
   b *suggestions made by the doctors themselves, and by the British Medical Association, to improve the situation;*
   c *the government's reaction;*
   d *the feelings of a typical junior doctor after a weekend on duty.*
3 *Translate the last paragraph of the report into German.*
4 *Look at the photographs, and say how Keith Altman might comment on them. Use the present perfect:* 'This is a picture of me at eleven o'clock in the evening. I've ...' *Go on.*

2 The new evangelism GG 58; GhE 191–193

Translate into English. These words will be useful: high point (or: big day) (l. 4) – the teachings of Christianity (8-9) – to be born again (9) – to take on a new meaning (12) – interpretation (14) – to prove effective (16) – highly emotional (17-18) – fraud (20) – dishonesty (20) – to appear in an unfavourable light (20-21)

‚Schon seit meiner Kindheit gehe ich regelmäßig in die Kirche', sagt Patty Schwarz aus Nashville, Tennessee. ‚Der Sonntag war für mich schon immer der Höhepunkt der Woche. Ich habe durch die Kirche auch viele Freunde gewonnen.'

Patty und ihre Familie sind, wie etwa 25 Millionen andere Amerikaner, ‚evangelists'. Nach *(in)* ihrem Glauben genügt es nicht, einfach die christliche Lehre zu akzeptieren; man muß ‚neu geboren' werden. Erst wenn man Christus persönlich als Herrn erkannt hat, ist man auch ‚neu geboren' worden – und das Leben hat einen neuen Sinn bekommen.

Seit einigen Jahren gebrauchen führende ‚evangelists' das Fernsehen, um ihre Auslegung des Wortes Gottes unter die Bevölkerung zu verbreiten. Dies hat sich als sehr wirkungsvoll erwiesen. Aber die sogenannten ‚tele-evangelists' und ihre emotional geladenen Sendungen sind in letzter Zeit häufig kritisiert worden. Einige bekannte ‚tele-evangelists' sind sogar wegen Betrugs und unehrenhaften Verhaltens ins Zwielicht geraten.

‚Das alles hat aber mit meinem Glauben nichts zu tun', sagt Patty. ‚Für mich persönlich und für meine Freunde hat sich nichts geändert.'

3 The tooth GG 58; GhE 191–193

Some well-known saying (it doesn't make much difference what) is proved by the fact that everyone likes to talk about his experiences at the dentist's. For years and years little articles have been written on the subject, little jokes have been made, and people in general have been telling other people just what emotions they experience when they crawl into the old red plush guillotine.

If there are more than two people at the experience-meeting, everyone will chip in and tell what he or she considers to be the worst phase of the dentist's work, all present enjoying the narration hugely and none so much as the narrator who has suffered so.

This sort of thing has been going on ever since the first mammoth gold tooth was hung out as a bait to folks in search of a good time. (By the way, when *did* the present obnoxious system of dentistry begin? It can't be so very long ago that the electric auger was invented. Yet you never hear of Amalgam Filling Day, or any other anniversary in the dental year. There must be a conspiracy of silence on the part of the trade to keep hidden the names of the men who are responsible for all this.)

However many years it may be that dentists have been plying their trade, in all that time people have never tired of talking about their teeth. This is probably due to the inscrutable workings of Nature who is always supplying new teeth to talk about.

From *One Minute Please* by Robert Benchley

8 **plush** soft material often used for covering seats – **guillotine** [ˌɡɪləˈtiːn] – 10 **to chip in** to interrupt – 16 **bait** s.th. used to attract people – 18 **obnoxious** [əbˈnɒkʃəs] very unpleasant – 20 **auger** [ˈɔːɡə] instrument for boring holes – 22 **conspiracy** [kənˈspɪrəsɪ] secret plan – 23 **the trade** all the people in a certain job or profession – 26 **to ply** *here:* to work at – 28 **inscrutable** [ɪnˈskruːtəbl] mysterious, impossible to understand

1 *Use the present perfect to explain the meaning of a) a well-known saying (l. 1); b) (a person's) experiences at the dentist's (3); c) a conspiracy of silence on the part of the trade (22-23).*
2 *Explain the use of the progressive form in ll. 15 and 25-26, and compare it with the simple form in ll. 13-14 and 26-27.*
3 *Rewrite ll. 4-5 ('For years … have been made'), using the active instead of the passive, but without changing the meaning.*
4 *Complete these sentences sensibly, using verbs in the present perfect:*
   a *'I'll have to make an appointment with the dentist. One of my fillings …'*
   b *'I'm not afraid of the dentist. I … twice a year ever since I can remember, and … so far.'*
   c *'Your face looks very swollen!' – 'One of my wisdom teeth …'*
   d *'I really ought to go to the dentist's for a check-up. I … for ages.'*
   e *'Going to the dentist's isn't nearly so bad now that those modern drills …'*
   f *'The right toothpaste makes all the difference. I … for years, and I really can recommend it.'*

Advanced Exercises

1 The present perfect without adverbials of time GhE 192, 193

Compare these examples of simple and progressive forms of the present perfect – without adverbials of time:

Dad **has been teaching** Jane to swim.	(= They have been at the swimming-pool together – probably more than once, and he has helped her to learn, but she isn't perfect yet.)
Dad **has taught** Jane to swim.	(= Thanks to Dad, she can swim now.)
You look hot! **Have** you **been playing** football with the kids?	(= Have you been busy playing with them all this time?)
I've kicked a ball through the neighbours' window.	(= The window is broken. The 'event' was quickly over.)
What's wrong with Jim and Susan? They**'ve been fighting** again.	(= Until a short time ago, they were shouting and hitting each other.)
Jim **has knocked** Susan over.	(= She's on the floor now.)

Now decide which form is more suitable in the following situations.

1 'Don't let him drive home. He …' (drink)
2 'I'm afraid I … one of those new plates.' (break)
3 '… you … the book you were looking for?' (find)
4 'Where have you been all this time?' – 'I … the dog for a walk.' (take)
5 'What's the matter? … you …?' (cry)
6 'Do you know those French irregular verbs now?' – 'Yes, I … them all.' (learn)
7 'My father … German at evening classes. He's slowly picking it up.' (learn)
8 'Can you lend me £5? I … all my pocket money.' (spend)

2 Summing up the situation
GG 58; GhE 192, 193

Look carefully at the situations in the cartoons and comment on them, using the present perfect.

'Phrase-book.'

4 Past Tense and Present Perfect Contrasted

Check-up

Form questions in the correct tense: past tense or present perfect (simple forms only). (Maybe you can answer them, too!)

1 It's common knowledge!

Example:
Which continent – Columbus – discover – in 1492?
▸ Which continent did Columbus discover in 1492? – He discovered America in 1492.

1 When – the Normans – conquer – England?
2 Since when – the present British government – be – in power?
3 How many times – Britain – be invaded – since the Norman conquest?
4 Where – the potato plant – come from – originally?
5 Where – the Summer Olympics – take place – in 1972?
6 How long – the present British monarch – be – on the throne?
7 Who – first – climb – Mount Everest?
8 In which century – the USA – become – independent of Britain?
9 Which American president – be shot – in 1963?
10 How many people – land – on the moon – so far?
11 In what year – the first German – win – the men's singles championship at Wimbledon?
12 What city – be chosen – for the next Summer Olympics?

2 Meetings

Choose the correct verb form: past tense or present perfect (simple or progressive).

wait / get / stand / get / not leave / ring put keep / not get arrange

1 *Mark:* There you are at last! I … for absolutely ages.
Jo: Sorry! – When … you … here?
Mark: At least quarter of an hour ago. I … about in the rain all this time, and as you can see, I haven't got an umbrella. Look how wet I …! Why … you … home earlier?
Jo: Suzanne … up just as I … my coat on. She … me on the phone till nearly half past. You know what she's like. Anyway, I'm sorry I … here at the time we …, Mark.

read / give / start / not finish like

2 *Author:* Nice to see you. Er – … you … the book yet?
Friend: Which book? Oh, you mean the one you … me a month or so ago. Your first novel. Ah yes, well, I … reading it last week, but I'm rather a slow reader really, so I … it yet. So far, I … it very much, though.

get / start / meet say

Author: How far … you …?
Friend: Oh, not very far yet, I'm afraid. – But tell me now, … you … work on another book yet? Last time we …, you … you might write another.

collect be / come bath

Author: Well, actually, I … ideas most of the time since then, so I … *very* busy. One of my best ideas … to me while I … the dog in the kitchen sink last weekend. I –
Friend: Sorry – I must rush. Tell me about it another time though, won't you?

Past tense	Present perfect
My brother **moved** to Leeds three years ago.	We'**ve moved** house. (Have you got our new address?)
We often **went** to the theatre when we **lived** in London.	**Have** your visitors **gone** yet?
When **did** you last **see** Tom? I **saw** him in Harrod's last week. **Did** you **hear** from Nancy at Christmas?	**Have** you **seen** Stuart lately? I **haven't seen** him for ages. **Have** you **heard** from the Smiths since they left?
The past tense is used for events and states in the past that are over, and are **not seen as related to present time.** Stress is laid on **the time or period of time at which the event took place.**	The present perfect is used for events and states that happened or began at some time in the past, but are **closely related to present time. The result of the past event is important**, not the time when it took place.
Time adverbials that signal 'past tense': *yesterday, last week, a year ago*, etc.; clauses with *when;* questions with *when*	**Time adverbials that signal 'present perfect':** *so far, up to now, (not) yet, lately, since ..., for ...*

Progressive forms

What **were** you **doing** last night between nine and ten o'clock? – I **was watching** television.	What **have** you **been doing** all the time since supper? – **I've been writing Christmas cards.** (I've still got a lot left to do.)
The past progressive stresses what was **in progress at a certain time in the past.**	The present perfect progressive is used for activities that began in the past and **have continued into the present** (and may still continue further).

4

1 Acid mist pollution GG 61; GhE 194, 195.1

Scientists have blamed the Continent for Britain's worst case of acid mist, which damaged thousands of trees along the east coast last month. Although Europeans have repeatedly blamed Britain for causing acid rain on the Continent, reports say that fumes from cars and heavy industry in East Germany, Poland and West Germany were responsible for the acid mist which severely affected Norfolk and Lincolnshire on September 9th. There has not been a worse case of air pollution in this country since Chernobyl.

The mist that rolled in over the east coast affected 1,000 square miles, and killed the leaves on thousands of trees overnight. There have also been repeated cases of black cloud water from eastern Europe and Germany appearing over the hills of the Lake District and Scotland.

Dr David Fowler, of the Institute of Terrestrial Ecology, was working in Norfolk when the mist arrived. He said: 'A week later, we started getting reports that hedges and trees were turning brown on their windward side.'

Fowler and his team have been investigating for the Department of the Environment. They have discovered the cause and extent of the pollution by studying records of wind and weather patterns in the days before the incident.

Naturally, people have been wondering how damaging acid mist may be to their health. Some local people have blamed the mist for colds and irritation of the skin and eyes, although doctors have not been able to say if there were any direct links.

Adapted from *The Sunday Times*, October 22, 1989

acid chemical term for 'sour' – **mist** another word for 'fog' – 5 **fumes** smoke, dirty air, etc. – 8 **to affect** to have an effect on – 17 **terrestrial** having to do with the Earth – 25 **pattern** *here:* formation

1 *Collect all the examples in the text of past tense and present perfect forms. Compare them with the Basic Rules, and explain why the forms are used (referring either to the adverbials of time connected with them, or to the context).*

2 *Use the past tense and the present perfect in your answers to these questions:*
   a *What happened on September 9th 1989, and what caused the incident?*
   b *How did it affect plant life (and, possibly, people's health)?*
   c *What other incidents of air pollution do you know of? (Refer to those mentioned in the text, and any others you have heard of.)*
   d *Has anything been done (or planned) recently to prevent air pollution in Germany (or other parts of the world)?*

2 The great moment GG 61; GhE 194, 195.1

Form sentences to describe the situation in the cartoon. Choose carefully between past tense and present perfect forms.

1 The scientists – work – laboratory – since nine o'clock in the morning
2 They – do – experiments – all day
3 They – know – each other – for years
4 Now at last – make – revolutionary discovery
5 When – start – work – in the morning – sun – shine – weather – seem – good
6 None of them – notice – when – storm – start – because – all – work – so hard
7 Now – the strong wind – uproot – the tree outside their laboratory
8 But – still – not notice – anything – yet

to outsmart to be cleverer than

'Well, we've outsmarted Mother Nature this time!'

3 Indian girls in Britain
GG 61; GhE 195.1

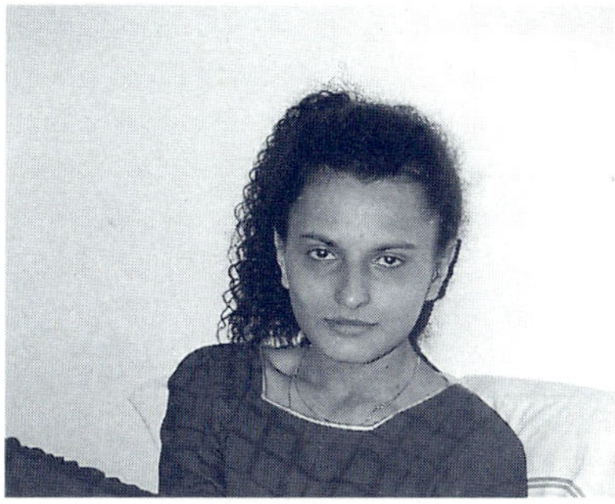

Eyes fixed on Western horizons: Indian girls in Britain have changed in ways that would have seemed unthinkable ten years ago.

Choose the most suitable verb forms: past tense or present perfect (simple or progressive).

change
arrange
begin

not be allowed hate
be assert
be forced
talk
have tell be

work leave
finish not like
get
overhear
talk
say

The situation of Indian girls in Britain ... dramatically in recent years. Not so long ago, parents ... their daughters' marriages, but now the majority of Indian mothers and fathers ... to realize the importance of a career for their daughters. Simi, aged 25, remembers being a teenager: 'Because my friends ... to go out in the evening, I ... going down the street with a boy, even if he ... a cousin. But now most teenage girls ... themselves, and parents ... to see that by being too strict they will lose their children. Of course, it *is* hard for parents. Yesterday I ... to mine about the future while we ... our evening meal. I ... them I never want to get married, and it ... an awful shock to them.'

Suki, 19, a friend of hers, says: 'I ... as a management trainee since I ... school. I ... the second year of my course now. At first my parents ... the idea of me having a career, but they ... used to it by now.'

'In their heart of hearts they feel proud of us,' says Simi. 'I ... my mother a day or two ago, while she ... about me to a friend. "Look how well my daughter is doing" – that's what she ....'

Adapted from *The Guardian*, September 9, 1988

6 **to assert oneself** to defend one's rights and opinions; to act positively –
14 **to overhear** to hear by chance

4 Adrian, the runaway GG 61; GhE 194, 195.1

Sue Townsend's humorous books about Adrian Mole, written in diary form, quickly became bestsellers. In this extract from the second book, Adrian, who has been having trouble at home and is feeling generally unhappy and unwanted, has finally run away. He has now been away from home for four days ...

Saturday April 2nd

Manchester Railway Station.

Got here by fish lorry. Pretended to be asleep in order to avoid driver's conversation.

10.31 a.m. I wonder what my mum and dad have bought me for my birthday. I hope they are not too worried. Perhaps I ought to ring them and convince them that I am well and happy.

12.15 p.m. We have been ordered out of the railway station café by a bad-tempered waitress. It's the stupid dog's fault. It kept going behind the counter and begging for bits of bacon. Yet I bought it a bacon roll all to itself this morning.

3 p.m. Nobody has said 'Happy Birthday' to me.

3.05 p.m. I'm not well (I've got a cold) and I'm not happy. In fact I'm extremely unhappy.

5.30 p.m. Bought myself a birthday card. Inside I wrote:

To our darling first-born child on his sixteenth birthday.

With all the love it is possible to give,

From your admiring and loving parents.

PS. Come home son. Without you the house is devoid of life and laughter.

6.15 p.m. There was nothing about me on the six o'clock news.

7.30 p.m. Can't face another night in the open.

9 p.m. Park bench.

I have asked three policemen the time, but none of them have spotted me as a runaway. It's obvious that my description hasn't been circulated.

9.30 p.m. Rang the police station, using a disguised voice. I said, 'Adrian Mole, a sixteen-year-old runaway, is in the vicinity of the Blood Transfusion Headquarters. His description is as follows: small for his age, slight build, mousey hair, disfigured skin. He is wearing a green school blazer. Orange waterproof trousers. A blue shirt. With him is a mongrel dog, of the following description: medium height, hairy face, squint in left eye. Wearing tartan collar and matching lead.'

The desk sergeant said, 'April Fool's Day was yesterday, sonny.'

10 p.m. Waited outside the Blood Transfusion place but there wasn't a policeman in sight. There is never one around when you need one.

11.39 p.m. I have walked past the police station twenty-four times, but none of the cretins in blue have given me a second glance.

11.45 p.m. I have just been turned away from an Indian Restaurant on the grounds that I wasn't wearing a tie, and was accompanied by a scruffy dog.

Sunday April 3rd Easter Sunday

Still in Manchester. (St. Ignatius's church porch.)

1 a.m. It is traditional for the homeless to sleep in church porches so why don't vicars make sure that their porches are more comfortable? It wouldn't kill them to provide a mattress, would it?

7.30 a.m. Got up at six. Had a wash in a bird bath. Read the inscriptions on the gravestones. Then went in search of a shop. Found one; bought two Cadbury's creme eggs. Ate one myself, gave the other to the dog. The poor thing was so hungry, it ate the silver paper as well.

Monday April 4th

St Ignatius's church porch, Manchester.

6 a.m. For two days I have had the legal right to buy cigarettes, have sex, ride a moped, and live away from home. Yet, strangely, I don't want to do any of them now I'm able to.

Must stop. A woman with a kind face is coming through the gravestones.

10 a.m. Mrs Merryfield, the vicar's wife, has phoned my parents and asked them to come and fetch me. I asked Mrs Merryfield for my parents' reactions. She crumpled her kind face up in thought, then said, 'Angry relief is the nearest I can get to it, dear!'

I haven't seen the vicar yet. He is having a lie-in because of being so busy yesterday.

From *The Growing Pains of Adrian Mole* by Sue Townsend

24 **devoid of** without – 30 **to spot** to notice – 32 **to use a disguised voice** [dɪs'gaɪzd] to speak in a different voice (so as not to be recognized) – 34 **vicinity** [vɪ'sɪnətɪ] neighbourhood – 36 **slight build** *here:* not very strong-looking – **disfigured** made ugly (e.g. by acne) – 39 **mongrel (dog)** ['mʌŋgrl] dog of 'mixed' parents – 40 **to have a squint** *schielen* – 41 **lead** [li:d] long thin piece of leather (to tie to a dog's collar) – 48 **cretin** ['kretɪn] person of very low intelligence – 49 **glance** a quick look – 51 **on the grounds that** because – 52 **scruffy** untidy-looking – 55 **porch** covered entrance-way – 57 **vicar** rector of a church – 63 **Cadbury's creme eggs** chocolate Easter eggs with creamy filling – 77 **to crumple (up)** *zerknittern* – 80 **to have a lie-in** to sleep later than usual

1 *Compare Adrian's diary entries at 3 p.m., 9 p.m. and 11.39 p.m. on Saturday with the one at 7.30 a.m. on Sunday, and explain the reason for the different tenses.*
2 *Translate the sentence beginning 'For two days ...' (Monday, 6 a.m.), and the one beginning 'Mrs Merryfield ...' (Monday, 10 a.m.). What do you notice?*
3 *Look carefully at the text, and say what Adrian was doing at the following times:*
  a *10.30 a.m. on Saturday;*
  b *9 p.m. on Saturday;*
  c *1 o'clock on Sunday morning.*
  (You won't be able to quote from the text for this!)
4 *Now write a short account of what happened to Adrian in Manchester (up to 1 a.m. on Sunday), using the simple form of the past tense only. (Keep to a summary of the facts for this; do not try to include Adrian's thoughts and opinions.)*
5 *Imagine what Mrs Merryfield might say to her husband about Adrian. Use the present perfect and the past tense to explain what (has) happened.*

5 Northern Ireland – land of troubles GG 61; GhE 194, 195.1

Translate into English. The following words will be helpful:
driving seat (l. 2) – to be part of everyday life (5-6) – decade (7) – (bomb) attack (8/9) – to set off (a bomb) (12) – to suppress (20) – to keep order (27) – a solution (to a problem) (28) – mistrust (29)

‚Ein 36jähriger Polizist starb gestern in der Nähe von Belfast, als eine Bombe unter dem Fahrersitz seines Autos explodierte. Seine 8jährige Tochter, die er gerade zur Schule fuhr, wurde schwer verletzt.' Solche Berichte über Gewalt gehören in Nordirland schon längst zum Alltag. Auch in Großbritannien hat es in den letzten zwei Jahrzehnten schreckliche Anschläge gegeben. 1974 sind beispielsweise bei einem Bombenanschlag in Birmingham 21 Menschen ums Leben gekommen. Im Dezember 1983 hat die IRA vor dem Londoner Kaufhaus ‚Harrod's' eine Autobombe gezündet; die Explosion, die sich zu einer Zeit ereignete, als viele ihre Weihnachtseinkäufe machten, hat 5 Menschen getötet und 91 verletzt.

Die Probleme Irlands hatten im 16. und 17. Jahrhundert ihren Anfang. Damals besiedelten protestantische Engländer und Schotten vor allem den Norden des Landes und begannen, die irischen Katholiken zu unterdrücken. Die Republik Irland – [zu] 95 % katholisch – ist seit 1921 vom Vereinigten Königreich unabhängig, aber Nordirland ist – mit einer protestantischen Mehrheit von 65 % der Bevölkerung – ‚britisch' geblieben. 1969 brach in Londonderry und Belfast Gewalt auf beiden Seiten aus. Seit dieser Zeit versuchen britische Soldaten in Ulster für Ordnung zu sorgen, aber bisher wurde eine Lösung der Probleme nicht gefunden. Das Mißtrauen zwischen Protestanten und Katholiken ist mehr oder weniger unverändert geblieben.

4 Advanced Exercises

1 Past tense or present perfect with certain adverbials of time and frequency

GhE 195.2

Certain adverbials of time or frequency can be a signal for either the past tense or the present perfect, depending on the context.
Look at these examples:

	Past tense	Present perfect
already	The children **were *already* sitting** at the table *when we came in.*	No more cake, thanks. I**'ve *already* had** three pieces!
just	We **were *just* having** tea *when Paul and Joanna called round.*	Are your visitors still here? – No, they**'ve *just* left.**
always	*When I was little,* I ***always* woke up** early on Christmas morning, but I don't now!	Of course we're not going out for Christmas dinner. We**'ve *always* had** it at home.
never	They ***never* served** Sunday lunch at the golf club *until a year or so ago.*	Let's have lunch at the Rose and Crown. We**'ve *never* been** there for a meal.
today	I **didn't go out** at all ***today*** – the weather was so bad! (It's too late in the day to go out now!)	No one**'s taken** the dogs out ***today.*** Let's have a quick walk over the fields with them now. (The day isn't over yet!)
for (+time):	We **lived** in London ***for six years*** *before we moved here.*	I**'ve been looking** forward to this trip ***for weeks.*** Now the great day is here at last!

Now complete these dialogues so that the tense fits the context.

wait	1 – You're back early! – Yes. I … for 20 minutes, but Julie didn't turn up, so I decided to come home.
go/just	2 – Where's Dad? – He … out into the garden.
hate/always	3 – Why isn't John coming to 'The Magic Flute'? – It's not his cup of tea. He … opera, you know.
see	4 – … you … Greg today? – Not yet, but he may call round later.
come/just be/always	5 – Sally must have missed her train this morning. – No, she didn't, actually. It … in when we got to the platform. It was five minutes late! She … lucky with things like that.
go love/always know/never be go/never have/always be/never	6 – Where … you … for your summer holiday this year? – Greece. We … Greece. But another time we'll go there in the spring. I … it as hot as it … this time. – All these holidays abroad! When I was a boy, we … to the Continent. We … three weeks in Cornwall, and it … too hot there, I can tell you!
see/already	7 – Let's watch 'Rebecca' on TV tonight. – That old film? I … it at least twice.
write/just sit	8 – What's happened to Sylvia? Where is she? – When I last saw her, she … some letters in her room. I'll call her. She … up there for hours now.

2 Past tense or present perfect in sentences without time adverbials GhE 195.3

When no adverbial of time is used, choice of past tense or present perfect depends on other 'clues' from the context – or on the personal 'perspective' of the speaker.
Compare these examples:

Past tense (connection with past time)	**Present perfect** (connection with present time)
I **met** Paul at the tennis club dance. (*meaning:* when I was at the dance)	**Have** you **met** Nancy? (*meaning:* Do you know her?)
Mary's father **was** in the Army. (*meaning:* before he retired)	He **has been** all over the world. (*meaning:* He has a lot of travelling experience/ is very cosmopolitan.)
We **parked** the car outside the library. (*meaning:* when we went down into the town)	Someone **has parked** their car in front of the garage. (*meaning:* I can't drive in/out.)
How many eggs **did** you **put** in the cake? (*meaning:* when you made it)	I **haven't put** any sugar on the strawberries. (*meaning:* You can still add some if you like.)

Now comment on the choice of tense in the following sentences, by explaining the speaker's meaning.

1 Have you seen Samantha anywhere?
2 I bought these jeans at a little shop on the King's Road.
3 I'm afraid I forgot to post your letter.
4 Don't worry – I haven't forgotten what you said.
5 I'm surprised Jerry hasn't written.
6 We caught the train from Exeter, and we were in London for lunch.
7 Didn't you hear the telephone?
8 Someone's taken my camera.
9 Why haven't you packed your tennis shorts?
10 I've put some cheese and tomato sandwiches in the fridge.
11 You and Frank were at primary school together, weren't you?
12 Why didn't you put any onions in the salad?

'He was one of the best stuntmen in the business.'

'To be honest, I have been to better office parties.'

5 Forms of the Future

Check-up

1 The family noticeboard

Will-future or going-to-future? Decide which form fits best.

be stay on
have

Sam! I expect I … back late this evening – I … at the office all afternoon to get through all the work that's been building up. Could you take some steaks out of the freezer for supper? Don't worry about vegetables – we … a tomato salad, that's quick.

Love, Jenny

book
be mean

Mum! The travel agents rang up about your trip to Paris next Wednesday. As there are no seats left on the 10.30 flight, they … one for you on the 8.20. Hope that … O.K! (It … getting up early!!)

Tina

sail
be
take

Tina – Freddy and I … out to the island this evening. Want to come with us? Ring me (at Freddy's!) if so. (There … room in the boat for Foxie, too, if you want to bring her along.) We … a picnic.

Jack

come
be

Dad! Pete Richards rang. He says he … round when he finishes work. (That … probably … at about six, he thinks.)

Jack

spend show
come

Jack!! Thanks for your note. I … the evening at Moira's. She … me her photos of Austria (as planned – or didn't I tell you?). Enjoy your picnic. Perhaps I … next time!

Tina

2 It's all arranged

Present progressive, simple present, or will-future? Fill in the most suitable form.

go
go
be set off
leave change arrive
start
show
do not be
be
have reach
be go spend

Ted: David and I … skiing for a week after Christmas. Like to come too?

John: … you … to the Alps?

Ted: No – the Cairngorms. It … super! We … on Boxing Day. The train to Edinburgh … in the morning. We … trains at Edinburgh, and we … at Aviemore in the early evening. Our ski course … at ten the next morning. Look – I … you the catalogue.

John: Hmm. What … you … if there … any snow – like last year?

Ted: There … plenty of snow, you just wait. According to the long-range forecast, we … a really hard winter this year. Temperatures … all-time lows!

John: Well, as long as you believe it. Anyway, I can't come with you. My French penfriend … here when you … . He … Christmas and New Year with us.

Will-future

I can post that parcel after work. The Post Office **will** still **be** open. I expect Tom **will do** the shopping on Saturday morning. I'm ready! – Right, I**'ll get** the car out. I**'ll drive** carefully – don't worry!	1 for predictions, and future events not influenced by the speaker's plans 2 for what the speaker supposes (often with *I expect, I'm afraid, probably,* etc.) 3 for spontaneous decisions and promises

Going-to-future

Are you **going to book** a seat on the train?	for plans and intentions, mostly in the near future

Present progressive

We**'re collecting** Suzanne at half past eight this evening.	for definite arrangements (often with an adverbial of time)

Simple present

Our flight to Dublin **leaves** at 11.40. The meeting **starts** at 9 a.m. I*'ll ring* up when we **arrive.** If we **don't leave** soon, we*'ll be* late.	1 for timetable information, and programmes of events 2 in clauses with *if, when, as soon as,* etc. referring to future time. (Note the *will*-future in the main clause. See also Basic Rules p. 53.)

'Whether you like it or not, we are dining with the Watsons.'

'They'll be unbearable when they get the swimming-pool.'

5 1 An unexpected invitation GG 63–66, 68–69; GhE 198–201, 203–204, 208

Erskine Childers' novel 'The Riddle of the Sands' was published in 1903. At the beginning of the story Carruthers, a diplomat, hears from an old friend, who invites him to go sailing with him. A pleasant invitation, it seems … Yet once he arrives in the marshes of northern Germany, Carruthers discovers a network of spies and treachery. Britain is in danger of invasion, and his own life is at risk. The great adventure begins with a harmless letter …

Yacht Dulcibella
Flensburg, Schleswig-Holstein, Sept. 21

Dear Carruthers,

I expect you'll be surprised to hear from me, as it's ages since we met. Probably, what I'm going to suggest won't suit you, as I know nothing of your plans and you probably won't be able to get away from the Foreign Office. So I'm just writing to ask on the off-chance. Can you come out here and join me in a little yachting and duckshooting? There will be plenty of duck here soon, if it gets cold enough. My friends here are having to leave shortly, and I'll badly need someone else to help me, as I'm not putting the boat into dock for a bit. If you can come, a telegram to me at the PO here will find me. Flushing, and on by Hamburg will be your best route – your boat for Flushing goes from Queenboro'.

I'm going to have a few repairs done here this week, and will have them ready by the time your train arrives. Bring your gun and some oilskins. I know you speak German like a native, and that will be a great help. Forgive this hail of instructions, but I've a feeling that you'll come. I'll be here when you get here. Goodbye.

Yours ever, *Arthur H. Davies*

Adapted from *The Riddle of the Sands* by Erskine Childers

Childers [ɪ] – **riddle** puzzle, mystery – **Carruthers** [kəˈrʌðəz] – **marsh** *Sumpfgebiet* – **network** *here:* complex organization – **spy** person whose job is to find out secret information about another country or organization – **treachery** [e] *Verrat* – 4 **to suit s.o.** to fit in with s.o.'s plans – 6 **Foreign Office** government department responsible for working with other governments – **on the off-chance** just in case (it may be possible) – 8 **yachting** [ˈjɒtɪŋ] sailing – 10 **badly** *here:* very much – 13 **PO** Post Office – **Flushing** *(Vlissingen)* a town in Holland – 18 **oilskins** waterproof clothes – 20 **hail** *here:* bombardment

1 *Collect all the examples of future forms and explain why each form is used.*
2 *Use suitable future forms in your answers to these questions:*
   a *What are Davies's immediate plans?*
   b *Why does he so badly want Carruthers to join him?*
   c *What makes him think his suggestion may not suit Carruthers?*
   d *Why does he tell Carruthers to bring oilskins?*
3 *Carruthers decides to go to Flensburg. Think of:*
   a *questions he might want to ask at the railway station, about times, places, etc.*
   (These words will help you: London station, leave, arrive, change, sleeping car, restaurant car, reservation, seat, …)
   Example:
   Which London station does the train to …
   b *thoughts he may have about things to take with him and things to do there.*
   (cold weather, warm clothes, map, camera, sailing shoes, writing paper, books, clothes for the evening, …)
   Example:
   The weather will probably … so I'll need …

2 Are you coming this evening? GG 63–66, 68–69; GhE 198–201, 203–204, 208

Translate this conversation into English. Refer to the Basic Rules whenever you are unsure about which future form to use. You will sometimes find that more than one form is possible.

Sandra: Kommst du heute abend zum Clubhaus? Es gibt nächstes Jahr wahrscheinlich eine neue Damenmannschaft, und wir wollen uns alle treffen, um die Einzelheiten zu besprechen.
Julia: Leider schaff' ich's diesmal nicht. Ich gehe heute abend zum Chor. Wir proben (*to rehearse* [ɜː]) mit dem Orchester für das Konzert am Samstag. Es gibt Ärger, wenn ich nicht hingehe.
Sandra: Wann fängt denn eure Probe *(rehearsal)* an?
Julia: Um halb acht. Sie geht vermutlich bis neun oder halb zehn. Bis dahin ist die Besprechung im Clubhaus sicher schon vorbei.
Sandra: Glaub' ich nicht! Wir treffen uns erst um halb neun. Wenn du also nach der Probe zum Clubhaus kommst, ist die Besprechung wahrscheinlich noch voll im Gange *(in full swing).*
Julia: Also gut. Ich komme, sobald die Probe vorbei ist.

3 He's leaving home GG 63–66, 68–69; GhE 198–201, 203–204, 208

Benjamin Braddock has just finished college. All his life he has done what he's told: been successful at school, passed exams, done what people expect. Now everyone expects him to go to a graduate school and become a teacher. But Ben has other ideas …

In the morning, Benjamin got up earlier than usual. Mrs Braddock was in the kitchen. 'You're up early,' she said.

Benjamin sat down at the table in front of his grapefruit. 'I'm leaving home,' he said.

'What?'

'I said I'm leaving home,' he said. 'I'm clearing out after breakfast.'

'You're going away?'

'That's right.'

'Well, where are you going?' she said.

'If you want the cliché,' Benjamin said, looking up from his grapefruit, 'I'm going on the road.'

'What? I don't understand this. You aren't just planning to throw your things in the car and leave, I hope.'

'No. I'm hitchhiking.'

'What?'

'Don't get excited, Mother. I'll be all right.'

'You mean you're just going to pack your bag and go?'

'I'm not taking any luggage.'

'What?'

'I'm taking what I have on.'

'Are you serious?'

'Yes.'

'Well how much money are you taking?'

'Ten dollars.'

'Oh,' she said. 'Then you won't be gone more than a day or two. – How long will you be gone?'

'I don't know. Maybe five years. Maybe ten. I don't know.'

'What?'

Mr Braddock came into the kitchen carrying the morning newspaper. 'You're up early,' he said.

'Ben, tell your father. Because I know he won't let you do it.'

'What's all this about?' Mr Braddock said.

'I'm leaving after breakfast on a trip,' Benjamin said, sprinkling sugar on his grapefruit. 'I have no idea where I'm going. Maybe just round the country or the continent. Maybe if I can get papers I'll work around the world. So that's that.'

Mr Braddock frowned at him. 'This doesn't sound too well thought out,' he said. 'You just plan to work around? Bum around?'

'That's right.'

'Meet all kinds of interesting people I suppose.'

'That's right.'

'Well Ben,' his father said. 'I don't see anything wrong with taking a little trip. But this is the wrong way to go about it. How's this for an idea, Ben. Spend the summer picking out a graduate school in the East, then throw your things in the car and take a week or two driving back.'

'No.'

'What's wrong with that?'

'Because I'm finished with schools, Dad.'

A section of grapefruit fell off his spoon and onto the table. 'I never want to see another school again. I never want to see another educated person again in my life.'

'Come on, Ben.'

'Come on!' Benjamin said, standing up. 'Now I have wasted twenty-one years of my life. And that is a hell of a lot to waste.'

'Sit down.'

'Dad,' Benjamin said, 'for twenty-one years I have been shuffling back and forth between classrooms and libraries. Now you tell me what the hell it's got me.'

'A damn fine education.'

'You call me educated? Well, I don't,' Benjamin said, sitting down again.

'Ben?' his mother said. 'What are you talking about?'

'I am trying to tell you,' Benjamin said, 'that I am through with all this. I don't know what it is but I'm sick of it. Do you know what I want? Simple people. I want simple honest people that can't even read or write their own name. I want to spend the rest of my life with these people.'

'Ben.'

'Farmers,' Benjamin said. 'Truck drivers. Ordinary people who don't have big houses. Who don't have swimming-pools. Real people, Dad. – I know how I feel.'

They finished breakfast quietly. When it was over, Mr Braddock pulled a checkbook out of his pocket and began making out a check. He signed it and tore it out of the book. 'Here,' he said. 'Take it.'

'I won't.'

Mr Braddock reached over to stuff it in the pocket of Benjamin's coat. Benjamin removed it, read the amount, then returned it to his pocket.

'Cash it if you have to,' his father said.

'I won't have to.'

'All right. But Ben?'

'What.'

'I have a feeling you'll be back here before you think you will.'

'I won't'. Benjamin stood. 'Goodbye,' he said, holding out his hand.

His father shook it.

'Ben?' Mrs Braddock said. 'Do you think you might be back by Saturday?'

'Mother.'

'Because I invited the Robinsons over for dinner.'

From *The Graduate* by Charles Webb

graduate school ['grædʒʊət] senior department of a US university – 7 **to clear out** *(slang)* to go away – 44 **to frown at** [aʊ] to look critically at – 46 **to bum around** *(US slang)* to fool around wasting one's time – 69 **to shuffle** to walk (aimlessly, without lifting one's feet) – 94 **to remove** to take out or away

1 *Sum up Benjamin's arrangements and plans:*
He's leaving after breakfast. He …
2 *Why do you think Benjamin doesn't want to stay at college and become a teacher? Suggest some reasons.*
Examples: If he stays at college, he'll just spend all day … / he won't …
If he becomes a teacher, …
He's afraid that …
He feels that … probably …
By breaking away, he expects that …
3 *Imagine what will happen to Benjamin when he leaves home. How soon do you think he'll be back? Do you think he'll need the check? Why?*
4 *What future form does the author use most, and why? What other form could have been used instead?*

Advanced Exercises

More ways of expressing future time

Tomorrow at this time, I**'ll be flying** over the Atlantic. Barry **will be coming** back from New York next month. I expect he**'ll be staying** with us for a few weeks.	1 The **future progressive** expresses a that an activity will be in progress at a certain time in the future; b what the speaker expects to happen 'anyway', whether it is planned or not.
The waiter can't speak any English. It**'s going to be** difficult to explain what we want. It's still quite a long walk to the theatre. We**'re going to miss** the beginning of the show.	2 The ***going to*-future** can be used to express a logical conclusion (the speaker feels certain that s.th. will happen because there are already signs that it is inevitable).
By the end of this year, we**'ll have moved** into our new house.	3 The **future perfect** expresses that something will have happened by a certain time in the future.

1 The future of the world GG 64.2, 67A, 70; GhE 202, 205, 207

A

The sun is never going to hurt us very badly. It's a very friendly star. It varies, but we can rely on it to rise and set every day and, I think, to provide most of our needs. In the very long picture, our sun will do what the other stars in the sky do. In many billions of years into the future, it will gradually get bigger and bigger, grow redder and thereby become so bright that it will end life on Earth. That time is so far away, however, that only poets need think about it. (Jack Eddy, National Center for Atmospheric Research, USA)

B

Eddy says 'The 100 years during which we have studied the sun very closely have been a time of relative calm. We can say for certain only that this will not last forever'. Could we be coming to another ice age? Tom Wigley, of the Climatic Research Centre, thinks we could, within the next 500 years.
(Fred Pearce, news editor of New Scientist Magazine)

C

We must prepare for the possibility of a sudden, totally unexpected change in climate. It would be like a drought starting and never ending. We're thinking this may happen between 2040 and 2100. That's the time when there are going to be 10 billion people on the Earth. It's going to be hard to feed those people, to keep them happy and to stop them shooting nuclear weapons at each other.
(Wally Broecker, Lamons-Doherty Geographical Observatory, USA)

D

Tuvalu (the Ellice Islands) is the smallest country in the world. It became independent from Britain in the 1970s, but probably won't enjoy even 100 years of independence. It will disappear beneath the waves as the sea level rises. In 1988, its prime minister said, 'There is nothing we can do. Maybe all of us will have to go to Australia.' Many other islands will become uninhabitable if the sea level rises. (Fred Pearce)

1 **to vary** to change – 9 **calm** [kɒ:m] a still, quiet time – 13 **drought** [draʊt] a time of no rain – 18 **Tuvalu** [ˌtu:və'lu:] – 20 **wave** movement of seawater

Adapted from *Climate and Man* by Fred Pearce

1 *Find examples of the* going to-*future in texts A and C, and explain why this form is suitable here.*
2 *What will be happening between 2040 and 2100, according to Wally Broecker (text C)?*
3 *What will have happened, according to Jack Eddy (text A), to …*
   – *the sun, by 10 o'clock this evening?*
     (The sun will have set.)
   – *the sun, by 9 o'clock tomorrow morning?*
   – *the sun, in billions of years?*
   – *life on earth, in billions of years?*
4 *Can you make other predictions? (Think of the earth's population, the earth's climate, Tuvalu and its people, other islands, nuclear weapons, food, energy, water reserves, automobile factories, etc.)*
   Imagine what will be happening or will have happened by – say – 2040. Use examples from the texts and add your own ideas.

2 It's inevitable! GG 64; GhE 202

What might you say in these situations?
Example:
Big black clouds are coming across the sky from the west.
► 'It's going to rain in a few minutes'./'I think we're going to have some rain'.

1 A car is overtaking a lorry on a narrow road. Another car is coming the other way.
2 There is a lot of blossom *(viele Blüten)* on the apple trees in your garden.
3 England has to play against Germany in the final of the World Cup.
4 There is a very strong wind. You have just got on the cross-Channel ferry at Dover.
5 It has been a very dry, hot summer, with practically no rainfall.
6 You are waiting for the London train. Crowds of other people are also on the platform.

'Before we start, I'll bet you fifty pounds I'm going to fail this test.'

3 Gone! A Victorian melodrama
GG 67A, 70; GhE 205, 207

Cook: Here, dear, drink some of this! *(She holds out a glass of water.)*
Henry: Louisa's gone! She's gone! She'll never come back. *(He groans.)* She said she hated me. She threw my presents out of the window. Look! *(He points with great drama to some jewels lying in the dust.)* We were going to be married next month!
Cook *(patting him on the shoulder):* There, there.. Don't worry. Where's she gone, then?
Henry: She's just gone on without me. I had to jump out of the cab to get the jewels. The cab was going quite fast, and I fell over. Look at my clothes!
Cook: Don't you worry about her. She's no good. Forget her. *(The young man sighs.)* Why don't you come into the house? I'll make you a nice cup of tea. *(She helps the young man to his feet, picks up the jewels for him, and they go slowly into the house.)*

4 **to groan** to make a noise in pain – 11 **cab** taxi *(here:* horse-drawn).

Look carefully at the picture, and at the scene describing what it might be about. Then say:
1 *what will be happening in one minute/in five minutes;*
2 *what you think will have happened an hour later/six months later. What will Louisa be thinking and doing then? And what about Henry?*
Use your imagination to think of as many possibilities as you can.

6 Sequence of tenses

Check-up

1 In town

Put in the missing verb forms. Think carefully before deciding which tense to use.

come
park
discover
close
leave have
arrive

look not get
have
serve
get be

1 'When Dick Randall ... out of the cinema last Thursday evening, he couldn't remember which street he ... his car in.'
2 'I wanted to walk back along the river, but when I got to the bridge, I ... that they ... the public footpath.'
3 'The play starts at 7.30. If we ... here at half past six, we ... plenty of time. I expect we ... at the theatre shortly after seven.'
4 'There were so many people waiting for the Underground at Waterloo, it ... as if we ... onto the train at all!'
5 'You ought to try the King George. I ... lunch there several times recently. They ... excellent pub food.'
6 'Sorry we're late. We ... to the station in good time, but the train ... late.'

2 Jenny's A-level results

Our holiday in Normandy was over, and I knew what would await me when we got home. My A-level results. A little white envelope – or would it be a postcard? – from the school would be on the mat with all the other letters that had come while we'd been away.

All through the holiday, I had been trying to forget all about it. But now the day of truth had finally arrived! I worked out in my head what I would do when we got home. I'd take the envelope up to my room, then I'd lock the door and read the results on my own.

I knew my parents were expecting me to do well, but I also knew that my Biology teacher hadn't been very impressed with my efforts before the exams ... The worst thing in a way was that I knew I hadn't done as much revision as some of my friends. Would they pass? Would I fail? I didn't think I would, of course, but if my marks weren't good enough, I wouldn't get into University – which had always been my dream.

Answer the questions, referring in detail to the lines given in brackets, and using the present as the basic tense.
Example: Why is Jenny nervous about coming home from holiday? (1-4)
▶ She knows what will await her when she and her parents get home. Her A-level results. A little white envelope – or will it be a postcard? – from the school ... *Go on*

1 *Why is Jenny nervous about coming home from holiday?* (1-4)
2 *Has she often thought about her exam results during the holiday?* (5)
3 *What does she plan to do when she and her parents get home?* (7-8)
4 *What do other people think of her chances?* (9-11)
5 *What worries Jenny most?* (11-12)
6 *What have her results to do with her future – and why are they so important to her?* (13-14)

Basic Rules and Exercises

The two **basic tenses** in English are the **present tense** and the **past tense.** The use of all the other tenses depends on which **basic tense** is chosen. This fundamental relationship is called the **sequence of tenses.**

1 Present tense sequence

past tense: *before*	present perfect: *up to now*	basic tense = present tense: *now*	*will*-future: *later*

Example:

It **is** hard to believe that the young woman of today – or tomorrow – **will** ever **return** to the hampering clothes of her great-grandmother. She **is** a different sort of person and **lives** in a different world. Women in the 1920s **were thought** very daring to expose their legs to the knee, but we **have reached** a degree of permissiveness in society which even the Twenties never **attained.** It **is** fairly certain that the main lines of 'emancipated' costume **will remain.**

From *A Concise History of Costume* by James Laver

The present tense sequence is used when referring to present time, e.g. in everyday conversation. It is also often used in summaries, comments, essays, etc.

2 **to hamper** to hinder –
4 **to expose** *here:* to show –
6 **to attain** to reach, to achieve

2 Past tense sequence

past perfect: *before that time*	past perfect: *up to then*	basic tense = past tense: *then/at that time*	conditional (*would* + infinitive): *later*

Example:

Maxim **was not** in love with me, he **had never loved** me. Our honeymoon in Italy **had meant** nothing to him, nor our living here together. What I **had thought** was love for me, for myself as a person, **was not** love. He **did not belong** to me at all, he **belonged** to Rebecca. He still **thought** about Rebecca. He **would never love** me because of Rebecca … Rebecca, always Rebecca. Wherever I **walked** in Manderley, wherever I **sat,** even in my thoughts and in my dreams, I **met** Rebecca.

From *Rebecca* by Daphne du Maurier

The past tense sequence is used to describe real past events. It is also used in most novels, short stories, and in other fictional narratives.

2 **honeymoon** *Flitterwochen*

Note 1

'Work **has begun** on the new school hall. It **will be finished** in the spring.'
The headmistress **said** that work **had begun** on the new school hall, and that it **would be finished** in the spring.

The past tense sequence is also used in reported speech if the introductory verb is in the past tense. (See Basic Rules p. 61.)

Note 2

The Princess Royal **is opening** the new town hall tomorrow. The Mayor **is going to make** a speech.
Clare and Johnny were glad. They **were flying** back to Cape Town the next morning. Uncle Bill **was going to take** them to the airport.

Other forms of the future (see Basic Rules p. 37) have equivalent forms in the past tense sequence.

1 Sleep: How much do you need? GG 57–61, 66, 72; GhE 179, 186–195, 199

Complete the sentences with verbs forms belonging to the present tense sequence.

go off	Millions of Americans wake up feeling tired when the alarm … in the
	morning. In Europe, too, countless people try to manage regularly on six
be proved need	hours sleep or less, although it … by recent tests that most adults … about
get	eight hours – teenagers at least nine! A simple test to check that you … the
need have	sleep you …: You don't need an alarm clock to wake you if you … enough
	sleep.
allow	People mistakenly believe that as long as they … themselves more time
compensate lose	in bed at weekends, their bodies … for the sleep they … during the week.
	Everybody knows that people sometimes feel irritable simply because
have	they … too little sleep the night before. More seriously, fatal road accidents
fall	can be caused by exhausted drivers – especially truck drivers – who …
drive not remember	asleep while they … . When questioned later by police, they often simply …
happen	how it … .
	Another common problem is insomnia: many people find it difficult to
have hate	sleep after they … a very active or stressful day. Some people even … the
be sleep	thought of going to bed because they … so afraid that they … badly. Instead
suffer	of sleeping-pills, doctors recommend that people who … regularly from
go	insomnia should do something really relaxing before they … to bed.
feel do	Why not have an early night tonight? You … fitter tomorrow if you …!

2 A bright idea

GG 60, 62, 71, 72; GhE 179, 189, 196–197, 210–211

Look at the pictures, then tell a story based on them, using the past tense sequence.
Use these words and phrases to guide you:

lovely summer afternoon – Mr Bright – go – garden; weather – last few weeks – very hot and dry – so – decide – water – flowers – big flowerbed; after – get – hosepipe – garage – switch on – water; when – start – spray – plants – notice – hole – develop – hosepipe; at first – annyoyed – because – realize – hosepipe – have to be repaired; then – suddenly – have – bright idea; go back – house – fetch – corkscrew (which) – use evening before – to open – bottle – wine; as soon as – switch – water – off – start – work; make – neat row – little holes – hosepipe; enjoy – job – because – all the time – think – the work (that) – save himself; after – finish – job – switch – water – back on – then – stand back – to admire – results; water jets – work – beautifully; Mr Bright – nothing else to do – so – think – relax – rest of the afternoon; fetch – deckchair – shortly after – sit down – eyes – close – fall asleep.

3 The newcomer GG 57–62, 66, 71, 72; GhE 179, 186–197, 199, 210–211

This extract is taken from the beginning of Jack London's short story 'To Build a Fire', in which a man fights – unsuccessfully – to survive in the bitter cold of the Yukon.

Day had broken cold and gray, exceedingly cold and gray, when the man turned aside from the main Yukon trail. He paused for breath. It was nine o'clock. There was no sun nor hint of sun, though there was not a cloud in the sky.

The man flung a look back along the way he had come. The Yukon lay a mile wide and hidden under three feet of ice. On top of this ice were as many feet of snow. It was all pure white, rolling in gentle undulations where the ice-jams of the freeze-up had formed.

He was a newcomer in the land, a *chechaquo*, and this was his first winter. The trouble with him was that he was without imagination. Fifty degrees below zero meant eighty-odd degrees of frost. Such fact impressed him as being cold and uncomfortable, and that was all. That there should be anything more to it than that never entered his head.

As he turned to go on, he spat speculatively. There was a sharp explosive crackle that startled him. He spat again. And again, in the air, before it could fall to the snow, the spittle crackled. He knew that at fifty below spittle crackled on the snow, but this spittle had crackled in the air. Undoubtedly it was colder than fifty below – how much colder he did not know. But the temperature did not matter. He was bound for the old claim on the left fork of Henderson Creek, where the boys were already. They had come over across the divide from the Indian Creek country, while he had come the roundabout way to take a look at the possibilities of getting out logs in the spring from the islands in the Yukon. He would be in to camp by six o'clock; a bit after dark, it was true, but the boys would be there, a fire would be going, and a hot supper would be ready. As for lunch, he pressed his hand against the protruding bundle under his jacket. It was also under his shirt, wrapped up in a handkerchief and lying against the naked skin. It was the only way to keep the biscuits from freezing. He smiled agreeably to himself as he thought of those biscuits.

The trail was faint. A foot of snow had fallen since the last sled had passed over, and he was glad he was without a sled, traveling light. He was surprised, however, at the cold.

At the man's heels trotted a dog, a big native husky. The frozen moisture of its breathing had settled on its fur in a fine powder of frost. The animal was depressed by the tremendous cold. It knew that it was no time for traveling. Its instinct told it a truer tale than was told to the man by the man's judgment. In reality, it was not merely colder than fifty below zero. It was seventy-five below zero.

From *To Build a Fire* by Jack London

the Yukon ['ju:kɒn] part of Canada, east of Alaska; also the name of a river – 1 **exceedingly** extremely – 6 **to fling/flung/flung** to throw – 9 **gentle** soft – 10 **undulation** wave – 13 **trouble** *here:* fault – 15 **zero (Fahrenheit)** = –17.8°C (–50° F= ca –46° C) – **eighty-odd degrees of frost** about 80°(Fahrenheit) below freezing point (=32°F) – 19 **to spit/spat/spat/** *spucken* – **speculatively** ['spekjʊlətɪvlɪ] *here:* in order to form an opinion – 20 **crackle** sound like dry sticks burning – **to startle** to shock, to surprise – 27 **bound for** on the way to – **claim** piece of land 'belonging' to a (gold) miner – 28 **creek** (AE) small river – 29 **divide** line of high land between two rivers – 31 **roundabout way** long way round – 37 **to protrude** *here:* to swell out – **bundle** small parcel – 38 **wrapped** packed – 39 **naked** ['neɪkɪd] uncovered – 42 **faint** unclear, hard to see – 43 **sled** *Schlitten* – 46 **heel** back of the foot – 47 **moisture** ['mɔɪstʃə] slight wetness – 48 **fur** (animal's) thick hair – 49 **tremendous** [trɪ'mendəs] great, extreme – 52 **merely** only – 53 **seventy-five below zero** = ca –60° C

1 *Pick out the past perfect forms in the text and explain why they are used.*
2 *Why are conditional forms used in lines* 33-36?
3 *Why didn't the man realize the danger he was in on his journey? Refer to the weather, the man's past experience, his character, and the length of time he expected the journey to take.*
These words will help you:
extremely cold – man – never – be – Yukon – before – not realize – temperature – not imagine – what – happen – if – walk – long way – not know – how foolish – outside – nine hours
4 *The dog with him was a 'native' of that part of Canada. In what way did this make it wiser than the man?*
Use these words to help you:
live – cold climate – for years – know – because – experience – low temperatures – before – also – know by instinct – dangerous
5 *Decide which are the most important points in the text, and arrange them freely as a summary, using the present tense sequence. Start like this:*
A man is walking through the icy cold of the Yukon. He has left the main trail, and he wants ...

6 Advanced Exercises

The past tense as an alternative to the past perfect

David was tired when he arrived home that evening. It **had been** a long day. He **had left** London early in the morning, and heavy traffic on the motorway **(had) made** the journey seem longer than ever. The weather **(had) turned** wet in the afternoon, and then it **(had)** even **started** to snow.	It is sometimes possible to use the past tense instead of the past perfect: Once the 'time before' relationship to the narrative has been made clear, it is common to change back to the past tense in order to avoid a long run of past perfect forms.
They went to bed *as soon as* their visitors **(had) left.** A few moments *after* she **(had) switched** the light off, the baby started crying again.	In clauses with *as soon as, once, before* or *after,* the past tense is often used: As the time relationship is made clear by the conjunction, the past perfect is not absolutely necessary.

1 The party dress GG 60, 62, 71, 72; GhE 179, 189, 196–197, 210–211, 323.2a

Clara, 17, has grown up under the thumb of a mean and disapproving mother. She is now in Paris on a school trip, which her mother surprisingly allowed her to take part in.

On the last night of the trip there was a dance. Some of the girls had been looking forward to this as to the highlight of the trip, but Clara had been dreading it, and for a classic reason, which was that she had nothing nice to wear. Since her social life in Northam did not exist outside school, she had no evening clothes, and had had nothing resembling a party dress since the age of six, when she had possessed a fetching little garment of pink satin. All the other girls had at least a best dress, and some of them were burningly anxious to display clothes bought by extravagant parents especially for the occasion. Clara had had the sense not to try to ask her mother about a possible purchase, as she could only too clearly imagine the responses to which such a request would expose her, and the abuse which would be cast upon those girls fortunate enough to have a use for party dresses. Her mother tended to see all expenses as a sign of innate vulgarity, and had tried to instil into her children the view that the truly refined can manage without toys, clothes and entertainments. Nevertheless, Clara had been obliged to raise the subject of a best dress, because the brochure about the school trip had clearly stated that it would be expected. Her mother had reacted to the subject in a predictable way, and had expatiated at some length about the absurdity of taking a dress all the way to Paris and back for the sake of one evening's amusement, but in the end she had consented to do something about it. What she did was to go through her cupboards, where she discovered a dress which had once belonged to Clara's cousin, and which had been enclosed before in a charitable parcel of hand-ons. She came downstairs with this garment, triumphant, not unwilling to please with pleasure so cheaply bought. And at the sight of it, Clara's spirits faintly rose, because the colour – a blue-green – was one which, at that age, she rather fancied. But once she had tried it on, her spirits sank once more to unprecedented depths.

For the dress was quite impossible.

From *Jerusalem the Golden* by Margaret Drabble

under the thumb of s.o. dominated by s.o. – 3 **to dread** [e] opposite of 'to look forward to' – 6 **fetching** attractive, 'sweet' – **garment** article of clothing – 8 **to display** to show – **extravagant** [-'---] spending too much money – 10 **purchase** ['pɜːtʃəs] (the act of) buying – 11 **to cast abuse (up)on** to criticize violently – 13 **expense** the spending of money – **innate** inborn – 14 **to instil** *here:* to 'drill' – **refined** *here: vornehm* – 18 **to expatiate** [ek'speɪʃɪeɪt] *(formal)* to speak in great detail – 21 **to consent** to agree – 23 **charitable** kind and helpful towards people in need – 24 **hand-ons** second-hand clothes – 27 **to fancy** to like (and want) – 28 **unprecedented** [ʌn'presɪdəntɪd] never experienced before

1 *In narrative texts such as novels or short stories, it is common to refer back to periods of time before the events of the actual plot (here: the last night of the trip to Paris). This technique is called 'flashback'.*
Pick out the parts of the text that refer back to:
   a *Clara's – and the other girls' – feelings before the dance;*
   b *Clara's early childhood;*
   c *her mother's efforts in the past to teach her children the 'right' attitudes;*
   d *her mother's reaction to Clara's request for a dress.*
2 *Comment on the author's use of tenses in lines 20-28 ('but in the end … unprecedented depths'):*
   a *Where could the past perfect be used instead of the past tense?*
   b *Can you find an example of a 'flashback within a flashback' in this passage?*
   c *Can you find an example of the past perfect where the past tense could be used instead?*
3 *Replace the expressions in italics by phrases that contain verbs belonging to the past tense sequence:*
   a anxious to display clothes *bought by extravagant parents (l. 8);*
   b not to try to ask her mother *about a possible purchase (9-10);*
   c Her mother had reacted to the subject *in a predictable way (17-18);*
   d about *the absurdity of taking* a dress all the way to Paris *(19);*
   e not unwilling to please *with pleasure so cheaply bought (24-25).*
4 *Imagine what Clara might reply to these questions from a friend:*
   a 'You don't seem to be looking forward to the dance. What's wrong?'
   b 'Why didn't you ask your mother for a new dress?'
   c 'Doesn't she like you to have nice things?'

'Poor Eric, he had got within two yards of the Princess when her private detective stamped on him.'

6

Changing from one tense sequence to another

The tenses of the **present tense sequence** all show a **relationship to present time.**
The tenses of the **past tense sequence** show that **no relationship to present time** is intended.

However, it is often possible to change from one sequence to the other.
This is done when there is a change of focus from present to past time, or from past to present time.
The use of corresponding time adverbials usually makes the change clear.

Example:	
Graham Fagg *yesterday* **became** the first Briton since the Stone Age to reach France without wearing a bear skin, sniffing the sea breeze or taking to the air. Mr Fagg, aged 47, a tunneller from Dover, **had** *never* **visited** France *before. At 2.15 pm* the first trainload of English and French Tunnel workers **travelled** from one shore to the other . They **emerged** triumphant at Folkestone to meet Customs officers who **had been manning** Britain's newest frontier *since midnight.*	**Past sequence** (focus on past events)
The Eurotunnel project, which **will cost** about £7.5 billion **is expected** to be completed *in June 1993.*	**Present sequence** (focus on present time, looking towards the future)
From *The Sunday Telegraph,* December 2, 1990	

2 South coast anglers ready for Jaws GG 57–62, 72; GhE 179–180, 186–197

Bob Williamson was in no doubt. 'It was savage, a vicious thing,' he said. 'But we're ready for it now.'

Mr Williamson, a veteran fishing boat skipper, was talking about a giant shark he believes is prowling off the Devon coast. And although he and other South coast game fishermen are in competition to catch the beast, he is not only worried that a rival boat may scoop his prize, but also fears that a shark may soon attack a swimmer in British waters.

Last year, in a little-reported incident, a lifeguard hustled bathers from a British beach after seeing a shark swimming among them. Some shark fishermen believe such incidents – or worse – could be repeated if warmer weather alters sea temperatures and brings changing marine life to Britain.

A month ago, Mr Williamson, 63 and for 19 years a fishing boat skipper sailing out of Plymouth, was returning from a trip on his boat Gay Girl IV, when the anglers realised they were being followed.

'It was a Mako shark,' Mr Williamson recalls. 'The boys had been gutting the fish they'd caught, and throwing the waste over the side. That was what the shark was following.'

Makos are not uncommon in British waters, where their speed and fighting qualities make them prized targets for game anglers. What made this shark remarkable, however, was its apparent size.

'I've never seen one so big,' Mr Williamson insisted. 'At one point it was alongside the boat and we estimated it at 18ft. I'd say it could have been a 1,000-pounder, easily.'

Marine biologists and many other sea anglers have ridiculed Williamson's claims as just another fisherman's tale. The British record for a line-caught Mako is 500lbs, and few are thought to exceed 12ft. But he is adamant.

Jaws der weiße Hai (jaw = *Kiefer)* – 1 **vicious** ['vɪʃəs] violent and evil – 3 **veteran** old and experienced – **skipper** captain – 4 **to prowl** [aʊ] to wander about searching for victims – 5 **game** *here:* sporting (game = animals hunted for sport or food) – 6 **to scoop** to get (before s.o. else) – 8 **to hustle** ['hʌsl] to send off in a hurry – 11 **to alter** ['ɔ:ltə] to change – 15 **Mako** ['mɑ:kəʊ] – **to gut** to take the insides out of – 19 **prized** loved and wanted – **target** ['tɑ:gɪt] an object you aim at – 22 **to estimate** ['---] to guess (e.g. the size of s.th.) – 24 **to ridicule** ['---] to laugh at – 25 **claim** *here:* what s.o. says is true – 26 **to exceed** to be more than – **adamant** ['ædəmənt] certain, not to be persuaded against one's opinion

'Since then, divers have seen a Mako they said was nearly 15ft here in Plymouth Sound,' he said. 'I've no doubt it's out there. But I tell you, I wouldn't have wanted to be in the water with it. The fishermen in the boat – they all agree they were scared, and I'm not surprised.'

Salcombe, Devon, employs Australian lifeguards, who presumably know a thing or two about sharks. It was one of them, 21-year-old Jason Close, who hustled bathers out of the sea at Challaborough, Devon, last June, when a shark came too close for his comfort.

Mr Graham Hannaford, the skipper of another Plymouth boat, said: 'Sharks do come a lot closer to shore than people think. I've caught 350-pounders within 70ft of the shore off north Cornwall.'

Sharks are perennially good for trade in the West Country. In Plymouth's early morning fish market crowds gathered last week as five men struggled to lift a netted porbeagle shark onto the market scales. As it lay on the quayside, its fearsome-looking mouth bloodied grotesquely, small boys looked on in awe.

Jaws has been bad news for the sharks. Conservationists believe it has encouraged excessive angling of the fish, which are slow to reproduce. Mr Nigel Merrett, senior ichthyologist at the Natural History Museum, believes it has also encouraged an unhealthy fear. 'The sad thing about sharks is that people are all too ready to regard them as savage animals which are a threat to humans. In fact, they are simply top predators in their environment. I don't think they are really a threat to us. After all, I think there are barely half-a-dozen fatal shark attacks a year in the whole world. My personal view is that it is very unlikely that dangerous sharks will get into our bathing waters.'

From *The Sunday Telegraph,* June 3, 1990

28 **sound** narrow area of seawater – 31 **presumably** most probably – 38 **perenially** [-'---] year after year, all the time – 41 **quayside** ['ki:saɪd] stone landing-place by the sea – 42 **in awe** [ɔ:] deeply impressed – 44 **to reproduce** to have young – 45 **ichthyologist** [ˌɪkθɪ'ɒlədʒɪst] an expert on fish – 48 **predator** ['predətə] animal that kills others for food

1 *This article contains a mixed report of incidents, facts and opinions. How many different incidents involving sharks in British waters are described? Sum up what happened in each case.*

2 a *What does Mr Williamson believe – and fear?*
  b *Is he alone in his opinion? Summarize the other attitudes stated in the text. Say whose opinion you find most convincing, and why.*

3 *Replace these three participle constructions by clauses. Decide carefully which tense sequence to use.*
  Last year, in *a little-reported incident,* a lifeguard hustled bathers from a British beach *after seeing* a shark *swimming* among them. (ll. 8-9)

4 *Rephrase the following expressions, using verbs in the tense demanded by the context.*
  a a veteran fishing boat skipper (l. 3): a skipper who ...
  b for 19 years a ... skipper sailing out of Plymouth (ll. 12-13): a skipper who ...
  c their (...) fighting qualities (ll. 18-19): the way ...
  d 350-pounders (ll. 36-37): fish that ...
  e a netted porbeagle shark (l. 40): a porbeagle shark which ...

5 *Have you read 'Jaws' – or seen the film? If so, describe briefly what it is about. Then say what impression the story/film made on you. Has it influenced your attitude to sharks in any way?*

7 Conditional Sentences

Check-up

1 Sunday trip to the seaside

Fill in the correct verb forms.

look go	*Mother:* Listen, all of you. If the weather ... nice tomorrow, we ... to the seaside.
be look	*Father:* All right. But if I ... you, I ... at the forecast on TV tonight to make sure.
not be able go	*Daughter:* Well, I'm afraid I ... to get up all that early if I ... to Dan's party tonight.
not go do	*Mother:* You and your parties. If you ... to so many parties, you ... a lot better at school, you know.
not complain feel	*Daughter:* Oh, Mum! If you ... all the time, I ... much more like trying!
give work	*Son:* I'm sick of hearing about school. – What about Whitby then? If you ... me the map now, Dad, I ... out the best route.
	12.30 next day:
leave not get	*Mother:* If we ... earlier, we ... stuck in that awful traffic jam back there.
be able not spend	*Son:* Well, we ... to start in time if 'Sleeping Beauty' ... so long in the bathroom.
not get listen	*Daughter:* I like that! Anyway, we ... into that stupid traffic jam in the first place if we ... to the traffic news on the radio like I suggested.
not forget not need not waste	*Father:* Now then, now then. If Junior here ... his bathing trunks, we ... to go back, and we ... that hour.
	Mother: And who forgot to fill the tank up yesterday?
stop have	*Father:* Well, let's not worry about whose fault it all was. We've still got a nice day – hm, afternoon – on the beach to look forward to. If this rain ..., we ... a great time, I'm sure!

2 In the news today

First read the text, then complete the sentences below.

There was a catastrophic accident on the M6 near Birmingham last night, in which 40 cars and lorries were involved. The police say that the drivers were surprised by sudden fog, and so were unable to slow down in time. The road was icy, making driving conditions extremely difficult. A lorry had broken down shortly before, so one of the lanes was blocked. A Ministry of Transport spokesman said after the accident: 'Drivers simply don't take enough notice of weather conditions. That's the reason for so many road accidents. People must learn to be more responsible behind the wheel. Otherwise drastic fines will be the only answer.'

1 *If the drivers hadn't been surprised by the fog, ...*
2 *Driving conditions wouldn't have ...*
3 *If the lorry ...*
4 *There would be fewer accidents if ...*
5 *Drastic fines will be the only answer if ...*

Type I	This condition may be fulfilled
If Tom **practises** a lot,	he **will get** very good at tennis.
But if he **doesn't play** regularly,	he **won't improve** much.
if-clause: **present tense**	main clause: **will future**

Type II	This condition cannot be/isn't likely to be fulfilled
If Tom **was** a year younger,	he **would** still **be** in the junior team.
If he **played** in the tournament next month,	he **would** perhaps **do** quite well.
if-clause: **past tense**	main clause: **conditional**

Type III	This condition can no longer be fulfilled
If he **had won** more matches last year,	he **wouldn't have lost** interest so easily.
If he **hadn't broken** his leg in the autumn,	he **would have had** more practice.
if-clause: **past perfect**	main clause: **conditional perfect**

Note 1

If Tom wins against Ralph on Sunday, he **can** really **be** proud of himself.
In Type I, can, must, needn't *or* may *can be used instead of* will.

Note 2

If he tried hard enough, he **could get** really good.
If he hadn't injured his leg, he **might** have **won** the tournament.
In Types II and III, might *or* could *can be used instead of* would.

1 I'm in a 'What if' mood today GG 73; GhE 215–217

to raise kittens to look after young cats while they are growing up

7

1 *Which of the three types of conditional sentences does Garfield use? Why does he use this one?*
2 *Use the other two types instead. In what way does the situation change?*
3 *Can you add any further ideas to Garfield's thoughts?*

Example:
If we had a huge wedding, it would cost a lot of money / … we'd get all sorts of useless presents …
If we had some kittens … If I stayed on my own …
If Arlene wasn't so beautiful …
Go on.

2 Do you know this joke? GG 73; GhE 215–217

Fill in the correct verb forms.

pull / say / pull / say / happen / pull / fall

Salesman (selling parrot to young boy): If you … the string on his right leg he … 'Good morning', and if you … the string on his left leg he … 'Good night'.
Boy: What … if I … both strings together?
Parrot: I … off the perch, you idiot.

prefer / pull

Patient: What do you charge for pulling a tooth?
Dentist: Ten dollars.
Patient: What! Ten dollars for only two minutes' work?
Dentist: Well, if you …, I … it very slowly.

serve / forget

Betsy had forgotten a schoolmate's birthday and sent this note of apology: 'I have no excuse for forgetting, and it … me right if you … my birthday, which will be next Wednesday.'

stand / flow

'If I … on my head,' said the science teacher, 'all the blood … to it. Why doesn't it rush to my feet when I'm standing on them?
'Because,' replied a student, 'they're not empty.'

have / not hurry

'Don't apologize,' said the baby-sitter to the parents who came back late. 'If I … a kid like yours, I … home either.'

not / come

A night watchmann heard noises in the dark warehouse. Drawing his revolver, he went to the door and called, 'Come out with your hands up, so I can see who you are. If you …, I … in and see who you were.'

4 **perch** branch etc. on which a bird can rest – 5 **to charge** to ask for money (in return for goods or services) – 9 **note of apology** short letter saying 'sorry'

3 Things would be much better if …

GG 73, 76; GhE 214–217

1 *Complete the conditional sentences below and say how things could be/could have been improved.*
Example:
I would be much happier if Kevin didn't always complain about everything.

a You might look much better if …
b If we hadn't bought that expensive car, …
c If we go on like this, …
d If you weren't so lazy, …
e If you hadn't eaten up all the biscuits, …
f People would like you much better if …
g If we'd got up a little earlier, …
h If I had washed my jeans yesterday, …
i You won't pass your driving-test if …

'If you didn't spend so much money on cameras we might be able to afford a real holiday.'

2 *Now use conditional sentences to express complaints or regrets in the following situations:*
a Your little brother keeps using **your** tennis balls.
b Your father forgot to wake you up in the morning.
c Your English teacher never calls on you.
d Your friend didn't want you to copy her homework.
e Tom didn't pass the ball to **you.**
f Your little sister has worn your pullover **again.**
g You didn't get any tickets for the pop concert – you forgot to ring up.
h You have had a nasty fall – the brakes on your bike didn't work.

4 Once upon a time GG 73; GhE 217

1 *Do you still remember the old fairy tales you used to know so well? First put together a simple summary of the story of Little Red Riding Hood. Then think –*
It all might (could/probably would) have happened quite differently if ...
If Grandmother hadn't been ill, Little Red Riding Hood's mother wouldn't have baked a cake for her. If Little Red Riding Hood hadn't stopped to pick some flowers, she might not have met the wolf in the first place.
Go on.

Think of: the Wolf speaking English; Little Red Riding Hood talking to him; Wolf being frightfully hungry; Wolf wearing Grandma's night-clothes; Little Red Riding Hood being rather naive; Hunter coming to the rescue ...
Use conditional sentences; you needn't be too serious.

2 *Choose one of the following fairy-tales and comment on it, using conditional sentences:*
Snow White, Sleeping Beauty, Hansel and Gretel, Rumpelstiltskin, Cinderella *(Aschenputtel), ...*

5 Writing to an English penfriend GG 69, 73, 129; GhE 208–209, 216–217, 317

You might want to express these ideas in English. Be careful with the German wenn *– decide whether to put* when *or* if *in English.*

1 Wenn Du ankommst, holt Dich meine Mutter am Flughafen ab.
2 Wenn Du dann bei uns bist, kannst Du Dich erst einmal ausruhen.
3 Wenn ich am Samstag aus der Schule komme, können wir etwas zusammen unternehmen.
4 Wenn das Wetter am Sonntag schön ist, gehen wir schwimmen.
5 Wenn Du nichts dagegen hast, können wir am Abend in eine Disco gehen.
6 Wenn Du vor zwei Wochen gekommen wärst, hätten wir uns eine tolle Picasso-Ausstellung *(exhibition)* anschauen können.
7 Wenn ich ‚Adrian Mole' gelesen habe, schicke ich es Dir zurück.
8 Oder willst Du es mitnehmen, wenn Du im Juni kommst?
9 Wenn Du Dir das Foto ansiehst, merkst Du, wie groß Jens geworden ist.

7 Advanced Exercises

In both written and spoken English you will also come across other types of conditional sentences. Look at the following combinations.

Compare these combinations of if-clauses and main clauses to the three basic types (p. 53). Say in what way they differ in structure and meaning.

1 If you **want** more information, **write** to the address below.
2 If you **should not like** the book, we'**ll take** it back.
3 If you **buy** on credit, you **have** more time to pay.
4 If you **had ordered** the car in June, you **would be** able to drive it now.
5 If I **were** you, I **wouldn't wait** any longer.

1 The language of advertising GG 73–75; GhE 214–218

Try to put the two parts together correctly – so that these advertisement slogans make sense.

1 If a man has money
2 And if we may draw a conclusion from five generations of experience
3 If and when 'Your 6 numbers' come up
4 If all this seems like yesterday
5 Wouldn't it be better
6 If you think it's expensive
7 If you should see furniture like this in a shop
8 If I were you
9 How can you meet the right person
10 If this doesn't tempt you
11 If you prefer to drive

a think again.
b it would probably cost at least twice as much.
c you'll find a free parking space reserved for you.
d nothing will.
e if you're not even meeting the right people?
f see what tomorrow could bring.
g it will be this: choose once but choose well.
h you will share in a guaranteed minimum of $1.000.000.000 in tax-free cash.
i if you had control over your payments rather than the other way round?
j it's usually a sign that he knows how to take care of it.
k I wouldn't be satisfied with second-best.

'You'll have heard about our new sales policy – if you don't want the encyclopaedias all you have to do is say No.'

1 *Can you guess what these slogans advertise – or what sort of person they are trying to attract? Example:*
I think slogan number 1 might advertise … / could be from an advert for … / is supposed to attract people who want …
2 *Explain the use of the verb forms in these adverts. Which forms are used most often? Why is this so?*
3 *Now make up your own advertising slogans. Use conditional clauses. You want to advertise:* jeans – toothpaste – a mountain bike – a personal computer – instant coffee – a sportscar – …

2 Tough Jobs GG 73, 74; GhE 214, 217

How to Tell If You're Stressed – And What to Do About It

Only recently have doctors and psychologists begun to study workplace tension in depth. They've discovered the most trying professions are those involving danger and extreme pressure – or that carry responsibility without control.
The symptoms of stress have been found to range from frequent illness to nervous tics and forgetfulness. The most common tips for dealing with it centre on relaxation. But sometimes the only answer is to fight back – or walk away.

Tough Jobs	Warning Signs	Ways to Cope
Inner-city high-school teacher	Rapid pulse	Maintain a sense of humor
Police officer	Frequent illness	Get a massage
Miner	Insomnia	Exercise regulary
Air-traffic controller	Irritability	Eat more sensibly
Junior doctor (in a hospital)	Nail biting	Limit intake of alcohol and caffeine
Journalist	Lack of concentration	Take refuge in family and friends
Waiter/Waitress	Increased use of alcohol and drugs	Stand up to the boss
Secretary	Hunger for sweets	Quit

SOURCES FOR THE 8 TOUGHEST JOBS: THE NATIONAL INSTITUTE ON WORKERS COMPENSATION: AMERICAN INSTITUTE OF STRESS

tension feeling of nervousness, worry and pressure – **trying** difficult and annoying – **insomnia** sleeplessness – **irritability** a mood in which you get very easily annoyed – **to quit** to stop doing, to give up and leave

Look at the list of tough jobs above. Talk about the jobs mentioned in the table, the warning signs and symptoms, and about possible cures.
Examples: If I was a police officer, I might suffer from insomnia.
If you (should) suffer from lack of concentration, try to eat more sensibly.
If I worked as an air-traffic controller and was frequently ill, I would quit and look for a different job.

3 The 'ifs' of history GG 73; GhE 217

Say what 'would', 'could' or 'might' have happened 'if' …
Example: If the Romans hadn't conquered Britain, many names of places in Britain would be different today. / Hadrian's Wall wouldn't have been built / …

1 If Harold had defeated the Normans in 1066, …
2 If Columbus hadn't discovered America, …
3 Henry VIII might not have broken with Rome if …
4 If the Great Armada hadn't been defeated in 1588, …
5 If the American colonists had been represented in the English Parliament, …
6 If all the Indian tribes had united against the white man, …
7 If the economy of the Southern states of the USA had not depended on cotton, …
8 Britain would not have been able to found so many colonies if …
9 Slavery in the United States might have continued even longer if …
10 The Americans might not have landed on the moon if …

Go on. Talk about other 'ifs' of history.

4 'Fifteen' GG 73, 74; GhE 214, 217

... is the story of one summer in the life of fifteen-year-old Jane Purdy. She is quite an ordinary sort of girl, with quite ordinary hopes and fears. What is different about her is that she is an American; which also means that quite a lot of things happen to her a little bit sooner than they happen in other countries. If she had been a British girl, for instance, she wouldn't have had such long holidays, or spent so much of them earning money by baby-sitting. And Stan would not have been delivering dogs' meat to help pay his way through college. In fact he would not have been allowed to drive a van at all, because he wouldn't have been old enough to have a licence, and Jane and Stan would probably not even have met each other until a year later.

But whether Jane is British or American, or fifteen or sixteen, what she feels through this summer and how she copes with the first pangs of growing up are very delicately and truly set down in this book.

Foreword to the British edition of *Fifteen*

Mrs Purdy looked curiously at her daughter. 'What's come over you tonight?'

'Oh, nothing,' said Jane, realizing that she had better be careful what she said, or her mother would start asking a lot of tiresome questions like who was the boy's family and what did his father do and a lot of things she couldn't answer until she got to know him. If only she knew the boy's name she could look him up in the telephone book and just happen to walk by his house, and he might just happen to be outside washing the car or mowing the lawn or something. She would glance at him with a faintly puzzled expression as if she had seen him someplace but couldn't quite remember where. And he would look up from whatever he was doing and say, 'Why, hello. Aren't you the girl who was baby-sitting at the Nortons'?' And she would say ... But she did not know his name and even if she did, he was probably so new in town that his family would not be listed in the telephone directory yet. Or he might not even live in Woodmont. He might live in some other town and when school started he would be part of the school-bus crowd.

Or she could find out where the Doggie Diner was located and just happen to walk past about the time he might be through work. Jane considered this idea and discarded it as being too obvious. A business that cut up horse meat would not be in a part of town where she could go for a walk without having people wonder what she was doing there.

Or she could happen to walk by the Nortons' house about three o'clock on Friday afternoon when he might be delivering Cuthbert's food again. Jane thought this over and decided the plan had both advantages and disadvantages. She could easily go for a walk in the Nortons' neighbourhood without looking out of place. However, the truck would not arrive at exactly three o'clock and she could not very well walk up and down in front of the Nortons' as if she were picketing their house. The neighbours would begin to wonder what she was doing. Nevertheless, a leisurely stroll up their street next Friday afternoon could do no harm. He might happen to drive by and see her and think, 'Why, there's that girl I spoke to at the Nortons'. He would stop the truck and say, 'Hi, there. Going to Sandra's house? If you are I'll give you a lift.' And she would say ...

And then Jane had an even better idea. If she were baby-sitting with Sandra she would be sure to see him. She turned this over in her mind. Could she stand another afternoon of Sandra – another afternoon of trying to manoeuvre her into doing what she was supposed to do when Sandra was so clever at outwitting sitters? To see that boy again, yes. It would not be easy but she could do it. The boy would arrive with Cuthbert's food and say, 'Hi! I didn't expect to see you here again,' and of course he would look as if he were glad she was there again. And she would laugh and say ...

From *Fifteen* by Beverly Cleary

18 **to cope with** to deal with a problem successfully – **pang** a sudden sharp feeling of pain – 24 **tiresome** annoying, irritating – 32 **puzzled** surprised and confused – 46 **to discard** to get rid of, to set aside – 59 **to picket** to guard, to watch in order to prevent people from going in or out – 61 **a leisurely stroll** ['leʒəlɪ] an unhurried walk – 74 **to outwit** to defeat s.o. or to gain an advantage over s.o. by behaving in a clever or tricky way

1 *Use conditional sentences to say what would/could/might happen or be the case*
if Jane wasn't very careful what she said (l. 23),
if she knew the boy (26-27),
if she just walked past his house (28-29),
if the boy's family was new in town (38),
if he didn't live in Woodmont (40),
if she knew where the place was where he worked (43-44),
if she went for a walk in the Nortons' neighbourhood (54-55),
if he saw her there (62-63),
if she said she was going to Sandra's house (66).

2 *Pick out the conditional sentences in the extract from the novel and in the foreword and comment on the verb forms.*
3 *Sometimes several main clauses in the text depend on one if-clause only, or the if-clause is only implied. Find examples.*
4 *What does the use of the many conditionals tell us about Jane's state of mind, her way of thinking, her character?*
5 *Translate from 'Or she could happen to ...' (l. 50) to 'And she would say ...' (l. 66)*

5 The greenhouse effect GG 73–75; GhE 214–218

Translate the text. These words will help you:
ice age (l. 7) – sea level (12) – icecap (14) – ice-sheet (15) – Antarctic (16) – carbon dioxide [daɪ'ɒksaɪd] (22/35) – nuclear power (station) (26/31) – fossil fuels (27) – to calculate (34) – sycamore (tree) (38)

Wenn die Verschmutzung der Atmosphäre nicht gestoppt wird, könnte sich die Durchschnittstemperatur auf der Erde in den nächsten 50 Jahren um *(by)* zwischen einem und vier Grad Celsius erhöhen. (Vier Grad ist ungefähr der Unterschied zwischen den Temperaturen jetzt und denen während der letzten Eiszeit.)

Verheerende klimatische Veränderungen wären die Folge einer solchen Entwicklung.

Wenn man den gegenwärtigen Vorhersagen glauben kann, sollte sich die Welt auf einen Anstieg der Meeresspiegel um etwa einen Meter irgendwann im Laufe des 21. Jahrunderts vorbereiten. Wenn die polaren Eiskappen schnell genug schmelzen, könnten es zwei Meter sein. Und falls auch die Eisschicht der westlichen Antarktis schmelzen sollte (obwohl dies als unwahrscheinlich gilt), könnten die Meeresspiegel um weitere *(a further)* sechs Meter ansteigen. Schlechte Nachrichten für die Menschen, die auf *(at)* Meeresspiegelhöhe leben. Manche Wissenschaftler warnen schon seit vielen Jahren davor, daß die Menge von Kohlendioxyd in der Atmosphäre ständig ansteigt. Wenn die Politiker früher auf sie gehört hätten, wäre die Situation jetzt vielleicht nicht ganz so schlimm.

Was kann man tun? Eine Möglichkeit wäre, Kernenergie anstelle von fossilen Brennstoffen zu verwenden. Aber falls die Länder der Erde versuchen, fossile Brennstoffe durch Kernenergie zu ersetzen, müßten sie in den nächsten 40 Jahren zwischen 3 und 16 Atomkraftwerke in der Woche bauen.

Ein amerikanischer Wissenschaftler hat berechnet, daß es eine einfache Möglichkeit gibt, einen Teil des Kohlendioxid in der Atmosphäre zurück in Holz zu verwandeln: Man müßte nur ein Gebiet in der Größe von Australien *(the size of A.)* mit Bergahorn bepflanzen.

'What worries me is who's going to conserve us if they become extinct?'

8 Reported Speech

Check-up

An interview

First read the text, then complete the sentences below.

Sue wants to work for a few weeks during the summer holidays. She sees an advert in the local paper for a temporary job at a rest home, and decides to apply for it. Mrs Beale, who is in charge of the home, invites her to come for an interview.

Mrs Beale: Sit down, Sue. Right. Before I can promise you the job, I'd like to ask you one or two questions. – Why did you apply for this kind of work?
Sue: Well, firstly, I like the idea of helping other people. And I think I'd enjoy the work.
Mrs Beale: Have you ever worked with elderly people before?
Sue: No, I haven't. But I don't think I'll have any problems.
Mrs Beale: Where do you live? Will you be able to start work at seven-thirty most mornings? That's when the night nurse goes off duty.
Sue: I'll easily be able to manage it by then. I live quite near.
Mrs Beale: Fine. – Can you cook?
Sue: Er... well! I often help to get meals ready at home, but I haven't often cooked a whole meal by myself.
Mrs Beale: Don't worry. You won't have to cook whole meals without help. But I do need someone with a bit of experience in the kitchen. You would also have to do jobs like vacuum-cleaning, washing, setting tables and so on.
Sue: I see. – When will you be able to tell me whether I can have the job, Mrs Beale?
Mrs Beale: Well, a young man's coming to see me in the afternoon, so naturally I can't make a decision until I've talked to him, too. Ring up tomorrow morning and I'll let you know then.

2 **temporary** opposite of permanent – **rest home** home for old people – 9 **elderly** old (of people)

That evening, Sue talks to her friend Belinda about the interview. 'What happened?' Belinda asks.
'Well, Mrs Beale told me to ..., and then she asked me why ..., and so I told her ... and ... Then she asked ..., and of course I said ..., but that ... She also wanted to know ..., and asked ... I told her ... as ... Then she asked me ..., so I said ..., but that ... She told me ... about that, and explained that ..., but that ... She also told me ...'
'When will you know if you've got the job?' Belinda asks.
'Well, Mrs Beale said ..., so ... She told me ... to find out.'

'It looks bad: the boss asked me this morning whether I'd ever thought of emigrating.'

Direct speech	Reported speech *(introductory verb in the past)*
'I **like** your new jacket.' 'I'**m looking** for a pair of warm boots for the winter.'	She said that she **liked** my new jacket. He said he **was looking** for a pair of warm boots for the winter.
present tense →	**past tense**
'Dad **looked** at hundreds of pullovers, but he **didn't buy** one.'	She told me that her father **had looked** at hundreds of pullovers, but that he **hadn't bought** one.
past tense →	**past perfect**
'You'**ve spent** enough on clothes for one day!'	I told her she **had spent** enough on clothes for one day.
present perfect →	**past perfect**
'The shops **will be** open till 6.'	He told us the shops **would be** open till 6.
future →	**conditional**
'**Where**'s the cash-desk, please?' 'Will you take a cheque?'	I asked the assistant **where** the cash-desk was. I asked them **whether/if** they would take a cheque.

Questions:
Repeat the 'question word' *(where/when/*etc.). If there is no 'question word' use *whether* or *if.*

'**Try** on the trousers you like best.' '**Don't buy** them if they're too tight.'	She told me **to try** on the trousers I liked best. She advised me **not to buy** them if they were too tight.

Imperatives: Use the infinitive with *to/not to.*

Note 1
'Saturday morning **is** the worst time for shopping.'
→ I reminded her that Saturday morning **is/was** the worst time for shopping.

If the speaker states a fact that does not change (or is generally accepted as true), the tense in reported speech need not necessarily be changed.

Note 2
'I **hadn't thought** of that.'
→ She said she **hadn't thought** of that.
'I **would prefer** to go to town on Monday.'
→ I told her I **would prefer** to go to town on Monday.

Past perfect and conditional remain unchanged in reported speech.

'We didn't say it would look good. We merely said you wouldn't have to iron it.'

1 Waiting GG 150–152; GhE 320, 322, 327

Mrs Foster was always terribly afraid of missing a train or a plane. Her fear was made worse by her husband, who had a habit of keeping her waiting unnecessarily. Mrs Foster, who was too afraid of her husband to complain, sometimes wondered if he did this intentionally. On the day of her long-awaited journey to Paris to visit her daughter and grandchildren, her flight from New York was put off because of fog, and was finally arranged for eleven o'clock the next day. A car was ordered for nine o'clock, to take Mrs Foster to the airport and to drop Mr Foster at his club on the way …

Next morning, Mrs Foster was up early, and by eight-thirty she was downstairs and ready to leave.

Shortly after nine, her husband appeared.

'Did you make any coffee?' he asked.

'No, dear. I thought you'd get a nice breakfast at the club. The car is here. I'm all ready to go.'

'Your luggage?'

'It's at the airport.'

'Ah yes,' he said. 'Of course. And if you're going to take me to the club first, I suppose we'd better get going soon, hadn't we?'

'Yes!' she cried. 'Oh, yes – please!'

'I'm just going to get a few cigars. I'll be right with you. You get in the car.'

She turned and went to where the chauffeur was standing, and he opened the car door for her.

'What time is it?' she asked.

'About nine-fifteen.'

Mr Foster came out five minutes later. As on the day before, he paused to examine the sky. The weather was still not quite clear, but there was a wisp of sun coming through the mist.

'Perhaps you'll be lucky this time,' he said as he settled himself beside her in the car.

'Hurry, please,' she said to the chauffeur. 'Please get going. I'm late.'

The man went back to his seat behind the wheel and started the engine.

'Just a moment!' Mr Foster said suddenly. 'Hold it a moment, chauffeur, will you?

'What is it, dear?' She saw him searching the pockets of his overcoat.

'I had a little present I wanted you to take to Ellen,' he said. 'Now, where on earth is it? I'm sure I had it in my hand as I came down.'

'I never saw you carrying anything. What sort of present?'

'A little box wrapped up in white paper. I forgot to give it to you yesterday. I don't want to forget it today.'

'A little box!' Mrs Foster cried. 'I never saw any little box!' She began hunting frantically in the back of the car.

Her husband continued searching through the pockets of his coat. Then he unbuttoned the coat and felt around in his jacket. 'Confound it,' he said. 'I must've left it in my bedroom. I won't be a moment.'

'Oh, please!' she cried. 'We haven't got time. Please leave it! You can mail it.'

'Stay here!' he commanded. 'I'm going to get it.'

'Be quick, dear! Oh, please be quick!'

She sat still, waiting and waiting.

'Chauffeur, what time is it?'

'I make it nearly nine-thirty.'

'Can we get to the airport in an hour?'

'Just about.'

At this point, Mrs Foster suddenly spotted a corner of something white wedged down in the crack of the seat on the side where her husband had been sitting. She reached over and pulled out a small paper-wrapped box, and at the same time she couldn't help noticing that it was wedged down firm and deep, as though with the help of a pushing hand …

From *The Way Up to Heaven* by Roald Dahl

20 **a wisp of sun** a little sunshine – **mist** fog – 31 **to wrap up** to pack (in paper) – 34 **frantic** excited (with worry) – 36 **Confound it** Damn it – 47 **to spot** to notice – 48 **to wedge** to squeeze or push tightly – **crack** *Ritze* – 50 **she couldn't help noticing** it was impossible for her not to notice

Retell what happened, using reported speech. You need not always give a word-for-word report.

When Mrs Foster's husband came downstairs, he asked her ... (l. 4), but she explained that ... She told him that ... and that ... (ll. 5-6). He wanted to know ... (7), and she reminded him that ... (8). Just when they seemed ready to leave, he told her that ... (12). So he went upstairs again, telling her that ... and instructing her ... (12-13).

By the time Mr Foster reappeared, it was 9.20. When he had got in the car, she told the chauffeur ..., because ... (23). But no sooner had the man started the engine than Mr Foster ordered him ... (25-26). Mrs Foster wanted to know ... (27), and he explained that ... (28). He felt sure that ... (29). His wife asked him ... (30), and he explained to her ..., which ... (31-32). After searching through his pockets, Mr Foster announced that he ... probably ... (37). He wanted to go and look for it, but his wife begged him ..., reminding him that ... (38-39). He took no notice of her, however, and said ... (40). By this time, it was almost 9.30, and Mrs Foster was wondering ... (45). While her husband was in the house, Mrs Foster suddenly noticed the box in the crack of the car seat. When she saw it wedged down so deep, she wondered ... (51).

2 Disappointments and misunderstandings

GG 150–151; GhE 320, 322

Things don't always turn out as we expect, do they? Sometimes other people disappoint us – or we misunderstand what they meant in the first place, or ...

Complete these pieces of dialogue with your own ideas. Use reported speech.
Examples: 'I won't be able to get to your party till ten at the earliest.' – 'But **you said you would come** at eight-thirty.'
'Donna's been dropped from the volleyball team.' – 'But **I thought she was** their best player!'

1 'I've decided to give Betsy a box of chocolates for her birthday.' – 'But you told me ...'
2 'Your photos aren't ready yet, unfortunately.' – 'But when I brought them in, ...'
3 'Dr Singh is very busy this morning. Please take a seat in the waiting-room.' – 'But ...'
4 'Have you heard? Ted has failed all his A-levels.' – 'That's strange. ...'
5 'I'm going to stay with my aunt in Melbourne.' – 'Really? You never told me ...'
6 'John's getting married next Saturday.' – 'What! I never even knew ...'
7 'My Dad's in the USA on business. He's got a big meeting in Toronto.' – 'Uh? I thought ...'
8 'It's no good asking Steve what's the matter with your goldfish.' – 'Why not? ...'

Boy:
When I grow up, I'm going to be a policeman and follow my father's footsteps.
Friend:
I didn't know your dad was a policeman.
Boy:
He's not, he's a burglar.

'Excuse me, but did I hear you say you were a veterinary surgeon?'

3 The case of the young woman named Sherlock Holmes GG 150–152; GhE 320, 322, 327

The Case of the Young Woman Named Sherlock Holmes was a problem I solved the easy way a couple of years ago. George Spencer had told me that a guy he knew named Harry Huff was going to marry a girl named Sherlock Holmes. I said this was nonsense, because there isn't any girl named Sherlock Holmes. He said I didn't know anything about it. I said it was dangerous to believe everything one heard, and to go around repeating it.

I got out the phone book. There were two Henry Huffs listed, and I called the first one.

'Nah,' he said, 'I'm living in sin with Dr Watson. I thought everybody knew that.' He was obviously the wrong Henry Huff, and I hung up on him. The second one turned out to be the right one. I asked him to spell out the name of his fiancée. Without hesitation, he said he didn't want to, so I mentioned George Spencer and what he had said about Sherlock Holmes. Huff was annoyed, but he finally told me the name of the girl he was going to marry, one Shirley Combs.

9 **to live in sin** to live with someone without being married – 12 **his fiancée** [fɪ'ɑːnseɪ] the woman he is going to marry

From *Thurber Country* by James Thurber

1 *Read the text carefully, and pick out all the examples of reported speech.*
2 *Look at the text again, and try to reconstruct (in direct speech) the author's conversation with George Spencer, and his second telephone conversation, both described in the text in reported speech.*
Make them as lively as you can, by going beyond the text where it seems appropriate.

4 The giant ice-cream GG 150–152; GhE 320, 322, 327, 328.1

Look at the cartoon carefully. Then make a little story around it, using reported speech wherever you can. You could start like this:

One day, when Johnnie was out for a drive with his father, he saw … He **thought** … He **asked** … So his father **said** …, and parked the car. They got out together, and … **(asked/wondered/couldn't understand/explained …)**
Go on. End the story when Johnnie and his father have got back in the car.

5 Missing GG 150–151, **153**; GhE 320, 322, **325–326**

Mr and Mrs Bassett of Leeds gave the following statement to the police on August 3rd:

'Everything seemed quite normal this morning. Mark, our 15-year-old son, went out today, as he often does on Saturdays. He wanted to go to a football match, and we expected him back for tea this afternoon. But he hasn't come back. We didn't want to call the police unnecessarily, but when he still hadn't appeared by nine o'clock tonight, we decided to ring up and report him missing.'

At the beginning of November, Mrs Bassett was interviewed by a local newspaper reporter:

'Tomorrow it will be three months since Mark went missing. We have no idea what has happened to him. It was Mark's birthday last week. I bought him a present, as usual, hoping he would come home, but he still isn't here. We're going to talk to the police again next week, but they've discovered nothing up to now. It's the uncertainty that's so difficult to bear. One day I think to myself, "Perhaps tomorrow at this time he'll come walking in the door and everything will be all right." And another day I wonder if we'll ever see him again.'

Adverbials of time (e.g. *this morning, today, next week*) and place (e.g. *here*) sometimes have to be changed in reported speech. This is only necessary when the report is made at a time or place at which use of the original adverbials **would not apply.**

The following January, there was an article in the paper about young people missing from home:

Each year, over 90,000 young people in Britain go missing from their homes. Many of them return to their families of their own accord, others are found by the police; a few are found dead. But a large number of these missing youngsters disappear altogether. The following example is just one of many.

In August last year, Mr and Mrs Bassett of Leeds reported the disappearance of their son Mark. They told police that everything had seemed quite normal **that morning** ...

28 **of one's own accord** without being asked or told

Go on with the report, including the November interview with Mrs Bassett.

6 Hedgehogs as pets? GG 150–152; GhE 322

Translate the text. These words and expressions will help you:
the latest fashion in pets (ll. 1-2) – to appear for sale (4) – travelling dealers (6-7) – environment (10-11) – to breed (animals) (13) – to appeal as pets (15) – application (16) – to be made within Canadian law (17) – to lay down conditions (for) (18-19) – hedgehog lovers (20) – a spokesman for (21) – the British Hedgehog Preservation Society (21-22) – to be suitable as (25) – to roam (25-26)

Igel aus Europa sind in Nordamerika als Haustiere zur Zeit der letzte Schrei. Sie werden jetzt importiert und sind schon in einigen Zoohandlungen in den USA zum Verkauf aufgetaucht.

Mr Rick Sisco, der Besitzer eines Zoogeschäftes in Fort Lauderdale, Florida, berichtete, daß reisende Händler ihm junge Igel für 100 Dollar angeboten hätten, daß sie ihm aber nicht gesagt hätten, woher die Tiere kämen. Mr Sisco kaufte die Igel nicht. Er sagte, er könne ihnen nicht den natürlichen Lebensraum geben, den sie brauchten.

In Kanada sagte Mr Todd McBride, der Igel importieren und sie als Haustiere züchten möchte, er glaube, daß Igel besonders in ländlichen Gegenden als Haustiere Anklang finden würden. Er betonte, daß sein Antrag, die Igel einzuführen, dem kanadischen Recht entsprechend gestellt worden sei, welches strenge Bedingungen für die Einfuhr von Tieren aufstellt.

Igel-Liebhaber in Großbritannien sind gegen diese Exporte. Ein Sprecher der britischen Gesellschaft zur Erhaltung der Igel sagte, sie seien nicht gegen den Export der Igel an Zoos, wo sie gezüchtet werden könnten, aber sie glaubten nicht, daß Igel sich als Haustiere eigneten, da sie gerne herumwandern, besonders nachts.

Based on an article in *The Sunday Telegraph,* November 3, 1990

8 Advanced Exercises

Roger talking to Mark on the phone: Hello, Mark. Roger here. Look, I know this is a bit sudden, but I was wondering if you and Ann would like to come to Osmotherley and spend the weekend with us at the cottage? The weather forecast sounds quite promising, so it should be ideal for walking on the moors. Well, how about it?	*Mark later, talking to Ann:* Roger rang up this morning and invited us to spend the weekend with them at Osmotherley. He said they were planning to do some walking on the moors.

In most situations, it is natural **not** to give a word-for-word report of what has been said. Often it is enough to give a **summary** of the most important points.

1 Mr Van Huyten makes an offer GhE 319

Vic Brown is twenty. He works as a draughtsman (techn. Zeichner) *for a big engineering works in the North of England. On Saturdays he earns a little extra money working in Mr Van Huyten's record and music shop, a job he enjoys. One day Mr Van Huyten talks to him …*

'How do you like your work, Victor?' he asks me all of a sudden, and I give a shrug. I hate to admit it but I have to be honest with Mr Van Huyten. 'Oh, so so.'

'Only so so?'

'I liked it well enough for the first two or three years,' I tell him, 'but now, just lately … I've been a bit unsettled, as you might say.'

'You don't think it's just a change of scene you need? There comes a time in every man's life when he feels the need of a change.'

'I don't think it's that, Mr Van Huyten. I'm just tired of the work. I want something different altogether. I feel I want to meet different people …'

'You like it in the shop on Saturdays?'

'I enjoy it. It's grand.'

'Have you ever considered doing something like that full time?'

I'm a bit embarrassed at this. 'Well, to tell you the truth, Mr Van Huyten, I don't think the money's there. All the time you hear of shop assistants going to work in factories to get more money.'

He nods. 'I agree. The money isn't very good for the ordinary shop assistant. One must have er … an interest in the business for it to be worthwhile.'

He sits back in his chair. 'I'm an old man, Victor,' he says. 'Older than you probably think. I have a sound business which looks as though it will continue to prosper.' He smiles a bit. 'There's even room for expansion, but I'm past the age for striking out that way … I'm an old man,' he says again, 'and I have no living relatives. I was never fortunate enough to have children. I may have a few cousins or half-cousins in Holland, but I don't know them and they don't know me.' He stops for a minute. 'I don't want to say too much, Victor, because you're still a very young man, not yet of age … But I will say in all honesty that I'm very fond of you and have every faith in your character and ability. You've become rapidly familiar with the business even though you spend only one day a week with us …'

I'm wondering what he's driving at. Is he trying to tell me he wants to leave me the shop? I begin to feel excited, and a bit scared at the same time.

'The immediate problem, Victor, is that I'm going to be compelled to take on a full-time assistant in the shop. I want someone whom I can like and trust, someone to whom eventually, when I decide to retire and take things more easily, in a few years' time, I can hand over the day-to-day running of the business.'

1 **to give a shrug** to move one's shoulders up (as a sign of indecision, etc.) – 20 **sound** solid, financially safe – 21 **to prosper** to be a success – 26 **of age** over 18 (*here:* over 21) – 33 **to be compelled** to be forced – 35 **eventually** in the end – 41 **prospects** good chances for future success – 43 **to fancy** to feel keen on, to like

'What you're saying, Mr Van Huyten, is that you'd like me to come and work full-time in the shop.'

He nods again. 'Correct. Now assuming the money was, shall we say comparable, and there were prospects of a future when you wouldn't be just a shop assistant in a dead-end job, what would you say then?'

'I don't know, Mr Van Huyten.' I think about it for a minute. 'I rather fancy the idea. I've always liked working in the shop, as you know ...' I realize he's not expecting an answer off the cuff, and I say, 'Thanks very much for your offer, Mr Van Huyten, and I'd like to think it over, please.'

'Well done,' he says. 'A very reasonable answer. The last thing I wanted was for you to jump to a decision without considering every side of the matter.'

'I'll have to talk it over at home, you see.'

'Of course, of course. Naturally.'

From *A Kind of Loving* by Stan Barstow

Think out what Vic might say to his parents that evening. Before you start, pick out the most important points in the conversation, from Vic's point of view.

2 The anonymous letter GhE 321

When Ed gets home, his wife Greta shows him an anonymous letter, both unpleasant and threatening, which has come while he was at work. It is the third he has received ... All have been signed 'Anon'.

Many authors use **'inner monologue'** as a way of showing their characters' unspoken thoughts and feelings. For this style of writing, the 'backshift' of tenses is used, as in reported speech; but mostly, the introductory verb is left out and word order is the same as in direct speech.

As he let the water rinse away the soap, he thought, *I'm washing my hands of the subway and also of that damned letter.* Who was writing the letters? Someone who lived in his neighbourhood, probably. Ed two weeks ago had asked George, one of the doormen downstairs, if any stranger had asked for his name, if he'd seen anyone odd hanging around, male or female, and George had said no. Ed was sure George had asked the other doormen the same question. Was it someone in his office? Inconceivable, Ed thought. Yet one never knew, did one? A poison-pen letter-writer didn't necessarily stare at you, wouldn't be obviously an enemy. On the other hand, Anon's letters seemed genuinely dim-witted, not like anyone at C. & D., even the clean-up men. The letters annoyed Ed, but they frightened Greta, and Ed didn't want to show even his annoyance too much, lest it augment her fear. And perhaps he was a little afraid, too. Someone had singled him out to write to. Or was he the only recipient? Were there other people in his neighbourhood just as annoyed as he was?

7 **inconceivable** impossible to imagine – 10 **dim-witted** stupid, unintelligent – 12 **lest it happen** for fear that it might happen – **to augment** to make greater – 14 **recipient** person who receives s.th. (e.g. a letter)

From *A Dog's Ransom* by Patricia Highsmith

1 *Pick out all examples of direct speech, reported speech and inner monologue in the text.*
2 *Put the inner monologue into direct speech, then into reported speech, using suitable introductory verbs (e.g.* think/wonder/suppose/realize*). Explain the differences.*
3 *Try to describe the stylistic effect of inner monologue in this text. What impression does it make on you?*

9 The Passive Voice

Check-up

1 The by-pass

Change the active structures (in italics) into the passive. Decide where a 'by-agent' is necessary.

Last night the villagers of Botesdale in Suffolk met to protest against the Department of Transport's decision to postpone the building of the A143 by-pass between Wattisfield and Wortham. *The county council had agreed to the plan for the new road* two years ago. The construction of the by-pass was to begin next year, but now *the Department of Transport has informed the council* that *it cannot finance the project* until the late 1990s.

'We need the by-pass now,' said a speaker at the meeting. *'Enormous numbers of cars use the existing road through the village* on their way to the East Coast. *The constant noise of traffic badly affects people living on Botesdale High Street.* Over the past six years *lorries driving at high speed have killed or seriously injured nine people. Inhabitants no longer consider Botesdale a safe place for children,* who are especially at risk; not surprisingly, *house-owners are selling property here at an alarming rate. We must save our village community* before it is too late.'

At the end of the meeting, *the villagers decided on a course of action. They asked people* to sign a petition, *which they will send to the Department of Transport* before the end of the month.

by-pass a road leading traffic round a town or village instead of through it – 2 **to postpone** to put off until a later time – 13 **property** houses and land owned by s. o. – **rate** *here:* speed

2 Police kicked and beaten in quiet area of Canterbury

Add the passive forms (in the correct tense) to this newspaper article.

attack
start
shatter

do
beat kick not require
help
do arrest hear

carry out ask

Two policemen … as they tried to break up a fight in a quiet area of Canterbury in the early hours of Sunday. The trouble … by two rival gangs. Within seconds the peace and quiet of Surrey Road … by the noise of breaking glass and shouting. Police officers Sean Murphy and Bob Wilcox arrived at the scene only after considerable damage … . When they tried to make arrests, they … and … . Hospital treatment … , however, and they were able to remain on duty. They … by more police officers who arrived before any further damage … . So far, seven people … . They … in court next month.

Further investigations … still … , and witnesses … to pass on any information that might help the police.

3 **to shatter** to break, to disturb suddenly

How the passive is used

The question of the origin of the universe **is** often **discussed.**	1 The passive is preferred when the 'doer' is obvious, unimportant, or unknown.
Aristotle's idea of the earth as the centre of the universe **was** first **doubted** *by Copernicus* in 1514.	2 The 'by-agent' is used if it is important to say by whom (or by what) something is done.
At the London 'Planetarium', *visitors* **are shown** a vivid picture of how stars and planets are born – and die. Thanks to modern telescopes, fantastic new opportunities **have been given** *to scientists studying outer space.*	3 Certain verbs with two objects (e.g. *give, show* – see list 'Type *give*' on page 121) are often used with a 'personal' subject in the passive. The alternative construction with *to* is only used if the indirect object is emphasized, or especially long.
Signs of life on other planets **have** long **been searched for** with the help of radio telescopes.	4 Prepositions closely linked to verbs (e.g. *search for, look after, break into*) remain in the same position in the passive.
More research will need **to be done** before a manned mission to Mars can **be attempted.**	5 The passive also has an infinitive form (with or without *to*).
All the time, new discoveries about the nature of the universe **are being made.**	6 Progressive forms of the passive can be used in the present and past.

Note

A lot of science fiction stories are about spaceships that **get attacked** by aliens.

The passive with get *is often used in spoken English to express that an event is unintended or unexpected.*

'Doesn't it make you sick? Our baggage has been sent to Jupiter!'

'But Mars is in conjunction with Saturn, and I'm a Capricorn! I wasn't supposed to be knocked down by a car today!'

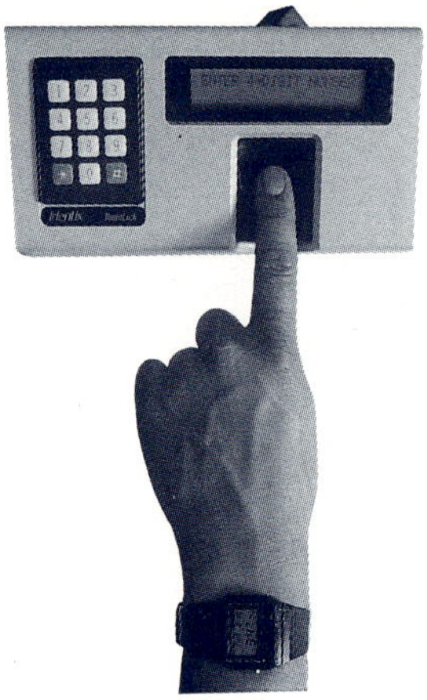

1 Biometric security? GG 77–80; GhE 178, 58–61

For many centuries, keys have been a common part of everyday life. But keys and combination locks could eventually be made obsolete by a new kind of technology: biometrics. Some time in the future, a person's entry into rooms and buildings will be controlled by special computers that will be designed to recognize personal characteristics such as fingerprints or voice. If the computer (or 'biometric' machine) is shown the correct 'personal data', the door will automatically be opened; but permission to enter will not be given to any 'unauthorized' person trying to work the machine.

The advantages of such a system are obvious. Copies can be made of keys, combination locks may be cracked, and the computerized cards that are sometimes used for hotel bedrooms are frequently lost or stolen. Biometric locks would mean that buildings could not be broken into so easily, and of course no more problems would be caused by 'forgetting your key'.

In the USA, biometric lock systems are already being produced – and sold. So far they have been invested in mainly by banks, research laboratories, and other institutions with a special interest in security. The most common version of the new computer is the 'fingerprint scanner', which is now being introduced for domestic use in Japan. Because of the high price, it is not expected to be installed in many American homes yet, but in time biometric security systems will probably be made widespread use of.

2 **eventually** in the end – **obsolete** outdated, no longer in use – 17 **scanner** machine used to examine things closely

1 *Find examples of the use of the passive as described in the Basic Rules.*
2 *Use the passive to explain briefly how the biometric security system works, and what its advantages are. Begin like this:*
A special kind of computer is designed to recognize the user's …
3 *Translate the text into German.*

2 Hallowe'en is being abused GG 77–80; GhE 178, 58–61, 63

Children throughout Britain have been asked not to play 'trick or treat?' pranks on old people on Hallowe'en. In recent years an increasing number of complaints have been made by older people about children and teenagers who abuse this traditional American custom. Now police warn that action will be taken against any young people who make hidden threats if their demand for money is not met. Last night on BBC TV a police spokesman for the West Yorkshire Constabulary, Inspector George Stevens, said: 'There have been incidents in the past in which flower-pots were kicked over or windows smashed. Sometimes fireworks even get thrown through letter-boxes. We don't think old people should have to put up with behaviour like that.' Inspector Stevens added that especially old people living alone could get badly shaken when doorbells were rung late at night – or if they opened their doors in the evening and were surprised by a group of youngsters wearing strange masks. 'The custom has been misunderstood by a lot of youngsters,' commented Inspector Stevens. 'Old people's helplessness is being taken unfair advantage of. It's an alarming sign of the times we're living in, I'm afraid.'

Hallowe'en October 31st, a 'party night', traditionally associated with ghosts and witches – **to abuse** to use in the wrong way – 2 **prank** foolish trick – 6 **demand** asking for s.th you expect to get

1 *Find the 'by-agents'. Say whether/why they are important.*
2 *Explain, using the passive,*
a *what complaints the police have received;*
b *what kind of incidents there have been;*
c *what will happen if there is more trouble.*

3 *Use passive forms choosing from the verbs on the left to complete what these people said about Hallowe'en when they were interviewed by a reporter for BBC television.*

deal with
hear of
look after
look into
make too much of
pay for
take advantage of

a 'Incidents of this kind ... never ... when I was a teenager.'
b 'I don't think hooliganism ... strictly enough – by parents or by the police.'
c 'Most of these pranks are harmless. They shouldn't ...
d 'Windows even got broken in our road last year. Damage of this kind must ...'
e 'It's no joke when old people ... like this.'
f 'Punishing these young people won't help. The real reasons for their behaviour need ...'
g 'This sort of thing wouldn't happen if kids ... properly. Parents these days don't give them enough of their time.'

3 Facing up to vandalism GG 77–80; GhE 178, 58–61, 63

What does vandalism mean to you?

Next time you're out take a good look around you. The chances are that somewhere you'll see the work of vandals. You may have to look no further than the shattered phone box; the broken windows in the bus shelter, the damaged trees in the park or street.
That's the unpleasant reality of vandalism, and it's something that most of us will suffer from at some time or other.
At best, vandalism may be unsightly or just inconvenient. At worst it may cause injury or even endanger life.
In an emergency, for example, that damaged call-box could lead to serious delay in summoning the fire brigade or an ambulance – a delay which could be fatal.

Vandalism is everyone's problem

If your home or car has ever been damaged, you know what an expensive business it can be. But think how much more vandalism costs the country as a whole.
Replacing telephones, repairing lifts, renewing seats on buses and trains, replacing young trees and shrubs. Each year the cost runs into tens of *millions,* and you pay for it – through rates, rents, taxes and higher prices. It's *your* money, money which might be better spent on new school buildings or hospitals. Once again it's the community which suffers.

The police need your help

Don't turn a blind eye to vandalism

If you see anything suspicious, don't hesitate – dial 999

Prepared for the Home Office by the Central Office of Information 1979. Printed in the UK for HMSO.

Dd 8934131 HOME J0262R 8/85.

4 **to shatter** *here:* to damage – 6 **shelter** place (protected from rain, etc.) where people wait – 10 **unsightly** unpleasant to look at – **inconvenient** causing difficulties – 13 **delay** a period of unwanted waiting – **to summon** to call – 20 **shrub** decorative bush – 22 **rates** a kind of tax – **suspicious** *verdächtig*

1 *What examples of vandalism – and its results – can you give? Use ideas from the text, and add more of your own. To start you off:*
Telephone boxes **are** often **damaged** so the telephones inside can't **be used** any more. Telephone books **are torn/get torn** ...
2 *What has to be done to restore order after acts of vandalism?*
Example: Telephones that **have been damaged** often have **to be replaced** by new ones.
3 *Has there been any vandalism in your area recently? Describe what was done – and where.*

9 4 The new Noah GG 77–80; GhE 178, 58–61

In 'The new Noah', Gerald Durrell describes his experiences as an animal collector in many parts of the world, and the unusual situations in which he found himself during his travels.

Before starting out on a collecting trip you have to know what wild animals are wanted by the zoos; then, knowing their whereabouts, you choose those areas in which not only the specimens required are to be found, but other rare creatures as well. Zoologists and biologists, generally, have not the time or the money to travel to these distant corners of the earth to find out about wild life on the spot. Therefore, the animals have to be caught and brought back to them, so that they can be studied more conveniently in the zoo. Now the larger and commoner creatures from most parts of the world are well represented in nearly all zoological collections, and quite a lot is known about them. So it was the smaller and rarer beasts, about which we know so little, that I wanted to collect.

From many points of view it is sometimes the small animals in a country that influence man more than the large ones. At home, for instance, the brown rat does more damage every year than any of the larger creatures. It was for this reason that I concentrated during my collecting trips on the smaller forms of life. For my first expedition I chose the Cameroons, since it is a small, almost forgotten corner of Africa, which is more or less as it was before the advent of the white man. Here, in the gigantic rain forests, the animals live their lives as they have done for thousands of years.

It is of great value to get to know and study these wild creatures before they are influenced by civilisation, for wild creatures can be affected just as much by change as people. One of the results of cutting down forests, building towns, damming rivers, and driving roads through jungle, is an interference with their way of life, and they have either to adapt themselves to the new conditions or die out.

I landed at the little port of Victoria and had to spend a week or so there, preparing for the journey into the interior. A great many things had to be done before I could start on the actual work of collecting. There were Africans to engage as cooks or house-boys, various stores to buy and a great many other things as well. Also the necessary permits to hunt and capture the animals I was after had to be obtained, for all the animal life in the Cameroons is strictly protected and, unless you obtain Government permission, you are not allowed to capture or kill any animals and birds. Eventually, when all this had been done, a lorry was hired and the food and equipment piled into it, and I set off.

From *The new Noah* by Gerald Durrell

3 **specimen** ['spesɪmən] a single animal or plant which is an example of a particular kind – 7 **conveniently** *here:* easily – 17 **advent** ['--] – 23 **interference** [ˌ--'--] unwanted attempt to influence others' affairs – 31 **to obtain** to get – 33 **to capture** to take as a prisoner, to catch

'Damned thing's been following us about all day hoping to be discovered.'

1 *Use the passive wherever possible in your answers to the following questions:*
a *What first has to be done before rare animals can be studied in zoos?*
b *Why did Durrel specialize in collecting smaller animals?*
c *Why were the Cameroons chosen as a collecting-ground for his first expedition?*
d *Why are so many wild animals in danger of dying out?*
e *What preparations had to be made before Durrell could set off into the interior of the Cameroons?*

2 *Put these sentences into the passive:*
a We know so little about the smaller and rarer beasts.
b Small animals sometimes influence man more than larger ones.
c The brown rat does more damage every year than any of the larger creatures.

3 *Using the information in the text, complete these sentences with passive infinitives:*
a The area in which the rare creatures are to … must … carefully.
b Animals' lives can … considerably by any changes that may … to their environment.
c No animal or bird may … or … without Government permission.

4 *What do you think? Should animals be kept in captivity? Use some of the verbs below – in the passive – to help express your opinion.*
Example: Zoos can be very educational. All sorts of interesting animals, which most people would normally never meet, **can be seen** in zoos.

see look after spend (money) be born improve lock up
feed keep (in natural/unnatural surroundings) allow transport
treat give show crowd (in small cages) leave

5 Having it done

GG 124; GhE 284, 64

'Has your house been repainted?' – Yes, we **had it repainted** last summer. We **had it done** by Carter's.'

A passive idea can sometimes be expressed with the '*have*-passive', which is used when a person causes an action to be done by someone else. The *'have*-passive' can also be used with a *by-agent.*

*Complete these mini-dialogues, using suitable forms of the 'have-*passive'.
1 'Your hair's getting a bit long.' – 'Yes, I really ought …'
2 'That big birch tree in front of the window makes this room very dark.' – 'Why don't you …?'
3 'There's something wrong with this stupid walkman!' – 'Well, don't throw it away! Perhaps you …'
4 'This is a nice photo of Sally! Who took it?' – 'We … by …'
5 'Don't look so worried – you're only going to the dentist's!' – 'I've got to …'
6 'Did you put up the wallpaper yourselves?' – 'Yes, we did. It would have cost the earth if we … professionally.'

9 Advanced Exercises

1 Other forms of the passive GG 77, 100.1, 112.1, 121.1; GhE 256

Look at the passive structures in the following sentences. What forms are used here?

1 Medical students sometimes feel faint when they watch an operation being done for the first time.
2 These instruments ought to have been sterilized, nurse.
3 Many people dislike being prescribed strong drugs, as they are afraid of being affected by unpleasant side-effects.
4 The cut on John's knee has healed well in spite of not having been stitched.
5 Having been given a local anaesthetic, the patient was able to carry on a conversation with the doctor while being operated on.
6 The girl being wheeled into the operating theatre just now was involved in a terrible road accident.

2 To wear or not to wear? GG 77, 100.1, 112.1, 121.1, GhE 256

Use the right passive forms to complete what these people say about furs.

see influence	*Kate (model):* I'm afraid of … in a fur coat now that everyone's started … by the animal rights movement.
threaten **close** **close sell**	*Sarah (London shop assistant):* Recently a lot of stores … with bomb attacks by animal liberationists. Our fur department is going … altogether now. It ought … last winter really – hardly any furs … here then either.
force **give**	*Liza (actress):* After … to wear a fur coat in my last film, I've now decided to make a written refusal before … any new role.
wear **bring up**	*Tom (animal liberationist):* I've never liked the idea of dead animals … on people's backs. … in a family that loved animals, I suppose that's not surprising.
farm **put off** **wear** **inform** **brainwash**	*David (in the fur trade):* Actually, furs … in just the same way as meat. There's absolutely no reason at all for … wearing furs. After all, since man's earliest days, furs … always … to keep out the cold. There's nothing better. If people … properly, they would see things in proportion. These days there's an enormous danger – especially for young people – of … by the media.

3 An unusual friendship GG 78–80, 125; GhE 58–61, 300–301

'The Ice House' is an unusual novel about familiar themes – love, marriage and friendship. The main characters, Daisy and Ruth, in spite of their very different personalities, have been friends since their schooldays. This extract is from the first part of the book, where their strange friendship is described.

That summer Saturday in 1951, Daisy Brown aged fifteen, going to tea with Ruth Perkin, also aged fifteen, had an unusual sense of adventure. The invitation, shyly offered, oddly phrased – 'My father says you may come to tea, Saturday', Ruth had said – was unique. No one that Daisy knew had ever been asked to the Perkin house. And although Ruth had been to tea with Daisy, her visits had been arranged more formally than the free and easy Brown household was used to: telephone calls at least a week in advance

4 **unique** [juːˈniːk] the only one of its kind – 13 **sympathetically** with understanding – **to dismiss** *here:* to pass over as unimportant – **extraordinary** [ɪkˈstrɔːdnrɪ] extremely unusual – **acute maternal anxiety** [əˈkjuːt] strong feeling of worry by a mother for her cild – 14 **as the fancy took her** whenever she felt like it, without any obvious reason – 15 **intriguing** [ɪnˈtriːgɪŋ] fascinating – 16 **casual** [ˈkæʒʊəl] relaxed and unworried – **restraints** controls, restrictons – **imposed** placed by some authority

between the two mothers, the exact time of Ruth's arrival, the exact time she was expected home, always stated and rigidly kept to. Ruth was not allowed out later than seven o'clock summer evenings, six o'clock in the winter.

'Nervous, poor soul, a hen with one chick,' Mrs Brown said of Mrs Perkin, sympathetically dismissing this extraordinary tyranny as acute maternal anxiety. Daisy, accustomed to coming and going as the fancy took her, found Ruth's situation more intriguing. Daisy was popular, she had plenty of friends that she made use of in a casual way, but the restraints imposed on this particular friendship made her value it more. Ruth never complained. Once, perhaps as an excuse, or an explanation, she said, 'My father was a Japanese prisoner during the war. He worked on the railway.' And another time, more seriously, 'My mother is always polishing under the mats in the hall.' Otherwise she seldom mentioned her home or her parents, keeping silent when other girls spoke of theirs, and, if they grumbled, smiled in a composed and secretive way that excited Daisy to romantic conjecture of an innocently snobbish and commonplace kind.

From *The Ice House* by Nina Bawden

1 *What complicated arrangements were made before Ruth was allowed to visit her friend?*
2 *What sort of up-bringing do you think the two girls had? Use the passive in your answer. Here are some verbs to help you:*
look after, protect, allow, give, watch over, love, force, encourage, expect.
3 *'The invitation, shyly* ***offered****, was unique.' (ll. 2-4). Find further examples in the text of past participles used in this way, and replace them by relative clauses.*
4 *The passive is sometimes used in literary texts to create an impersonal atmosphere. Do you think this effect is used here? Explain.*

4 The sense of smell GG 81, 100.3; GhE 62, 277 A1

Translate into English. Remember that passive constructions are sometimes used in English where you would find active constructions – especially with 'man' – in German.

1 Man sagt, daß der Geruchssinn Erinnerungen schneller heraufbeschwört als unsere anderen Sinne. *(to evoke)*
2 Man nimmt an, daß die meisten Menschen etwa 4000 Gerüche unterscheiden können. *(to differentiate between)*
3 Leute mit besonders empfindlichen Nasen sollen sogar 10.000 verschiedene Düfte erkennen können! *(sensitive)*
4 Frauen sind vermutlich geruchsempfindlicher als Männer. *(sensitive to smell)*
5 Man weiß, daß ein Baby von einem Monat seine Mutter an ihrem Geruch identifizieren kann. *(to identify s.o.by s.th.)*
6 Vor kurzem hat man auch entdeckt, daß Mütter in der Lage sind, die T-shirts ihrer Kinder am Geruch zu erkennen.
7 Bis zum 19. Jahrhundert hat man Körpergeruch nicht als unangenehm empfunden. Ob er je wieder in Mode kommt, bleibt aber abzuwarten. *(body odour, to consider)*
8 In der heutigen Zeit von Deos und Parfums ist eine solche Entwicklung [allerdings] kaum zu erwarten! *(in these days of deodorants and perfumes)*

Common phrases with the passive:
... is/are said to ...
... is/are supposed to ...
... is/are thought to ...
It is to be expected ...
It remains to be seen ...

9

Grave humour

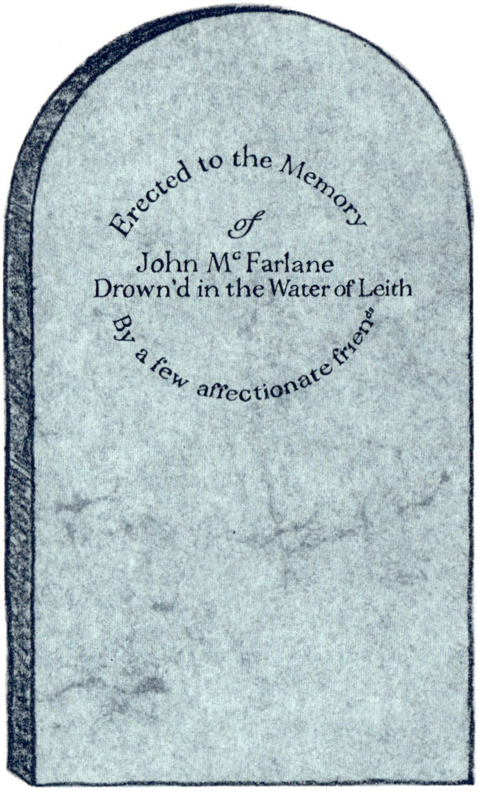

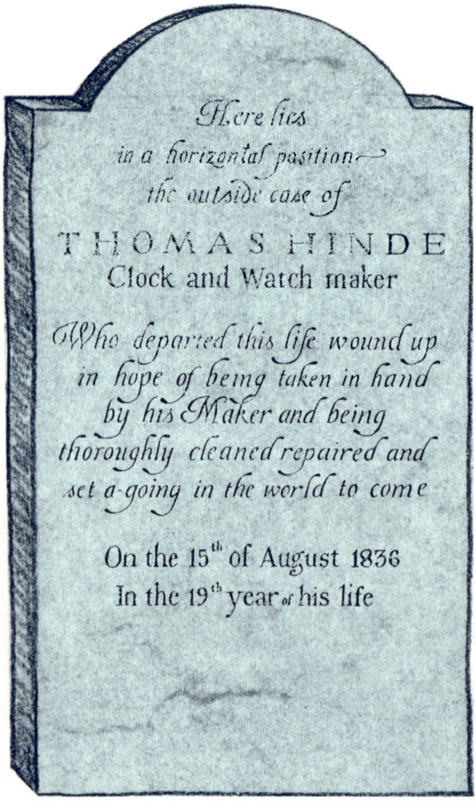

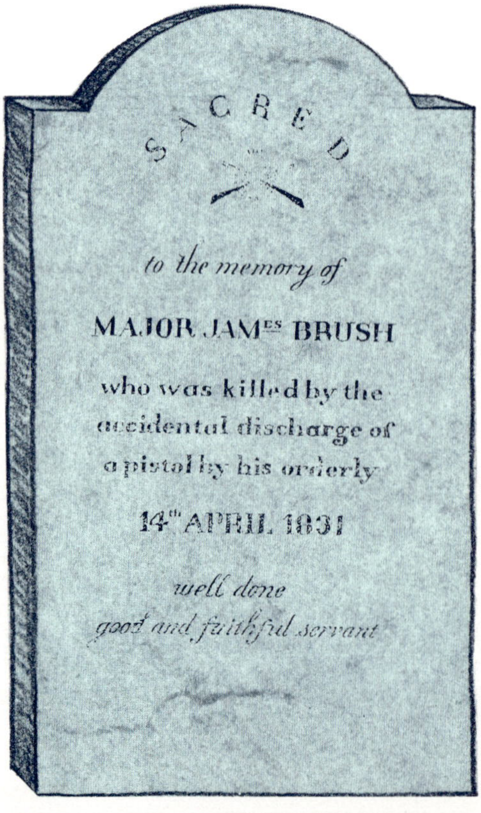

Modal Auxiliaries 10

Check-up

1 Summer time

Fill in suitable auxiliaries to fit these everyday situations.

1 *Choose between* can, can't, will, won't, may *and* may not.

- 'Let's go down to the beach now. It ... be so sunny this afternoon, you never know.'
- 'O.K. Wait – I ... find my sun-tan cream.'
- 'You ... use mine. – Hey, whose are those super flippers?'
- 'John's. But we ... take them. He ... let *anyone* borrow his things.'
- 'And this snorkel?'
- 'That ... be his, too, of course. Nobody else would have such a posh one. Come on – swimming ... be just as much fun *without* all this equipment.'
- 'O.K. You ... be right.'

2 *Now choose between* must, may, mustn't *and* needn't.

- 'How much further do you plan to go? We ... have walked miles along this beach by now!'
- 'All right. We ... go any further if you don't want to. Let's put our things down and go in the water straight away.'
- 'Have you seen that sign? "No swimming beyond this point." We ... swim in that direction, then. I wonder why.'
- 'I don't know exactly, but it ... be because of the river estuary. There ... be some reason.'
- 'I'll have a swim later. ... I borrow your camera to take a photo of those cormorants?'
- 'O.K., but you ... wade out to those rocks with it! I know what you're like.'
- 'You ... worry. I won't go near the water – even if you're drowning!'

4 **flippers** *Schwimmflossen* – 7 **posh** *here*: expensive-looking – 17 **estuary** ['estjʊərɪ] place where a river widens and joins the sea – 20 **cormorant** ['–––] sea-bird – 21 **to wade** to walk through water

2 Things were different then!

When Lucy's great-grandmother comes to stay, she notices how things have changed since she was a girl...
Put in suitable positive or negative forms of have to, be allowed to, be able to.

'You don't realize how lucky you are, Lucy! When I was a girl, we all ... wear thick black stockings for school, even in the heat of summer. We ... wear shorts at all – in fact, we ... even ... be seen in trousers!

'Nowadays, all you young people learn to drive. In my day, not many people ... afford a car. Luckily, my parents had one, but I'm afraid I ... often ... drive it. My father thought women ought not ... drive at all! Motoring was rather a hit-and-miss affair in those days. You ... take a driving test at all. You just bought your car, and you ... drive off in it without a single lesson. So of course quite a few accidents were caused by people that ... control their cars properly. There wasn't much traffic though, and when you went shopping, it was quite usual to ... park your car in front of each shop.

'When I was young, far fewer women ... go to university. Most of the places were reserved for men. I went into teaching, as you know, but when I got married, I automatically ... give up my job. I don't think many women would get married today if they ... do that, do you?'

10 Basic Rules and Exercises

1 What modal auxiliaries express

Common modal auxiliaries:	How to use them:	When to use them:
will / would can / could may	**Will / Would/Can/Could** you open the window, please? **May/Can** I sit here? – Yes, of course you **may**. You **can** have the window seat if you like. I **can** see the lights of New York already.	1 when asking someone to do something 2 when asking for permission 3 when giving permission 4 when talking about abilities
must / mustn't needn't	You **must** fasten your seatbelt. You **mustn't** smoke in here. I **must** apply for a new passport. You **needn't** show your ticket. Only your boarding card.	5 when instructing s.o. – to do s.th. – not to do s.th. 6 when talking about a duty or necessity 7 when explaining that s.th. is unnecessary
should / ought to shouldn't / ought not to	You **should/ought to** read this article. I really **should/ought to** send Judy a card. You **shouldn't/ought not to** spend so much money on souvenirs.	8 when giving advice 9 when talking about a moral obligation 10 when expressing a criticism
may / might / could must / will	There **may/might/could** be a good view from that bridge. Look at that ruin. It **must/will** be the castle mentioned in the guidebook. We **could** go to the National Gallery this afternoon.	11 when expressing – a possibility – a strong probability 12 when making a suggestion

Note 1

I've asked him twice, but he **won't** change his mind.

Refusal to do something can be expressed by won't / will not.

Note 2

We **ought to have left** earlier. / The train **may have arrived** by now.

Perfect forms (e.g. ought to have / could have / may have + *past participle) are also commonly used.*

Can you think of anyone who might have a grudge against you?

grudge *Groll, Haß*

2 Substitutes

Modal auxiliaries only have a present and/or past tense form.
For other tenses verbs with similar meanings are used as substitutes.

Modal auxiliaries:	Substitutes:	How to use them:
can/could	be able to	Perhaps we'**ll be able to** swim to the island tomorrow.
may	be allowed to	**Were** you **allowed to** look through the coastguard's telescope?
mustn't	not be allowed to	We **weren't allowed** to use the swimming-pool while it was being cleaned.
must	have to	The 'Beach Hotel' **has had to** close down.
needn't	not have to	The atmosphere's very informal here. You **won't have to** change for dinner.

Note

Guests **have to** sign the Visitors' Book.
The hotel staff **aren't able to** provide breakfast before 7.30.

Substitute forms can also be used in the present tense.

1 In human hands GG 86–90; GhE 221–230

Money can buy many things, including the basics to which every human being on the planet has a right, but there are lots of things it can't guarantee. Money alone can't guarantee our health and fulfilment, nor can it guarantee the future of the giant panda or the Bengal tiger, the fish in the sea or the quality of our drinking water.

Many things have to change, to ensure that life remains worth living. We have to stop believing that what we can take from the planet is limitless; that there will always be more. There are no new places to look for vast untapped resources.

In practical terms, this means using resources as carefully and sparingly as possible. If human beings didn't take more than their fair share, we wouldn't have chronic pollution and starvation. Left to its own devices, nature will not tolerate lasting imbalances. Far-reaching global imbalance such as currently exists is a uniquely human phenomenon.

Luckily, the chance of solving this dilemma is also in human hands. But we must act decisively, and act now. When faced with impending disaster, psychologists tell us, many people are able to continue functioning only by denying the signs of catastrophe. Part of the denial process is becoming numbed into a state where people believe that even though things aren't going as well as they should be, there is little they can do about it.

In fact, nothing could be further from the truth. And many of us are beginning to recognize that every action we take can affect the well-being of the planet. Some things we can do on our own, whereas others require groups of like-minded people. There is no end to the things we can do. And of course they don't all have to be done at once. You can begin in small ways, taking it one step at a time.

From *How to be Green* by John Button of 'Friends of the Earth'

9 **untapped** not yet made use of – 10 **in practical terms** expressed in a practical way – 12 **left to its own devices** left alone – 14 **currently** at the present time – 16 **impending** threatening to happen – 18 **to deny s.th.** to say s.th. is not true – 19 **to numb** [nʌm] to put in a state without feeling – 24 **like-minded** of the same opinion

1 *Go through the text and find as many examples of different modal auxiliaries (including substitute forms) as you can. Explain what they express, using the information in the Basic Rules to guide you.*

2 *What's wrong here? Correct the statements by changing the auxiliaries.*
a We needn't continue to take as much as we like from the planet.
b Nature may tolerate unlimited pollution.
c We mustn't save our world before it is too late.
d Some people think we shouldn't do much to improve the situation.
e Naturally, we must change our ways overnight; things ought not to be done step by step.

3 *Use modal auxiliaries or their substitute forms to explain the meaning of the following.*
Example:
There are no new places to look for vast untapped resources. (ll. 8-9)
▶ We **can't** expect to find new resources anywhere.
a This means using resources as carefully and sparingly as possible. (10-11)
b The chance of solving this dilemma is in human hands. (15)
c When faced with impending disaster… (16)
d Others (= other actions) require groups of like-minded people. (23-24)

4 *Use* can, could, should(n't), must(n't), *etc., to suggest ways of protecting the planet. Think of …*
energy in the home food the 'throwaway' mentality
free time and holidays respecting the countryside transport
chemicals …
Examples:
People should eat food that is grown locally instead of expensive imported food.
A lot of energy can be saved by insulating houses properly.

2 The right thing to say GG 87; GhE 222

'Do you think we could have the window open? After all, we came here for the sea air.'

Choosing the right auxiliary in everyday situations can be quite important. If you want someone to shut the door, for example, it is much more polite to say, 'Could/Would you shut the door, please?' than simply 'Please shut the door.' *Decide what to say if …*

1 … you are sitting in a non-smoking area, and someone gets out a cigarette.
2 … the shop assistant shows you a nice pair of jeans and you want to know if they'll fit.
3 … you want to recommend a book to someone.
4 … a friend gives you quite an expensive present, which you feel was unnecessary.
5 … someone is standing in your way, so it is difficult for you to get past.
6 … the coffee you have ordered is cold.
7 … you see a child putting her hand into a monkey's cage at the zoo.
8 … you haven't quite understood what someone means.

3 What can have happened? GG 86.2, 82 A2, 90 A2, 93; GhE 221.1, 228, 232.1

'H'm! The sleeping-bag must have shrunk a bit.'

The perfect forms *must have ..., may have ..., might have ...* are often used to express possible explanations of unexpected situations, while *should have ..., ought to have ...* and *could have ...* can express criticism or regret.
Think what you might feel like saying in the following situations. Try various possibilities.

Examples:
You go to meet your friend at the station, but she doesn't appear.
▶ 'She must have missed the train.'
You want to send a friend a card from holiday, but you don't know his address.
▶ 'I ought to have packed my address book.'

1 There is an unexpected tailback on the motorway.
2 You and a friend have decided to go to a concert, but when you get there, you are told the tickets are sold out.
3 You have arranged to meet a friend at the swimming-pool, and are disappointed when she doesn't turn up.
4 It is 11 p.m. There is no reply when you ring your friend's number.
5 You want to cut out an article you have read in yesterday's paper – but you can't find the paper.
6 Your cat likes to go out at nights. One morning, it does not come back home.
7 There is a delicious cake for tea, and you have five pieces. Later, you feel sick.

1 **tailback** long line of cars in a jam

Equivalents of German sollen

You really **ought to/should** try this cheese – it's delicious!	*Should/ought to* is used to give advice, etc. (see Basic Rules, p. 78).
Shall I put the flowers on this table? **Shall we** have wine with our meal?	*Shall I ...?/Shall we ...?* is used to ask what someone else would like or advise you to do, or to make a suggestion.
Dogs **are not to** be taken into the hotel dining-room. Our visitors **were to** arrive at six.	*Be to* expresses 1 a rule or obligation that someone else has decided on; 2 a previously arranged plan.
I don't like fish, although it'**s supposed to** be/**is said to** be very good for you.	*Be supposed to/be said to* are used to express what is generally accepted as true.

4 Doctor, doctor ... GG 93; GhE 231, 232, 233A2

Fill in the appropriate equivalents of sollen. *If you think more than one form is possible, say so.*

1 'Doctor, doctor, what ... I do? My little boy has swallowed my pen.'
'Use a pencil till I get there.'

2 *Patient:* Your advice last time was no good. I ... drink a glass of orange juice after my bath – but I just couldn't!
Doctor: Why on earth not?
Patient: Well, after drinking all the bath water, I couldn't manage anything else.

3 There were two snakes in the jungle. One snake said, 'Do you know if we ... be poisonous?'
'Why?' said the other snake.
'Because I've just bitten my lip.'

4 *Barber:* How much ... I take off this time, sir?
Man: Could you cut it very short on one side and not at all on the other, and with untidy bits sticking out at the back?
Barber: Oh dear, I really don't think I ... cut it like that!
Man: Why not? You did last time.

5 'Mums ... be experts on children, but that's nonsense in my opinion. After all, who else says you ... get up in the morning when you're sleepy, and then sends you to bed at night when you're wide awake?'

6 *Piano tuner:* Good morning, sir. I ... tune your piano.
Man: Oh? But we didn't send for you.
Piano tuner: No, sir, but your neighbours did.

7 *Sam:* One of my ancestors ... have died at Waterloo.
Ted: Really? Which platform?

8 *Teacher:* You're late! You ... have been here at nine o'clock.
Boy: Why, miss – what happened?

4 **barber** men's hairdresser

5 Complaints GG 93; GhE 231, 232, 233 A2

'Can't you read?'

'I know you can get it twopence cheaper down at the Supermarket – that's because here you have to pay for good old-fashioned personal service which you don't get there and if you don't like it you know what you can do!'

What else could they have said? Use equivalents of German sollen.

6 Unable to read GG 88, 90–92, 94; GhE 223, 229, 237, 239–242

Peter Ugarte left school unable to read a newspaper or comic book. He knew how to recognize a tin of baked beans in a shop but could not decipher names on new products. Cardiff, his home town, was the only city he could spell. He would bandage his hand before going to the dole office to avoid having to fill in forms.

Around four million British adults – far more of them men than women – have literacy problems. Around 300,000 cannot read or write at all; the rest might be able to read a simple sentence or might spell so badly that they cannot write a note to the milkman.

A Mori poll three years ago showed that 44 per cent of adults could not understand a simple fire notice. One in four had difficulty filling in a form correctly.

Peter, 29, was a late developer who started to play truant at the age of 10 to avoid reading. If he had to do an essay, he would write huge words to fill up the page. He left school at 15 with no qualifications.

By his early 20s, panic was starting to set in. He would get on the wrong bus rather than ask what the destination panel said. The crunch came when the dole office upbraided him for not wanting to work. He started his first adult literacy class unable to spell 'cat'.

From *The Sunday Correspondent*, January 7, 1990

4 **dole office** where unemployed people collect money from the government – 7 **literacy** ability to read and write – 10 **Mori poll** ['mɔːrɪ] questionnaire to discover public opinion, etc. – 13 **to play truant** ['truːənt] to stay away from school – 17 **destination panel** sign at the front of a bus saying where it is going – **the crunch** critical moment when action must at last be taken – 18 **to upbraid** to criticize

1 *Use suitable auxiliaries (or substitute forms) to complete these statements:*
   a When Peter Ugarte left school, he …
   b As a 10-year-old, he often missed school so that he wouldn't …
   c In order to fill in a form correctly, it is important to …
   d A fire notice describes what you …
   e A note to the milkman tells him how many bottles he …

2 *The auxiliary* would *is sometimes used in formal style to express past habits. Find examples of this in the text. What other expression could have been used instead?*

3 *Look up the use of* need *and* dare *in your English grammar (see GG 94; GhE 241-242).*
   Then use suitable forms to complete what Peter might say.
   a 'I always fixed a bandage round my hand so I … fill in any forms.'
   b 'I often got on the wrong bus simply because I … ask where it was going.'
   c 'Now that I've learnt to read, I … worry about things like that any more.'
   d 'It's a terrible situation when you can't read. You feel helpless, but you … admit it to people.'

4 *Comment on Peter's situation, using perfect forms of auxiliaries.*
   Examples:
   He **must have felt** very embarrassed about his problem/…
   He **ought not to have played** truant as a child/…
   His parents/teachers **should have** …
   The people at the dole office **may have** …/**might have** …
   His friends/wife …

10 Advanced Exercises

1 Vice versa GG 88–91, 93; GhE 221.1, 223–232, 235–236

Dick Bultitude is about to return to his hated boarding school after the Christmas holidays, and has come to say goodbye to his father, Paul. When Dick tells his father how he hates his school and does not want to go back, his father says, 'I only wish I could be a boy again, like you.' While speaking, Paul Bultitude is holding the mysterious 'Garudâ Stone', a talisman Dick's uncle once brought back from India. Though they do not know it, this is a wishing stone, and within seconds, Paul Bultitude has turned into a boy looking exactly like his son ...

'Dick,' said Paul faintly, 'what is all this? Could you see it coming on at all, eh?'

'It was all at once, just as you were talking about school and all that. You said you only wished – Why of course; look here, it must be the stone that did it! The Garudâ Stone! You've got it in your hand still. Don't you see? It's a real talisman after all! How jolly!'

'Oh, it's perfectly absurd! How can there be such things as talismans nowadays, eh? Tell me that.'

'Well, something's happened to you, hasn't it? And it must have been done somehow,' argued Dick.

'I was holding the confounded thing, certainly,' said Paul, 'here it is. But what could I have said to start it?'

'I know!' cried Dick. 'Don't you remember? You said you wished you were a boy again, like me. So you are, you see, exactly like me! What a lark it is, isn't it? But, I say, you can't go up to business like that, you know, can you? I tell you what, you'd better come to Grimstone's with me now, and see how you like it. I shouldn't mind so much if you came too. Grimstone's face would be splendid when he saw two of us. Do come!'

'That's ridiculous nonsense you're talking,' said Paul, 'and you know it. What should I do at school at my age? I tell you I'm the same as ever inside, though I may have shrunk into a little rascally boy to look at. Why on earth couldn't you let the stone alone?'

'You shouldn't have wished,' said Dick.

'Wished!' echoed Mr Bultitude. 'Why, of course – I never thought of that. The thing's a wishing stone; it must be! You have to hold it, I suppose, and then say what you wish aloud, and there you are. If that's the case, I can soon put it all right by simply wishing myself back again.'

He took the stone, and got into a corner by himself where he began repeating the words, 'I wish I was back again,' 'I wish I was the man I was five minutes ago,' 'I wish all this had not happened,' and so on, until he was very exhausted and red in the face. He tried with the stone held in his left hand, as well as his right, sitting and standing, under all the various conditions he could think of, but absolutely nothing came of it; he was just as exasperatingly boyish and youthful as ever at the end of it.

'I don't like this,' he said at last, giving it up with a rather crestfallen air. 'I can't make it work any more!'

'Perhaps,' suggested Dick, who had shown throughout the most unsympathetic cheerfulness, 'perhaps it's one of those talismans that only give you one wish, and you've had it, you know?'

'Then it's all over!' groaned Paul. 'What am I to do? What shall I do? Suggest something, for Heaven's sake. Can't you see what a terrible mess I've got into? Suppose – only suppose your sister or one of the servants were to come in, and see me like this!'

This suggestion simply enchanted Dick. 'Let's have 'em all up,' he laughed; 'it would be such fun! How they will laugh when we tell them!' And he rushed to the bell.

'Touch that bell if you dare!' screamed Paul. 'I won't be seen in this condition by anybody! What on earth could have induced that scoundrelly uncle of yours to bring such a horrible thing as this over, I can't imagine! I never heard of such a situation as this in my life. I can't stay like this, you know – it's not to be thought of! I – I wonder whether it would be any use to send over to Dr Bustard and ask him to step in; he might give me something to bring me round. But then the whole neighbourhood would hear about it! – I should be the laughing-stock of the city. Not a soul must ever guess that such a thing has happened. You must see that yourself.'

'Yes,' said Dick, 'I see that. It will be all right. I'm going to wish in a minute, and no one will guess there has been anything the matter. – Now, if I wish myself a man just like you were ten minutes ago, before you took the stone, that will put things all right again, won't it?'

'Is the boy mad?' cried Paul, horrified. 'I won't have it. Do you hear, I forbid you to think of any such thing. Give me back that stone. I can't trust you with it after this.'

'I can't help it,' said Dick doggedly. 'You've had your wish, and I don't see why I shouldn't have mine...'

From *Vice Versa* by F. Anstey

vice versa [ˌvaɪsɪ ˈvɜːsə] the other way round – 12 **confounded** damned – 17 **a lark** a joke, amusing situation – 20 **Grimstone** name of the headmaster of Dick's school – 27 **rascally** badly behaved (in a playful way) – 45 **exasperating** very annoying – 48 **crestfallen** disappointed and sad – 50 **unsympathetic** not showing any understanding – 58 **to enchant** to fill with joy or amusement – 64 **to induce** to persuade – **scoundrelly** good-for-nothing, 'bad' – 85 **dogged** [ˈdɒgɪd] very determined

1 *Pick out the examples of perfect forms of auxiliaries in lines 11-30. How would you express these forms in German?*

2 *Look carefully at Paul Bultitude's words in ll. 25-26 and 53-57, picking out the various equivalents of German* sollen. *Then find the equivalents of German* wollen *that he uses in ll. 38-40, 63 and 81-82.*

3 *Translate lines 62-74*

4 *Describe Paul's reaction to the new situation, and compare it with Dick's reaction. What are the reasons for their different points of view?*
Paul doesn't want to ..., because it means he won't be able to ... / he may have to ... / people might .... He thinks Dick ought to ... so that ... But Dick feels excited / ... because the change in his father means he may have to ... He realizes that if the stone 'works' for him, he'll probably be able to ... / allowed to ..., while his father ...

5 *At some time or other, most people imagine what it would be like to change places with somebody else. Think of a person you would like to (or would* **not** *like to) be for a day (or longer), and describe how the change would affect your life. Use forms of* have to, be able to *and* be allowed to.

2 Telecommuting: for stay-at-home workers GG 88–91, 93; GhE 223–235

Translate into English. These words and expressions will help you:.

to move to the country (l. 2) – the resulting loss of time (7-8) – to put an end to (9) – to have reservations (22) – to overlook (26) – human interactions (26) – to develop psychological problems (28) – home and work life (30) – to be distracted (32)

Nach dem zweiten Weltkrieg sind immer mehr Leute in Großbritannien aufs Land gezogen, weil sie dort ein attraktiveres Leben führen konnten als in den Großstädten. Da sie ihre Arbeit aber natürlich nicht aufgeben wollten, mußten sie jeden Tag in die Stadt fahren – sie wurden [zu] Pendlern ('commuters'). Verstopfte Straßen, überfüllte Züge und der damit verbundene Zeitverlust haben aber ihrer Freude am 'commuting' schon längst ein Ende gemacht. Für eine wachsende Anzahl von Menschen könnte 'telecommuting' – das Arbeiten für die Firma von zu Hause aus – die Lösung dieses Problems sein.

'Telecommuting' hat viele Vorteile – für Frauen mit kleinen Kindern, die zu Hause arbeiten wollen, ebenso wie für Manager, die effektiver arbeiten könnten, wenn sie wertvolle Zeit zwischen Arbeitsstelle und Zuhause nicht mehr vergeuden müßten. Viele Arbeitnehmer brauchen nicht jeden Tag tatsächlich im Büro zu erscheinen; sie können gut *(easily)* einen Teil ihrer Arbeit zu Hause erledigen.

Trotz des wachsenden Erfolges von 'telecommuting' soll es bei einigen noch Bedenken geben. ‚Wie soll ich wissen, ob meine Leute *(staff + plural verb)* überhaupt arbeiten?' fragt der traditionelle Manager. Man darf die Gefahren natürlich nicht übersehen. Zwischenmenschliche Kontakte sind sehr wichtig; wer ständig allein arbeiten muß, kann psychische Probleme bekommen. Eine weitere Gefahr besteht darin, daß *(is that ...)* der Unterschied zwischen Arbeitswelt und Zuhausesein verloren gehen kann; entweder arbeitet man zuviel, oder man wird zu Hause leichter abgelenkt, so daß man als 'telecommuter' weniger arbeitet als früher.

Based on an article in *The Sunday Telegraph*, July 15, 1990

11 The Infinitive

Check-up

1 The dinner party

Complete the sentences with infinitives. Decide whether to use the active or the passive infinitive, with or without to.

arrive
be deliver
get arrive
be
help
sit have

deliver inform
stop
turn ring

come let stay
say
come run
know
collect
stay
come
invite

The guests were expected … at eight o'clock. The Fergusons didn't want them … late as they had arranged for some delicious Chinese food … by that time. And, of course, they didn't want it … cold. The first … was Major Winterbottom. It was, of course, easy for him … on time as he was the Fergusons' next-door neighbour. He said he would love … in the kitchen, but Mrs Ferguson made him … down and asked him … a drink.

At 8.30 the Chinese takeaway rang up and said their driver had no idea where … the food and he would like … about the exact address. A few minutes later they heard a car … in their drive. But it was only someone that had used their drive … in. Then they heard the telephone … again. It was the MacAlisters, announcing that their babysitter had let them down. They were wondering whether … or not, as they didn't want … the children … at home on their own. At 9 the Chinese takeaway rang … that it was now impossible for them … because their driver had managed … into one of the poplar trees on the High Street and they wanted … if the Fergusons wouldn't like … the food themselves. By this time it was becoming more and more difficult for Mrs Ferguson … calm. A little later the phone rang again. It was the Joneses. They were not sure whether … at 7.30 or at 8 for the dinner party the following Wednesday. They added that they were delighted …

10 **drive** *Einfahrt* – 11 **to let down** to disappoint (unexpectedly) – 17 **calm** quiet, not nervous

2 Christopher Columbus

Replace the phrases in italics by infinitive constructions.

1 Christopher Columbus was not *the only sailor that explored* the oceans in the 15th century.
2 But while others had sailed south he was *the first explorer that thought* that west was *the direction one should take.*
3 At that time educated people *believed that the earth was round.*
4 But they thought it was *impossible that any ship could make* the 10,000-mile journey from western Europe to Asia.
5 Columbus, however, *decided he would travel* west and *expected that he would get* to India and China in the end.
6 He asked several European monarchs for help. A lot of money was needed *so that he could buy and equip* the ships for the expedition.
7 Columbus greatly underestimated *the distance that had to be covered.*
8 When they had sailed far beyond where they *had hoped they might find land,* Columbus' men *told him he should turn back.*
9 He *promised that he would give up* the search if they had not discovered land by October 12th.
10 When they finally sighted land Columbus *was overjoyed that he had reached* the 'East Indies'.

7 **to underestimate** to make a calculation that is too low – **to cover (a distance)** to travel

The infinitve without *to*

Manchester City *must* **play** Everton in the next round. The match *might* **be shown** on BBC 1.	– after most auxiliaries
The new coach *makes his players* **work** very hard. (= forces/tells/orders them to work …) Aston Villa *let their lead* **slip** away in the second half. (= allowed/permitted it to slip …)	– after *make* + direct object – after *let* + direct object
The home crowd were shocked when they *heard the referee* **blow** his whistle and then *saw him* **point** to the penalty spot.	– after verbs of perception + direct object

The infinitive with *to*

Leeds *hope* **to play** in their new stadium next year. It won't be *easy* **to get** tickets for the Cup Final. The fans couldn't understand Everton's *decision* **to sell** three of their best players.	after certain – verbs (*expect, want, would like,* etc.) – adjectives (*difficult, hard, ready,* etc.) – nouns (*attempt, plan, wish,* etc.)
At the press conference the team manager did not know *what* **to say.** (= what he should say.) Liverpool were *the first (team)* **to score** in a very exciting match. (= the first team that scored …) Some of the crowd stood on their seats *(in order)* **to get** a better view. (= so that they would get …) This is *the game* **to win** if we want to stay in the First Division. (= that we must/should win …)	instead of subordinate clauses: – after question words *(what, where, how,* etc.) – after *the first, the last, the only one(s)* – instead of a clause of purpose – instead of a relative clause with an auxiliary

Note

The coach *wanted all his players* **to take** fitness tests.
It is *unusual for local matches* **to attract** big crowds.

Want, wish, would like *and* expect *can be followed by an object + infinitive construction.*
After certain expressions, a construction with for *+ object + infinitive is used.*

'Hello! He's coming over to consult the linesman.'

'I never cease to be astonished at Lester's amazing will to win!'
to cease to be to stop being

There's plenty we don't tell disabled people in our care.

We don't tell them where to live.
We don't tell them what to wear.
We don't tell them what to eat.
We don't tell them what time to go to bed or get up.
We don't tell them what risks to take.
In fact, whether we're helping in their own homes, or one of ours, we say nothing that could in any way infringe on the basic human right to choose what to do, and when to do it.
For more details about our work please telephone or write to us at the address below.
The Red Feather can use all the help it can get.

THE LEONARD CHESHIRE FOUNDATION

26-29 MAUNSEL ST.,
LONDON SWIP 2QN.01-828 1822.

to infringe on to limit, to go against

1 Telling people what to do

GG 107; GhE 290–291

1 *First read the advert above. Then replace the infinitive structures by subordinate clauses. Example:*
We don't tell them where to live. ▶ We don't tell them where they must/should/ought to live.

2 *Many people are in the care of others – think of people in hospital, children, old people. Use infinitives with the question words below to complete the following ideas. Think of as many sensible variations as you can.*

when – whether – where – how – what

- Children should have the right to decide ...
- People in hospital would often prefer to decide for themselves ...
- Small children must be taught ...
- Doctors must tell patients ...
- Old people don't like being told ...

2 How they can help

GG 107; GhE 290–291

Say how the following people and things can help you. Use infinitive constructions with question words. Examples:
A travel agent advises people **where to go** on holiday.
If you don't know **which road to take** you can look at a map.

1 travel agent
2 map
3 recipe
4 careers officer
5 commercials
6 alarm clock
7 police officer
8 tourist guide
9 skiing instructor

3 Psychological warfare GG 100–103, 105, 107; GhE 264, 267, 268, 288

Describe what is happening in this cartoon. Use infinitive constructions, deciding whether to use an object or not.

score	1	Normally, it is easy for a player ... from the penalty spot.
score	2	And Kevin Robson hopes ....
get a goal	3	Of course, his teammates expect ....
succeed	4	But the Rovers' supporters don't want ....
be frightened	5	Those not directly behind the goal are pretending ....
be hit	6	They don't want ... by the ball.
win	7	They would like ....
make ... nervous miss	8	Their intention is ... and so to make ....
see ... score a goal	9	But the home fans directly behind the goal want ....
save	10	The goalkeeper hopes ... the ball.
make ... feel	11	The Rovers' supporters have managed ... unsure of himself.
take on	12	Kevin Robson looks as if he no longer wants ... the responsibility.
know do	13	He doesn't seem ... what ... any longer.

4 In and out of school
GG 101–103; GhE 259–260, 264, 268

Translate into English. Remember: German constructions with daß *sometimes correspond to infinitive constructions in English.*

1 ‚Wollen Sie, daß wir den ganzen Text übersetzen?'
2 ‚Ich möchte, daß Sie ein Gedicht aussuchen, das Ihnen wirklich gefällt.'
3 ‚Es ist wichtig, daß das Labor nach dem Unterricht geschlossen wird.'
4 ‚Meine Eltern wollen nicht, daß ich Kunst studiere. Sie erwarten von mir, daß ich den Familienbetrieb übernehme.'
5 ‚Ich will, daß du das Radio ausschaltest. Es ist unmöglich, daß du bei dem Lärm deine Hausaufgaben machen kannst.'

'Right! Now I want each of you to describe the weather in your own words.'

5 Dr Watson at work GG 106; GhE 281

In this short extract from 'The Hound of the Baskervilles', Dr Watson has been sent ahead by Sherlock Holmes to watch the house of the naturalist, Stapleton. Stapleton, the villain of the story, is preparing to attack Sir Henry Baskerville, his guest, with an enormous dog he has locked up in the outhouse. From his hiding-place, Dr Watson can look straight into the dining-room ...

As I watched them, Stapleton rose and left the room, while Sir Henry filled his glass again and leaned back in his chair, puffing at his cigar. I heard the creak of a door and the sound of boots upon gravel. The steps passed along the path on the other side of the wall under which I crouched. Looking over, I saw the naturalist pause at the door of an outhouse in the corner of the orchard. A key turned in a lock, and as he passed in there was a curious scuffling noise from within. He was only a minute or so inside, and then I heard the key turn once more, and he passed me and re-entered the house. I saw him rejoin his guest and I crept quietly back to where my companions were waiting to tell them what I had seen.

From *The Hound of the Baskervilles* by Sir Arthur Conan Doyle

naturalist botanist – **villain** the 'bad' character – **outhouse** shed – 4 **creak** groaning sound (e.g. of a door opening) – 5 **gravel** ['grævl] very small stones used to make paths – 6 **to crouch** [aʊ] kauern – 8 **orchard** ['ɔ:tʃəd] piece of land where fruit trees grow – 10 **a scuffling noise** sound like the quick movements of an animal

1 *Find examples in the text of object + infinitive after verbs of perception.*
2 *Use objects and infinitives where you can to describe more details of what Dr Watson saw/noticed/heard. Start like this:*
He watched Stapleton get up and ...

6 Chief Joseph GG 105; GhE 283,285

Chief Joseph's story is typical of the way American governments treated the native Americans. The Nez Perce were peace-loving Indians. For many years they had let white explorers and settlers travel through their land without ever attacking them. Chief Joseph never let his people sell any land to the whites because he believed the land was sacred. But when gold was found in the mountains of western Idaho in 1860, the government wanted to make the Nez Perce give up their land. They told Chief Joseph that he and his people had to leave within a month – to be resettled later on a reservation in Oregon. Joseph had only 55 men of fighting age. This made him realize that he would have no chance against the whites.

On their way to Oregon a few angry Nez Perce killed some white settlers. Troops were sent to capture them. Chief Joseph tried to escape to Canada with his small band. For months they managed to escape from thousands of soldiers. When, at last, they had reached the Bear Paw Mountains, only 30 miles from the Canadian border, Joseph let his exhausted people rest. It was then that the cavalry attacked. After holding out for four days the Indians were made to surrender. Rather than letting the children freeze to death and his people starve, Joseph decided to give up the struggle and let the government do with his people what they wanted. The government of the US made the Nez Perce settle on a barren reservation in Oregon, but they didn't let Chief Joseph stay with his people. He was made to live on a reservation in Washington state. There he died in exile. Officially he was said to have died of a broken heart.

They **made** him **do** it.
He **was made to do** it.

2 **Nez Perce** ['nez 'pɜ:s] – 7 **sacred** ['seɪkrɪd] connected with God, holy – 18 **to capture** ['kæptʃə] to catch – 27 **to starve** to die of hunger – 30 **barren** too poor in quality to grow anything on

1. *Replace the constructions with* let *and* make *by constructions with* allow, forbid, force, order, permit *or* tell.
2. *Translate the sentences with* let *and* make. *(Can you always use* lassen *in German?)*

7 The 'let and make thriller' GG 105; GhE 283, 285

Translate the 'thriller', using let *or* make *for German* lassen. *These words will help you:*
to sit up (l. 1) – ghostly (3) – torch (8) – to stop breathing (9) – throat (10) – to feel calmer (14) – to jump (16)

Ein plötzliches Geräusch ließ Bonner im Bett hochfahren. Das Licht der elektrischen Uhr ließ das Gesicht seiner Frau gespenstisch erscheinen. Bonner ließ sie weiterschlafen und ging nach unten. Die Holztreppe ließ seine Schritte schrecklich laut klingen. Die Angst ließ sein Herz schneller schlagen. Hatte der Hund Einbrecher hereingelassen? Das Licht einer Taschenlampe im Wohnzimmer ließ Bonner den Atem anhalten. Er ging zum Telefon. Seine trockene Kehle ließ seine Stimme unnatürlich klingen. ‚Lassen Sie den Einbrecher [ruhig] weitermachen', sagte der Polizist, ‚tun Sie nichts, was ihn veranlassen könnte, gewalttätig zu werden.' Die Stimme des Polizisten ließ Bonner ruhiger werden. Aber was war das? Ein Schrei ließ ihn zusammenzucken. …

'Oh, for Pete's sake let him dial it.'

11 Advanced Exercises

1 Why do the British drive on the left? GG 102, 103, 110, 111; GhE 264, 267, 268, 283, 296, 298

4 **scabbard** holder for a sword, hanging from the belt – 5 **to wield** to hold and use – 7/9 **the off/near side** the right/left side – 11 **contrary** ['---] opposite – 13 **arbitrary** ['----] based on chance or personal opinion rather than on facts or reason

The heart is (or, to be exact, appears to be) on the left side of the body. In the more primitive forms of warfare some type of shield is therefore used to protect the left side, leaving the offensive weapon to be held in the right hand. The normal offensive weapon was the sword, worn in a scabbard. If the sword was to be wielded in the right hand, the scabbard would have to be worn on the left side. With a scabbard worn on the left, it became physically impossible to mount a horse on the off side unless intending to face the tail – which was not the normal practice. But if you mount on the near side, you will want to have your horse on the left of the road, so that you are clear of the traffic while mounting. It therefore becomes natural and proper to keep to the left, the contrary practice (as adopted in some backward countries) being totally opposed to all the deepest historical instincts. Free of arbitrary traffic rules the normal human being swings to the left.

From *Parkinson's Law* by C. Northcote Parkinson

1 *True or false? Correct what is wrong, using infinitive constructions.*
   a In the Middle Ages men carried swords in order to protect their hearts.
   b The shield was used to attack enemies.
   c The scabbard was used to hold the shield.
   d Wearing a scabbard, a rider found it very difficult to mount a horse from the left.
   e Therefore it used to be common practice for a rider to face the tail of his horse.
   f Riders decided to stand their horses on the right of the road when mounting.
   g In backward countries it is normal to keep to the left.
   h Only arbitrary traffic laws make people drive on the right.

2 *Translate the text, paying particular attention to the way you render the infinitive constructions in German.*

2 Another April GG 100, 103, 105, 106, 110; GhE 264, 281, 286, 296–297

'How long has Grandpa been with us?' I asked Mom. 'Before you's born', she said. 'Pap has been with us eleven years. He was eighty when he quit cuttin' timber and farmin': now he's ninety-one.'

I had heard her say that when she was a girl he'd walk out on the snow and ice barefooted and carry wood in the house and put it on the fire. He had shoes but wouldn't bother to put them on. And I heard her say that he would cut timber on the coldest day without socks on his feet but with his feet stuck down in cold brogan shoes and he worked stripped above the waist so his arms would have freedom when he swung his double-bitted ax. I had heard her tell how he'd sweat and how the sweat in his beard would be icicles by the time he got home from work on the cold winter days. Now Mom wouldn't let him get out of the house for she wanted him to live a long time.

As I watched Grandpa go down the path toward the hog pen he stopped to examine every little thing along his path. Once he waved his cane at a butterfly as it zigzagged over his head, its polka-dot wings fanning the blue April air. Grandpa would stand when a puff of wind came along, and hold his face against the wind and let the wind play with his white whiskers. I thought maybe his face was hot under his beard and he was letting the wind cool his face. When he reached the hog pen he called the hogs down to the fence. They came running and grunting to Grandpa just like they were talking to him. I knew that Grandpa couldn't hear them trying to talk to him but he could see their mouths working and he knew they were trying to say something. He leaned his cane against the hog pen, reached over the fence, and patted the hogs' heads. Grandpa didn't miss patting one of our seven hogs.

There wasn't anything his dim blue eyes missed. He stopped under a redbud tree before he reached the garden to break a tiny spray of redbud blossoms. He took each blossom from the spray and examined it carefully.

'Gee, it's funny to watch Grandpa', I said to Mom, then I laughed. 'Poor Pap', Mom said, 'he's seen a lot of Aprils come and go. He's seen more Aprils than he will ever see again'.

From *Another April* by Jesse Stuart

1 **you's born** you were born – 3 **to quit/quit/quit** *here:* to stop – **timber** wood used for building – 8 **brogan (shoe)** heavy, ankle-high work boot – 10 **double-bitted** with two cutting edges – 11 **to sweat** [e] *schwitzen* – **icicle** long thin piece of ice – 15 **hog** AE pig – **pen** small piece of land enclosed by a fence esp. for keeping animals in – 17 **cane** walking stick – **butterfly** *Schmetterling* – **polka-dot wing** *getupfter Flügel* – 18 **to fan** *here:* to beat (the air) – 20 **whiskers** hair on a man's face, esp. on the sides – 23 **to grunt** to make the sound of a pig – 29 **dim** not bright – 30 **redbud (tree)** American tree with red buds *(Knospen)* – **spray** small branch with its leaves and blossoms – 31 **blossom** the flower of a tree or bush

1 *The author uses various infinitive structures to make the three characters in the story come alive. Say how he expresses that*
   a *Grandpa used to be insensitive to the cold;*
   b *the boy knows a lot from his mother about the time Grandpa was younger;*
   c *the boy's mother is worried about her father's health;*
   d *Grandpa loves nature;*
   e *the boy is amused by his grandfather's behaviour;*
   f *the boy's mother regrets the fact that her father is so old and will only have a few more years to live.*

2 *Talk about the story, using infinitive constructions.*
   The little boy is too young to …
   His mother tries to …
   His grandfather examines everything in detail in order to …
   The author manages to … *Go on.*

3 Fast food in America

GG 100, 103, 105, 107–110; GhE 264, 267–268, 281, 283, 290, 296–297, 300.2

Translate the text, using infinitive constructions where possible. These words will help you:

to be meant for (l. 1) – to overhaul (13) – to work efficiently (14-15) – to mass-produce hamburgers (15-16) – low income (17) – chain restaurant (20) – outskirts (23) – to dominate (24)

Fast food ist für Menschen gedacht, die keine Zeit haben, selbst zu kochen, oder die zu beschäftigt sind, sich gemütlich hinzusetzen und ein langes Mahl zu genießen. Sie wissen außerdem genau, was sie in Fast-food-Restaurants erwartet *(what to ...)*. Sie erwarten, daß das Essen immer gleich aussieht, gleich schmeckt und das gleiche kostet. Wenn man jedoch wirklich wissen möchte, was die Fast-food-Industrie so erfolgreich gemacht hat, braucht man nur den nächsten Zehnjährigen zu fragen, wo er denn gern essen würde – wenn er die Wahl hätte. Aber wie fing all dies an?

Maurice und Richard McDonald waren in den 40er Jahren Besitzer eines erfolgreichen Drive-in-Restaurants in San Bernadino, Kalifornien. Sie verdienten genug Geld, um sich jedes Jahr einen neuen Cadillac kaufen zu können. Aber im Jahre 1948 beschlossen sie, ihr Restaurant zu schließen, um es völlig zu überholen. Papierteller wurden eingeführt, um das Geschirr zu ersetzen. Die Brüder zeigten ihren Angestellten, wie sie ökonomischer arbeiten konnten. Sie brachten sie dazu, Hamburger wie am Fließband herzustellen. Das neue Restaurant wurde der Ort, wo man hinging. Denn zum ersten Mal konnten es sich selbst Familien mit geringem Einkommen leisten, ein Restaurant zu besuchen.

Die Brüder MacDonald waren die ersten, die die Chancen von Fast-food-Restaurantketten und Hamburger-Fabriken erkannten. Aber sie waren nicht die einzigen, die diese Idee nutzten. In den 50er und 60er Jahren begannen Fast-food-Restaurants das Gesicht amerikanischer Städte zu verändern. Besonders die Außenbezirke scheinen heute von den Fast-food-Restaurants beherrscht zu sein.

Fast-food-Restaurants scheinen wieder einmal zu beweisen, wie leicht es ist, den amerikanischen Traum zu verwirklichen: Man braucht nur zu wissen, wie man einen Hamburger anders herstellen kann und [schon] ist man Millionär.

Check-up

1 At the doctor's

Fill in suitable gerunds, together with prepositions when appropriate.

1 'Twenty cigarettes a day, Mr Miller?! I think it would be better if you stopped … altogether.
2 And you should also avoid … too much meat.'
3 'But I'm not keen … nothing but salad and vegetables. And I always look forward … a drink when I come home from work.'
4 'Well, well. How … muesli for breakfast now and then instead … egg and bacon every morning?
5 I'm afraid you're a bit overweight. Have you ever thought … weight? How … some exercise?'
6 'But I can't stand … round a track or … in some crowded pool.'
7 'Well, if you go on like this you might be in danger … a heart attack.'
8 'Hm, perhaps I'll give up … to work in the car. I might get used … my old bike again. I don't seem to get enough rest at night. I have difficulty … .'
9 'What … for a nice walk before you go to bed? That may help.
10 And carry on … those red pills. They'll also help you to relax. See you again on Wednesday then, Mr Miller.'

2 The successful politician

Rewrite the following sentences, using gerund constructions. Choose from the expressions on the right.
Example:

The successful politician has managed to become known all over the country.	*succeed*
▶ The successful politician has **succeeded in becoming** known all over the country.	**in**

The successful politician …

1 … doesn't find it difficult to remember people's names.	*avoid*
2 … is not nervous when she or he speaks in public.	*be afraid*
3 … expects to become a government minister after the next elections,	*be good*
and is very pleased about this.	*be good*
4 … is an expert hand-shaker and baby-kisser.	*enjoy*
5 … never disagrees with her or his party bosses. That is something she or he must	*get tired*
never do.	*have difficulty*
6 … likes it when she or he is seen together with famous film stars, athletes, etc.	*look forward*
7 … praises her or his party's achievements again and again.	*worry*
8 … is not frightened when she or he has to answer awkward questions.	**about at at**
9 … is a great actress/actor.	**in of of to**

12 Basic Rules and Exercises

	The gerund is used
Driving one's own car used to be very popular in the 20th and 21st centuries.	1 as a subject
People even *enjoyed* **going** on holiday in their cars.	2 as an object – after verbs without a preposition *(avoid, stop, suggest,* etc.)
Young people *looked forward to* **getting** a so-called 'driving licence'.	3 after verbs + prepositions
At the beginning of the 21st century people got *tired of* **waiting** in endless traffic jams and **breathing** the poisonous air.	adjectives + prepositions
They began to see the *danger of* **destroying** their own environment.	nouns + prepositions
Apart from causing pollution, cars had made city life very unattractive.	4 together with a preposition as an adverbial phrase *(instead of, by, without,* etc.)

Note 1

What about going by bike?

The gerund is also used after how about?/what about?, it's no use, it's no good, it's worth.

Note 2

Most people agreed with *the government('s)* **putting** more tax on petrol.
But many were against *them/their* **closing** city centres to private cars.

The gerund can have a ***subject of its own.***

1 Life's risks GG 112, 114, 116–118; GhE 257, 269–272, 288

Statistics show that the U.S. population has never been safer. But there is no such thing as a completely risk-free environment. According to *Science* magazine the annual risk of death from certain commonplace activities is as follows:

- Drinking ordinary city water treated with chlorine: 1 in 1,700,000;
- Eating four tablespoons of peanut butter per day: 1 in 125,000;
- An accident in the home, like falling down the stairs: 1 in 9,000;
- Breathing air pollution in the eastern United States: 1 in 5,000;
- Police killed on duty: 1 in 4,500;
- Motor vehicle accident: 1 in 4,000;
- Climbing a mountain (mountaineering): 1 in 1,700;
- Cancer from cigarette smoking (one pack per day): 1 in 300.

Adapted from *American Studies Newsletter,* January 1990

6 **chlorine** ['klɔ:ri:n] Chlor – 8 **peanut** Erdnuß

'Excuse me, but would you mind scratching my nose?'

1 *Talk about the statistics, using gerunds.*

- The risk of … is greater/smaller than …
- The chance of … is about as great as …
- People who … are in danger of …
- Driving a car …
- Mountain-climbing …
- People should avoid …
- If people want to reduce risks they should stop …
- Although … can be risky, many people don't seem to worry about …

2 *Of course, taking risks can be fun. Say what you personally enjoy doing and what risks there are in these activities.*
Example: I know that skiing is dangerous, but I simply enjoy doing it.
Use some of these expressions:

I like/love/enjoy ….	The risk of …
I'm very interested in …	As I'm no good at …
I've stopped … because …	I don't mind …
The idea of …	The danger of …
I'm fond of …	I've started …
… doesn't worry me.	

2 Parents and children GG 113; GhE 259, 261

Complete the sentences, using gerunds with subjects of their own.

1 Peter's parents are very strict and rather critical:

a They don't like TV much themselves. And they are very much against … all the time.
b They don't allow him to stay out late. They insist on …
c They don't want him to get a motor-bike. They are worried about …
d Peter is their only child. Understandably, this is the reason for …
e He has got a new girl-friend. But his parents object to …
f They are not looking forward to the time when Peter leaves home. They are keen on …

'George simply loves playing with the children.'

2 Sheila's parents are the very opposite:

a They allow her to stay out as long as she likes. They don't mind her …
b They don't mind when she sleeps as long as she likes on a Sunday. They don't object to …
c They think that their daughter is old enough to look after herself. They rely on …
d Sheila's opinions are sometimes extreme and her parents disagree. But they don't mind …
e They don't complain when Sheila spends weekends with her friends. They are quite happy about …
f They see that Sheila has become an independent person and realise that they can't prevent …

'Guess what? No more sitting up for her, no more Pop, no more teenage rave parties, no more being patronised by bearded boy-friends – she's eloped.'

to patronise s.o. to treat s.o. like an inferior –
to elope to run away with one's boy-/girlfriend

12 3 Rewards and punishments GG 119; GhE 292, 295

The danger in rewarding a child is not as extreme as that of punishing him, but the undermining of the child's morale through the giving of rewards is more subtle. Rewards are superfluous and negative. To offer a prize for doing a deed is tantamount to declaring that the deed is not worth doing for its own sake.

From *Summerhill* by A. S. Neill

2 **to undermine** [ˌ--ˈ-] to weaken or destroy gradually – **morale** [məˈrɑːl] – 3 **subtle** [ˈsʌtl] not immediately noticeable, difficult to explain – **superfluous** [suːˈpɜːflʊəs] unnecessary – 4 **tantamount to** having the same value or effect as

Use gerund constructions with prepositions to rewrite the following sentences. (Choose from the prepositions on the right.)
Example: Adults may think they can make children try harder if they promise them rewards.
▶ Adults may think they can make children try harder **by promising them rewards.**

1 Giving 'prizes' can create envy between children, and it can also cause big disappointments.
2 All true artists work 'for fun' – they do not think of financial rewards.
3 It is wrong to imagine that one can develop a person's interest in a thing if one offers a prize.
4 In the world of sport, successful people sometimes receive enormous sums because they have won a certain event.
5 But although they are worth so much money, these prizes are not the 'real' reward.
6 The winner of a sporting event takes pride in the achievement, but does not consider the prize important in itself.

as well as
by
for
in spite of
instead of
without

4 Ego war on the road GG 112, 114–120; GhE 257, 269–272, 288, 295

There is a war of the sexes raging on Britain's roads. Women drivers questioned in a major Gallup survey claimed they are constantly harassed by male drivers and they are terrified of breaking down at night.

More than 1,000 women were quizzed in the Gallup poll and 74 per cent named men as the major bugbear on the roads.

'Men have to be good at everything, especially driving … it's a big ego thing,' said one respondent.

One fifth of those questioned said the aggressiveness of male drivers was coupled with more confidence on the road.

Women, asked to assess their own driving, cited having patience and displaying more care as their main virtues. Indecisiveness and over-cautiousness were the most common vices. But their biggest fear was breaking down at night.

95 per cent were afraid of breaking down on lonely roads and 80 per cent said they worried about breaking down on the motorways.

Examples of macho behaviour experienced by the women questioned included:

Cutting in – experienced by 87 per cent; Speeding – experienced by 85 per cent; Dangerous overtaking – experienced by 83 per cent; Tooting horn and flashing lights – experienced by 72 per cent; Refusing to let you out of a side road – experienced by 53 per cent;

1 **to rage** to spread or go on with great force or violence – 2/5 **Gallup survey/Gallup poll** questioning of a wide group of people to find out the opinion of the public in general – 3 **to harass s.o.** [ˈ--] to trouble or annoy s.o. – 6 **bugbear** s.th. that worries or upsets people – 11 **to assess** [-ˈ-] to judge – **to cite** to mention – 12 **to display** to show – **virtue** [ˈvɜːtʃuː] good quality or good way of behaving – 13 **vice** the opposite of virtue – 22 **to toot the horn** *hupen* –

and 58 per cent of women said they were regularly criticised by their partners for their driving.

On drinking and driving they were adamant: There should be a total clampdown by the Government.

More than 80 per cent said drinking and driving should be banned completely, and 83 per cent said they never drove after drinking. The figure among under-25s was even higher at more than 95 per cent.

Women are becoming more independent according to the Gallup survey.

Just over three quarters of those interviewed (76 per cent) had their own or a company car and over half of these (54 per cent) bought the car themselves and paid for all the running and repair costs themselves.

Eight out of ten said they enjoyed driving, but over half (58 per cent) try to avoid driving in bad weather and more than a third (35 per cent) are nervous of night driving. About the same number (37 per cent) dislike motorway driving.

Gallup carried out 1,057 interviews for the poll in November 1989 throughout Great Britain.

From *The Daily Express,* January 5, 1990

26 **adamant** ['---] firm and determined – 27 **clampdown** sudden decision to stop or limit an activity – 28 **to ban** to forbid by law

1 *Explain the meaning of the following expressions, using gerunds in your definitions. (Your dictionary will be helpful.)*
Ego war, war of the sexes (l. 1), aggressiveness (9), confidence (10), patience (11), indecisiveness (12), over-cautiousness (13), macho behaviour (18), cutting in (20), speeding (20), running costs (35).
Examples:
Ego war **means fighting** to show how good or superior one is.
Confidence is **a feeling/an attitude of being** sure about your own abilities, qualities or ideas.

2 *Make a list of the different types of gerund constructions in the article according to the Basic Rules (p. 96).*

3 *Think of your own experience as a driver, a learner or a passenger and say what you think of male and female driving.*
Examples: My sister is very good at driving.
I enjoy being in the car when my mother drives because she is so much faster than my father.
Use some of the following expressions + gerunds:

enjoy/like/dislike/hate …	be good at/bad at …	be nervous about …
prefer …	be proud of …	have difficulty in …
not mind …	be afraid/frightened of …	worry about …
avoid …	be crazy about/keen on …	look forward to …

4 *Do you think this type of newspaper article is fair to women? – to men? Or does it simply repeat old clichés and prejudices?*
Use some of the following expressions + gerunds:

(Male) journalists should stop/ avoid/be ashamed of …	There's nothing wrong with …
I'm tired of …/I hate …	Statistics like these are a good way of …
It's no use/no good …	A lot of people are interested in …
Newspaper articles should concentrate on … instead of …	Why should we be afraid of/avoid …?
…	…

12 Advanced Exercises

1 'A Life in the Day' of Debra McArthur

GG 112–120; GhE 257, 261, 269–272, 295

On a school morning I usually manage to squeeze 10 minutes between my mother's and father's bathroom times. My father's reaction to anyone else being in the bathroom in 'his' bathroom time leaves much to be desired. It would be safer waving a red flag at a raging bull. I actually fear his reaction. Not that he would strike me or anything, but I think he feels both angry and hurt that he can't have the bathroom in his own home, and I wouldn't want to hurt him.

I admit I spend more than my fair share of time in the bathroom, but teenage girls need pampering time more than men. My father contradicts himself by portraying himself as an old man – too old for this and that – and then spends much time and money applying 'wet-look' styling gel to his greying locks. He unquestionably receives a fair number of jokes on this subject.

Fifteen minutes is spent on applying the Polyfilla and 15 on concreting my hair into place. No breakfast is consumed as I am far too busy for food. A rummage through the wardrobe finds my uniform and it's ready and set for action.

I usually enjoy school if I'm up to date with my schoolwork. I hate the feeling of being left behind with anything. I suppose I just hate missing out, even if avoiding this entails 'hard slog'. I enjoy school mainly because of the number of friends I have there. I also hate being alone. Another good reason for coming to school is to see my boyfriend, Craig, whom I meet every lunchtime. However, I do not let this interfere with my schoolwork. I believe that if I centre my full attention on either one or the other I will lose out somewhere.

At lunchtime I either go on a binge or I starve myself – never the happy medium. I usually starve for two reasons: either to make up for the binge which took place the previous day or to save money. At Christmas I save every penny I receive in order to buy people decent gifts. When I do find I have quite a lot of money for myself it seems to affect my logic. I either give it away or buy other people things, instead of spending it on the one who earned it – me! But I do love having money to spend on myself. My father would say I waste it but I relish the thought of taking the chemist's counter by storm. It's unbelievable how quickly I can spend £20 on make-up and other such junk!

After school it's either netball practice for the school team or it's off home and tarting up time once again. I see Craig almost every evening. He says he doesn't mind what I look like but I like to feel as though I've made an effort for him. I either fit my homework in before I see him, during the time I see him, or when he leaves for the bus at 11 pm – which would account for the lateness in my morning getting-up time. Either way, my homework gets done.

I really enjoy looking after young children. They are so interesting. It was an ambition of mine to be a nanny or nursery nurse, but efforts to dissuade me eventually succeeded. 'You're too bright.' 'There's no money in it.' 'You'd get bored.' 'You'd be able to get a far better job.' I suppose I could babysit as a hobby until I have children of my own. I am looking forward very much to having children. Not actually the pregnancy and birth, but the end product. I am not keen on the idea of being a stereotypical mother/housewife. I also want a career, and a good one, but doing what? I wish I knew! My father continuously asks whether I have made up my mind yet. Now I am concentrating on gaining good exam results so that I will have a solid base from which to move in any direction – preferably upwards.

I often think about possible careers, pick them to pieces in my mind, discard the confused ideas and replace them with fantasies. I am a demon for fantasising. I still maintain that I am going to be taken and made rich and famous due to an outstanding talent yet unrevealed (as you see in the movies). My bedtime thoughts consist of these two elements.

From *The Sunday Times Magazine,* March 27, 1988

'A Life in the Day' regular section in *The Sunday Times Magazine* – 12 **to pamper** to treat very kindly and pay a lot of attention to – 13 **to contradict o.s.** to say the opposite of what one has said before – 14 **to portray** to describe – 16 **to apply** *here:* to put s.th. onto s.th. – 19 **Polyfilla** equivalent of German 'Moltofill' – 20 **to concrete** ['--] to fix firmly into position – 22 **rummage** search for s.th. by moving things in a careless way – 26 **to miss out** *(coll.)* to miss an opportunity to take part in s.th. – 27 **to entail** to cause, to make necessary – **slog** hard dull work – 32 **to interfere with** to have a bad effect on – 34 **to lose out** *(coll.)* to be at a disadvantage – 35 **to go on a binge** [bɪndʒ] to eat and drink far too much – **to starve (o.s.)** to go hungry, not to eat anything – 37 **to make up for** to compensate for – 40 **decent** acceptable (i.e. not too cheap) – **gift** present – 41 **to affect** to influence – 45 **to relish** to enjoy – 48 **junk** useless things, rubbish – 50 **to tart up** to try and make oneself look attractive by applying make-up, etc. – 56 **to account for** to explain – 61 **nanny** a woman paid by parents to look after their children – **nursery nurse** person trained to look after very young children – **to dissuade** to persuade not to do s.th. – 62 **eventually** finally, in the end – 66 **pregnancy** the months before a woman's baby is born – 71 **to make up one's mind** to make a decision – 76 **to discard** to put aside, to throw away – 78 **to maintain** to say s.th. is true – 80 **unrevealed** undiscovered

1 *Write a summary of Debra's day. Use these expressions + gerunds:*
   a ll. 1-23: On a school morning her father insists on … and Debra is afraid of him … She admits … Her father spends a lot of time … in spite of … She normally goes to school without …
   b ll. 24-58: She enjoys … but hates … When she has some money she finds herself … She dreams of … when she has enough money. Craig doesn't mind her … but Debra is keen on … She often does her homework after … That is the reason for her …
   c ll. 59-82: She is fond of … At one time she was thinking of … But her parents succeeded in … She dreams of … although she is not actually looking forward to … She is not crazy about … Her father sometimes complains about her … But at the moment she is concentrating on … At bedtime she dreams of …

2 *Compare your own day with Debra's. What differences and similarities are there? These expressions might help you:*
I also have difficulty in …
I (don't) spend a lot of time …
I'm concentrating on …
The idea of …
I look forward to …
I (don't) enjoy …
I'm not keen on my friends/my parents …
I'm (not) interested in …
Whenever I have a lot of money I like/avoid …
My parents (don't) insist on me …

2 Brave New World GG 112, 114–120; GhE 257, 269–272, 295

At the end of Aldous Huxley's famous utopian novel Brave New World, *Mustapha Mond, one of the World Controllers, and the Savage, who was brought up on a 'reservation' on a mixture of Shakespeare and primitive customs, talk about the civilization of Brave New World.*

'My dear young friend,' said Mustapha Mond, 'civilization has absolutely no need of nobility or heroism. These things are symptoms of political inefficiency. In a properly organized society like ours, nobody has any opportunities for being noble or heroic. Conditions have got to be thoroughly unstable before the occasion can arise. Where there are wars, where there are divided allegiances, where there are temptations to be resisted, objects of love to be fought for or defended – there, obviously, nobility and heroism have some sense. But there aren't any wars nowadays. The greatest care is taken to prevent you from loving anyone too much. There is no such thing as a divided allegiance; you're so conditioned that you can't help doing what you ought to do. And what you ought to do is on the whole so pleasant, so many of the natural impulses are allowed free play, that there really aren't any temptations to resist. And if ever, by some unlucky chance, anything unpleasant should somehow happen, why, there's always *soma* to give you a holiday from the facts. And there's always *soma* to calm your anger, to reconcile you to your enemies, to make you patient and long-suffering. In the past you could only accomplish these things by making a great effort and after years of hard moral training. Now, you swallow two or three half-gramme tablets, and there you are. Anybody can be virtuous now. You can carry at least half of your morality about in a bottle. Christianity without tears – that's what *soma* is.'

'But tears are necessary. Don't you remember what Othello said? "If after every tempest come such calms, may the winds blow till they have wakened death." There's a story one of the old Indians used to tell us, about the Girl of Mátsaki. The young men who wanted to marry her had to do a morning's hoeing in her garden. It seemed easy; but there were flies and mosquitoes, magic ones. Most of the young men simply couldn't stand the biting and stinging. But the one that could – he got the girl.'

'Charming! But in civilized countries,' said the Controller, 'you can have girls without hoeing for them; and there aren't any flies or mosquitoes to sting you. We got rid of them all centuries ago.'

The Savage nodded, frowning. 'You got rid of them. Yes, that's just like you. Getting rid of everything unpleasant instead of learning to put up with it. Whether 'tis nobler in the mind to suffer the slings and arrows of outrageous fortune, or to take arms against a sea of troubles and by opposing end them … But you don't do either. Neither suffer nor oppose. You just abolish the slings and arrows. It's too easy. What you need is something *with* tears for a change. Nothing costs enough here.'

From *Brave New World* by Aldous Huxley

2 **nobility** admirable behaviour or attitude – 4 **inefficiency** working or performing in a badly organized way – 6 **thoroughly** completely – **unstable** not firm, likely to change or fail – 7 **occasion** opportunity, reason for doing s.th. – 8 **allegiance** [ə'li:dʒəns] support for a group, person or belief – 9 **temptation** attraction to s.th. forbidden – **to resist** to fight successfully against – 13 **to prevent** to stop – 15 **conditioned** influenced by training – **you can't help doing** it is impossible for you not to do – 22 **to calm** to make quiet, to soften – 23 **to reconcile** to make friendly again after a quarrel – 25 **to accomplish** to achieve, to manage – 27 **to swallow** to eat without chewing – 28 **virtuous** ['vɜ:tʃʊəs] well behaved and morally correct – 32 **tempest** storm – 37 **to hoe** to use a garden hoe *(Hacke)* – 40 **to sting** to hurt sharply – 46 **to frown** [aʊ] to draw one's eyebrows together – 49 **Whether 'tis nobler …** part of the famous 'To be or not to be' monologue in Shakespeare's 'Hamlet' – 50 **sling** catapult used in war – **outrageous** shocking, violent – **fortune** *here:* fate – **to take arms** to fight – 51 **to oppose** to fight (against)

1 *Contrast Mustapha Mond's arguments to those of the Savage. Use gerund constructions.*

Mustapha Mond claims/argues:

In a really civilized state there aren't any occasions for … (ll. 1-4)
The perfect state of today has succeeded in … and its people have no difficulty in … (ll. 12-16)
As people's instincts are allowed to run freely there is no point in … (ll. 16-19)
If people have any problems, they can solve them by … (ll. 19-24)
That's why … is so easy in Brave New World. (l. 28)
And anyone can get what they want without … (ll. 24-26, 42-44)

The Savage thinks/believes:

The young man in the Indian story that was able to bear … eventually succeeded in … (ll. 35-41)
The story shows that … something without … for it is too easy.
And only things that are won by … are really worth … (ll. 31, 54-55)
People should be given a chance of … and they ought not to be prevented from … (ll. 47-53)
… of everything unpleasant would make life too easy and perhaps not worth …

2 *Translate the gerund constructions in the first paragraph (ll. 1-30).*

Check-up

1 Proverbs

Complete these English proverbs with either present or past participles.

bark
save earn
roll
sleep
bite
serve
last
play
share halve
unite divide
do
begin do

1 A … dog never bites.
2 A penny … is a penny … .
3 A … stone gathers no moss.
4 Let … dogs lie.
5 Once … , twice shy.
6 First come, first … .
7 First impressions are the most … .
8 There's many a good tune … on an old fiddle.
9 A trouble … is a trouble … .
10 … we stand, … we fall.
11 If you want a thing … well, do it yourself.
12 Well … is half … .

2 Finnegan's rest

First read the text. Then rewrite it, using participle constructions where possible.
Example:
Having had a tough day at the police station, Inspector Finnegan felt exhausted.

1 Inspector Finnegan had had a tough day at the police station. He felt exhausted.
2 He had his supper and after that sat down on the sofa and switched on the TV.
3 On the screen he could see two men. They were getting into a car.
4 With heavy eyes he watched them as they drove slowly away.
5 The man who was driving the car looked very much like Franco Costellini.
6 Finnegan leaned back on the sofa and closed his eyes.
7 His beer stood on the table next to him. It was untouched.
8 He heard some soft voices. They were talking about something he couldn't quite make out.
9 There was this third man. He was standing in front of the bank. He was waiting for someone or something.
10 As Finnegan had never seen him before he tried to concentrate on the other two. – But where were they now? –
11 Suddenly he found himself in some dark room. He was lying on a bed.
12 He lay there and was covered with some sort of blanket.
13 He didn't know where he was. So he felt frightened.
14 Then he heard that someone was opening a door somewhere.
15 When he tried to get up he noticed that someone was standing in front of him. – Costellini!?! –
16 He jumped up in panic and screamed for help.
'Sorry, darling, I didn't mean to wake you up,' said his wife.

'… So if some character comes up to you offering you a cheap pocket TV, ring the police.'

Present participles (active in meaning)	Past participles (passive in meaning)	
The weather forecast for the **coming** week doesn't sound very **promising.**	The weather in Scotland was rather **mixed,** and we even had an **unexpected** fall of snow.	1 used as adjectives
We got back in the car and *sat* **waiting** for the rain to stop.	With so little snow most ski pistes will *remain* **closed.**	2 after verbs describing a position *(sit, lie,* etc.) or movement *(come, go,* etc.)
We *watched* the clouds **racing** across the sky.	When we got down to the beach, we *found* our boat **damaged** by the storm.	3 after verbs of perception and observation *(see, hear, notice,* etc.)
Rain **spreading** from the west will reach most areas tomorrow. (Rain which will spread ...)	A woman **hit** by falling branches was badly injured. (A woman who was hit ...)	4 instead of relative clauses
Knowing that the roads would be icy, we went by train. (As we knew ...) **Having reached** the top of the hill, they sat down in the sunshine. (After/When they had reached ...)	**Covered** in snow, the landscape looked quite different. (As it was covered in snow, ...)	5 instead of adverbial clauses or main clauses a without conjunctions (reason, time, circumstances)
The guide led us through the fog, **warning** us to keep to the path. (... He warned us to keep to the path.)	Rain will spread to most parts, **followed** by brighter weather later. (... It will be followed ...)	
While taking photographs of the enormous waves, a man was swept off a cliff.	**Though** badly **shaken** by the earthquake, the skyscraper did not collapse.	b with conjunctions *(while, when, though, if, as if,* etc.)

Note

There will be outbreaks of rain, *some of the showers* **falling** as snow over the Scottish hills.
It will be a cold day **with** *frost* **returning** to many places during the evening.
With *so many roads* **blocked** by the snow, traffic broke down in many areas.

Participle constructions can have subjects of their own. These constructions can also be introduced by with.

'The Joneses are having disappointing weather in Malaga!'

'It's considered a major breakthrough in man-made fibres.'

1 The Great Plague

GG 121, 123, 125–127; GhE 282, 293–295, 300

Samuel Pepys

A red cross was painted on house doors where the plague had struck

There were several disasters in the reign of Charles II. In 1665, a hot summer and the filthy streets caused a fever known as the Plague, or the Pestilence, to spread quickly, and thousands of Londoners died. A man named Samuel Pepys kept a secret diary at this time, written in shorthand. Here are some of the things he wrote down:

> June 7th.
> This day I did in Drury Lane see two or three houses marked with a red cross upon the doors and 'Lord have mercy upon us' writ there, which was a sad sight to see.

> June 21st.
> I find all the town almost going out of town, the coaches and waggons being all full of people going into the country.

People left the City in boats

People who were ill with the plague were taken away in closed litters or coaches to a kind of hospital known as a pest-house. At night men with carts collected the dead.

> Lord! how sad a sight it is to see the streets empty of people and two shops out of three, if not more, shut up.

The dead were taken outside the walls and buried in the fields

One day, Pepys saw a naked child being passed out of the window of a house:

> It was the child of a citizen in Gracious Street, a saddler, who had buried all the rest of his children of the plague, and he and his wife being now shut up in despair of escaping, did desire only to save the life of this little child; and so prevailed to have it received, stark naked into the arms of a friend, who brought it, having put it into new fresh clothes, to Greenwich; where we did agree it should be permitted to be received and kept in the town.

Returning after the plague

13 When the winter came, the plague grew less, but next year, 1666, another disaster happened: The Great Fire of London.

From *Looking at History* by R.J. Unstead

1 **reign** [reɪn] period of ruling (of a king, queen) – 5 **Pepys** [pi:ps] – 12 **mercy** pity and forgiveness – **writ** written – 15 **all the town almost** most of the town – 19 **litter** a kind of stretcher – 25/32 **(stark) naked** [ˈneɪkɪd] without clothes on – 30 **in despair of escaping** having given up all hope of escaping – 31 **to desire** to wish strongly – 32 **prevailed to have it received** managed to have it accepted, succeeded in handing it over

1 *Before you start this exercise make a list of all the participles or participle constructions in the text.*
   a *Find an example of a participle used as an adjective. What verb is it derived from?*
   b *Find one example each of present and past participles used after verbs of perception. What is the difference in meaning?*
   c *There are several participle constructions used instead of relative clauses. Change them into 'normal' relative clauses.*
   d *Change the clause with the perfect form of the present participle into an adverbial clause of time.*
   e *Translate the two sentences that include participle constructions with subjects of their own.*

2 *Look at the pictures and describe what you can see.*
Example: In the first picture you can see people painting red crosses on doors./People can be seen painting red crosses on doors.

2 My room GG 121, 125, 126, 146; GhE 293, 300, 341

In this extract from 'Room at the Top', Joe Lampton, the hero of the novel, has just arrived in Warley and is being shown his new room. Moving into a room of his own is the first step on the way from his working class background to the 'top'.

Complete the text with these participles:
burning – chosen – cream-painted – depressing – extending – feeling – fitted – following – hanging – impressed – leaving – meaning – wanting

Now, … Mrs Thompson into *my room,* I was moving into a different world. 'It's marvellous', I said, … the inadequacy of the words and yet not … to appear too … : after all, I hadn't been living in the slums. I looked at it with incredulous delight: wallpaper vertically striped in beige and silver, a bay window … for almost the whole length of the room with … cushions along it, a divan bed that looked like a divan and not like a bed with its … daylight intimations of sleep and sickness, two armchairs, and a dressing-table, a wardrobe and writing-table all in the same pale satiny wood. On the … book-case was a bowl of anemones and there was a fire … in the grate, … an aromatic smell, faintly acid and faintly flower-like, which I knew but couldn't quite place.

'Applewood,' Mrs Thompson said. 'Thanks to the coal shortage we're becoming connoisseurs. There's an electric fire but I thought a real one would be more cheerful on a miserable day like this.' There were three small pictures … on the far wall: *The Harbour at Arles,* a Breughel skating scene, and Manet's *Olympe.*

'Especially … in your honour,' Mrs Thompson said. 'Medici reproductions. We have quite a picture library – you just slip in new ones when you become tired of them.'

'I like the skaters,' I said, … I liked it best.

From *Room at the Top* by John Braine

to extend to stretch, to continue – **fitted** *here: genau passend* – 3 **inadequacy** if something is inadequate it is not good enough or fitting – 5 **incredulous delight** unbelievable joy – 6 **bay window** *Erkerfenster* – 8 **divan (bed)** [dɪˈvæn] *Liege* – 10 **intimation** suggestion – 14 **grate** *here: Kamin* – **acid** (unpleasantly) sour – 18 **connoisseur** [ˌkɒnəˈsɜ:] person who knows a lot about something

Now translate the first paragraph into German.

3 Get away from it all! GG 123, 125; GhE 282, 300

Write your own advertisement for a leisure break at one of the comfortable 'Castle Hotels' in Britain. Use present and past participles to make your advert sound effective.

Example:

Enjoy the view of the clouds **sailing** over the silent Yorkshire moors.
Appreciate the taste of our own **oven-baked** bread.

Use these ideas:

SIGHT	see	rainbow/sun	**rise/build up/form/set**	on the horizon
	watch	silvery moon	**shine**	on the sea
	look at	eagles	**fly**	over the Scottish hills
SOUND	hear	birds	**sing**	in the trees of Sherwood Forest
	listen to	village church bells	**ring**	in a Welsh valley
TOUCH	feel	soft wind	**blow**	in your hair
TASTE	enjoy	**locally grow/home–cook**	specialities	of our kitchen
	taste	**beautifully serve**	delicious meals	
	try	**specially pick**	fruit	from our own gardens
SMELL	find	lovely flowers	**beautifully arrange**	for you in your room
	be woken up by	aroma	**freshly make**	coffee or delicious chocolate
	rediscover	smell	open fire	**burn** in our bars
	be tempted	homely smell	**beautifully cook**	traditional English breakfast

4 Film of the week GG 123, 125–127; GhE 282, 293–295, 300

Shorten the text by turning the underlined clauses into participle constructions.

PHANTOM LADY

(Tuesday, C 4, 12.15 – 1.50 am)
Robert Siodmak, who was born in Germany, made his first impression with 'Piège', which was produced in France in 1939. But 'Phantom Lady' (1944) was his first real success in the US. The story is drawn from a novel by William Irish and it depends on the disappearance of an important witness – not a frightfully new plot, but its treatment here has unusual tension. The cast, which includes Franchot Tone, Thomas Gomez and Elisha Cook Jr., are particularly well chosen.

Alan Curtis plays a New York architect, who, after he has quarrelled with his wife, goes to a bar, gets to know a woman and goes to the theatre with her. She insists on anonymity, and they part without exchanging addresses. When he arrives home, he finds that his wife has been strangled and sees that the place is crowded with police. He is not afraid because he knows he has an alibi. The woman only has to be found. But as he does not know her name, he cannot trace her. People must have seen her when she sat with him at the bar and in the theatre. But there have been unfortunate accidents: the barman has been knocked down by a car and killed, and the drummer at the bar has had the bad taste to get strangled. Everyone insists that the architect was alone; he is tried for murder and found guilty, so he begins to despair. One hope remains: – his secretary (Ella Raines), who is convinced that he is innocent, searches and interviews.

Adapted from *The Sunday Times*, November 12, 1989

11 **witness** a person that is there when an accident or a crime happens – 13 **tension** a feeling of nervous excitement – **cast** the actors in a play or film – 21 **to insist on s.th.** to be very firm about s.th., to demand s.th. – 22 **to part** to separate, to say goodbye – 25 **to strangle** to kill by pressing the throat – 39 **to try s.o.** to examine s.o. in a court and decide whether he/she is guilty or not – 41 **to despair** to lose all hope – 43 **to be convinced** to be certain – 44 **innocent** not guilty

13 Advanced Exercises

1 Heroic failures GG 121–127; GhE 257.2, 292–295

The least successful home repairs

Home repairs offer immense scope to the right sort of person. In 1980 Mr Brian Heise of Utah showed the way when he woke up to find a burst pipe flooding his house. Deciding to hire a pump, he went out to his car only to find that a tyre was flat. Returning indoors to make a phone call, he received an electric shock so great that he was hurled across the room and ripped the telephone out of the wall. He then found that dampness had caused the floor to swell and the front door was jammed so he could not get out. A seminal figure in the world of home repairs, he spent some while screaming through the window for help. Only when a neighbour smashed down the front door did Mr Heise notice that his car had been stolen. Having informed the police, hired a pump, sealed the leak and cleaned up his flat, Mr Heise felt that the moment had come to relax. Displaying an impressive versatility, he went to a nearby civil war pageant and within minutes of arrival sat on a bayonet.

The least successful crime prevention

When his nightly stroll brought him face to face with a mugging, a young Brisbane doctor felt he had no alternative but to intervene. Seeing, in May 1982, a robust man struggling brutally with an old lady crying for help in the street, he cried, 'Stop at once', and leaped forward, grabbing her assailant by the shoulders. He had laid into the surprised mugger and was generally manhandling him, when the director of the television drama for which this was an outdoor sequence stepped forward to protect his cast.

The least successful jewellery raid

With a thoughtfulness that is rare nowadays, Paul Lassis alerted the staff of a Bristol jewellery shop to his forthcoming raid by sounding his car horn loudly while driving up on the pavement outside. With the entire staff watching, he reached out to smash the shop window. As his hammer bounced harmlessly off the toughened glass, he tried to reverse his car through it, but missed, crashed over a waste-paper bin and was stuck fast when a passing evangelical missionary, Mr Herbert Eaton, prevented a getaway by hurtling his bicycle through the car's windscreen.

From *The Return of Heroic Failures* by Stephen Pile

2 **scope** opportunity to act – 4 **to flood** to fill with water – 7 **damp** slightly wet – 9 **seminal** inventive and influencing future development – 12 **to seal** to repair by covering – **leak** hole through which water can escape – 14 **versatility** ability to change easily from one kind of activity to another – **pageant** ['pædʒənt] a splendid (often historical) show or procession – 15 **bayonet** ['beɪənɪt] – 17 **to mug** to attack in order to steal money – 18 **to intervene** [ˌ--'-] to step in, to take action in a special situation – 20 **assailant** attacker – 21 **to lay into** to start hitting – 22 **to manhandle** ['---] to treat very roughly – 23 **cast** actors – 24 **raid** sudden attack (e.g. in order to steal) – 25 **to alert** to warn – **staff** all the people working for a firm – 29 **to reverse a car** to drive backwards – 31 **to hurtle** to push violently

1 *Explain the meaning of these expressions: a burst pipe (l. 3); the surprised mugger (l. 21); his forthcoming raid (l. 26); Toughened glass (l. 29); a passing missionary (l. 30-31).*
   Example: A burst pipe is a pipe that has broken and lets the water out.

2 a *Find examples of participle constructions used instead of adverbial clauses or main clauses. Replace them by clauses. In what way does the style change?*
   b *Translate the first two sentences of the second text, paying particular attention to the participle constructions.*

3 *Write your own report of an amusing failure, using participle constructions where possible. (It can be something from your own experience, or a scene from a film or comedy show.)*

2 Sorrow floats GG 121–127; GhE 181–182, 292–294

In this scene from the novel 'The Hotel New Hampshire', we see the Berrys, an American family, flying to Vienna where they want to take over a hotel. They are flying on two separate planes because they think it safer. Sorrow used to be their family dog. When he died they had him stuffed. The stuffed animal accompanies the family everywhere, (symbolically) coming to the foreground at decisive moments in their history.

I think we took off about 7 or 8 p.m.: the lights of Boston, on a summer night, were half on and half off, and there was enough daylight left to see the harbor clearly. It was our first time on an airplane, and we loved it.

We flew all night across the ocean. Father slept the whole way. Lilly would not sleep; she watched the darkness, and reported sighting what she said were two ocean liners. I dozed and woke, dozed and woke again; with my eyes shut, I watched Elliot Park turning into a circus.

We landed in Frankfurt at quarter to eight in the morning. Maybe it was quarter to nine.

'Deutschland!' Frank said. He led us through the Frankfurt airport to our connecting flight to Vienna, reading all the signs out loud, speaking amiably to all the foreigners.

'We're the foreigners,' Franny kept whispering.

'Guten Tag!' Frank hailed all the passing strangers.

'Those people were French, Frank,' Franny said. 'I'm sure of it.'

Father almost lost the passports, so we attached them with two stout rubber bands to Lilly's wrist; then I carried Lilly, who seemed exhausted from her tears.

We left Frankfurt at quarter to nine, or maybe quarter to ten, and arrived in Vienna about noon. It was a short, choppy flight in a smaller plane. Lilly saw some mountains and was frightened; Franny said she hoped it would be smoother weather, the next day, for Mother and Egg; Frank vomited twice. 'Say it in German, Frank,' Franny said, but Frank felt too terrible to answer her.

The flight that Mother and Egg were taking was supposed to leave Boston slightly later in the evening of the next day and fly to Zürich; their connecting flight, to Vienna, would take about an hour, and Boston to Zürich – like our flight to Frankfurt – was scheduled for about seven hours. But Mother and Egg – and Sorrow – landed short of Zürich. Less than six hours out of Boston, they struck the Atlantic Ocean a glancing blow – off the coastline of that part of the continent called France. In my imagination, later (and illogically), it was some slight consolation to know that they did not fall in darkness, and to imagine that there might – in *their* minds – have been some hopefulness implied by the vision of solid ground in the distance (though they did not reach the ground). It is too unlikely to imagine that Egg was sleeping, although anyone would hope so; knowing Egg, he would have been wide-awake the whole way – Sorrow jouncing on his knees. Egg would have had the window seat.

And though we had moved to the city of Freud, I must say that dreams are vastly overrated: my dream of Mother's death was inexact, and I would never dream it again. She shot from the sky to the bottom of the sea with her son beside her screaming, Sorrow hugged to his chest.

It was Sorrow, of course, that the rescue planes saw. Searching for the sunken wreckage, trying to spot the first debris upon the surface of the gray water, someone saw a dog swimming. Closer examination convinced the rescue crew that the dog was just another victim; there were no survivors, and how could the rescue crew have known that *this* dog was already dead. This knowledge of what led the rescue crew to the bodies came as no surprise to my surviving family. We had learned this fact of Sorrow, previously, from Frank: Sorrow floats.

From *The Hotel New Hampshire* by John Irving

sorrow *Sorge, Kummer* – **to float** to stay on the surface, not to sink – **to stuff** to fill tightly *(here:* to restore the shape of a dead animal) – 6 **ocean liner** big ship – 11 **amiable** ['eɪmjəbl] friendly – 14 **to hail** to call to – 16 **to attach** to fasten – 7 **stout** strong – 17 **wrist** *Handgelenk* – 20 **choppy** rough – 22 **smooth** not rough – **to vomit** to be sick – 28 **to schedule** ['ʃedju:l] to plan, to time – 30 **to strike s.th. a glancing blow** to hit s.th. at an angle rather than directly – 32 **consolation** s.th. that makes you feel better at a time of sadness or disappointment – 37 **to jounce** to bounce, to jump up and down – 40 **to overrate s.th.** to attach too much importance to s.th. – 44 **debris** ['debri:] pieces of things that have been destroyed – **surface** ['sɜ:fɪs] top part of an area

1 *Imagine that you have seen the film in which these scenes are shown. Give a summary up to line 24, using participles after verbs of perception. Example:*
We see the Berrys flying to Vienna. On the plane the father can be seen …
Lilly watches …
At Frankfurt airport we find them … Frank can be heard …
Go on.
2 *Look at the participle construction 'knowing Egg' in line 36. In what way is it different from any other participle construction in this chapter? Try to explain what it means.*
3 *Translate from l.35 'It is too unlikely …' to l. 45 '… a dog swimming.'*
4 *Contrast the first part of the text (ll. 1–24) with the second part. These words may help you to formulate your impressions:*
surprising shocking unexpected amusing striking moving
well expressed detailed light-hearted in tone depressing

3 Journey of the Magi

'A cold coming we had of it,
Just the worst time of the year
For a journey, and such a long journey:
The ways deep and the weather sharp,
The very dead of winter.'
And the camels galled, sore-footed, refractory
Lying down in the melting snow.
There were times we regretted
The summer palaces on slopes, the terraces,
And the silken girls bringing sherbet.
Then the camel men cursing and grumbling
And running away, and wanting their liquor and women,
And the night-fires going out, and the lack of shelters,
And the cities hostile and the towns unfriendly
And the villages dirty and charging high prices:
A hard time we had of it.
At the end we preferred to travel all night,
Sleeping in snatches,
With the voices singing in our ears, saying
That this was all folly.

Then at dawn we came down to a temperate valley,
Wet, below the snow line, smelling of vegetation;
With a running stream and a water-mill beating the darkness,
And three trees on the low sky,
And an old white horse galloped away in the meadow.
Then we came to a tavern with vine-leaves over the lintel,
Six hands at an open door dicing for pieces of silver,
And feet kicking the empty wine-skins.
But there was no information, and so we continued
And arrived at evening, not a moment too soon
Finding the place; it was (you may say) satisfactory.

All this was a long time ago, I remember,
And I would do it again, but set down
This set down
This: were we led all that way for
Birth or Death? There was a Birth, certainly,
We had evidence and no doubt. I had seen birth and death,
But had thought they were different; this Birth was
Hard and bitter agony for us, like Death, our death.
We returned to our places, these Kingdoms,
But no longer at ease here, in the old dispensation,
With an alien people clutching their gods.
I should be glad of another death.

T.S. Eliot (1888–1965)

the Magi ['meɪdʒaɪ] the three wise men who brought gifts for the baby Jesus – 5 **the very dead of winter** the middle of winter – 6 **galled** [gɔ:ld] with their backs made sore by the saddle – **refractory** stubborn and difficult to control – 8 **to regret** *here:* to miss – 9 **slope** rising ground – 10 **silken** *here:* wearing silk *(Seide)* – **sherbet** kind of lemonade – 11 **to curse** to swear – 12 **liquor** ['lɪkə] any strong alcoholic drink – 13 **lack** absence – **shelter** covered place that protects against rain, wind, etc. – 14 **hostile** ['hɒstaɪl] unfriendly – 15 **to charge** to demand – 18 **to sleep in snatches** to sleep for short periods only and to wake up often – 20 **folly** stupidity – 21 **dawn** daybreak, sunrise – **temperate** neither too hot nor too cold – 25 **meadow** [e] field of grass – 26 **lintel** a piece of stone or wood across the top of a door (part of the frame) – 27 **to dice** *würfeln* – 39 **agony** great pain – 41 **at ease** feeling comfortable – **dispensation** a particular religious system or order – 42 **alien** ['eɪljən] foreign; strange and frightening – **to clutch** to hold very tightly

1 *Look at the structure of the sentences in the first part of the poem (ll. 1-20). Is there anything that strikes you as unusual? What effect is created by this style? How does the tone differ in the last part (ll. 32-43)?*
2 *Write a prose version of the first part. Do not use any participles. Start like this:* In his poem T.S. Eliot describes the 'Journey of the Magi' to Bethlehem: The weather was very bad. The camels did not want to go on and they lay down in the snow. The men …

14 Non-finite Verb Forms: Mixed Exercises

Check-up

1 96-year-old fined for speeding

Fill in the correct non-finite verb forms – infinitives, gerunds or participles.

speed
motor drive
take drive do
travel give
stop complain
go

operate
roar come
be
pass
take drive
motor
stop think
be caught have to do

need hear
think hand in drive

A motorist of 96 was fined £20 yesterday – for … – his first offence in 70 years of … . Mr Dale was warned … more carefully in future but was not ordered … a …-test. He was caught by a radar trap, … 49 m.p.h. in a 30 m.p.h. area, while … near his home in Folkestone. He refused … his age to police when … , but later wrote a letter to a newspaper, … about the radar trap. He said he was 96 and was looking forward to … around Brands Hatch on his 100th birthday.

Police Constable William Holton, one of the men … the radar trap, said: 'We heard an engine … and then saw him … round the corner. He appeared … in some hurry.'

Mr Dale said: 'Oh, I'm 96 all right, but I'm fit. I've no doubt that I could … any test they might have asked me … . I remember … my first motor-bike in 1902. More than 70 years of trouble-free … is not a bad record, and I've got no reason … … that I'm one of the safest drivers on the road. But I'm still annoyed about … . On that particular stretch of road, … … 30 m.p.h. is absurd. I take regular medical check-ups, and my heart and lungs are first-class. I do … glasses, and I don't … as well as I used to, but **that** won't make me … of … my licence. I'm still fit enough … .

Adapted from an article in the *Daily Mail*

to fine s.o. to make s.o. pay for breaking a rule or law – 1 **offence** breaking of a rule or law – 7 **Brands Hatch** a race track south-east of London

2 On holiday

Complete the sentences, using either infinitives or gerunds.

complain
get
send
see
shut
climb
get
go
get up
go
inform
buy

1 a Please stop … about the heat in here. I can't help it.
  b We'll have to stop … some petrol soon.
2 a We must remember … Aunt Agatha a postcard from the States.
  b I'll always remember … New York for the first time.
3 a Don't forget … the windows before we set off.
  b I'll never forget … Ben Nevis. What an experience!
4 a We should try … to the hotel before 8 p.m. if possible.
  b The motorways were so chaotic. Let's try … by train next time.
5 a The flight leaves at 8.20. That'll mean … quite early.
  b I've heard so much about Australia. I really mean … there soon.
6 a We regret … you that our hotel is fully booked for July.
  b I don't regret … that more expensive road map. It's so helpful.

'Let them have a bit longer to try to translate the menu, then start preparing steak and chips for three.'

Gerund and infinitve: no difference in meaning

The dog **started barking** when it saw the cat.	The cat **started to climb** the nearest tree.

Start, begin, continue and *like, love, hate, prefer* can be followed by a gerund or an infinitive.

Note

We **would like to have** a dog, but our flat is too small.

After would/(should) like/love/prefer *the infinitive must be used.*

Gerund and infinitive: different meaning

We must have annoyed our parrot. He has **stopped saying** 'Good morning' to us.	There's a pet shop over there. Let's **stop to get** some bird food.
The gerund after *stop* expresses an action which has come to an end.	The infinitive after *stop* expresses the intention to do something else.
I can't **remember taking** that photo of Bonzo. Do you know when I took it?	We must **remember to feed** the budgie before we go.
The gerund after *forget, remember* and *regret* expresses that something has been done/has happened.	The infinitive after *forget, remember* and *regret* expresses an intention to do something.

Note 1

Most budgie owners **try to teach** their birds to talk.
Sammy won't eat dog biscuits. – Why don't you **try mixing** them in with his meat?

The infinitive after try *expresses an attempt.*
The gerund after try *expresses a new method of doing something.*

Note 2

I **meant to take** the dog for a walk but I didn't have time. (Ich hatte vor, …)
Now that we've got that dog, it **means planning** our holidays much more carefully. (Das bedeutet, daß wir … müssen.)

The infinitive after mean *expresses an intention.*
The gerund after mean *expresses a consequence.*

'Oh, we could improve our image, I suppose. But that would mean we'd have to stop acting like rats.'

Present participle and infinitive after verbs of perception

We could **hear** the cats **fighting** and **screaming** all night.	We **saw** the cat **stop** suddenly and then **jump** on the mouse.
The present participle after verbs of perception describes an action in progress.	The infinitive after verbs of perception describes a completed action. The construction is mainly used to describe short actions or a series of actions.

1 The boxing match GG 99, 115, 116, 123; GhE 263, 276, 282

Complete the sentences, using infinitives, gerunds or participles.

spend / beat / see / fight / say become / stare / look frighten sound / dance / avoid throw / hit send / count hold / go drop / crash / yell / shout / use / tap stand / insult / annoy look / shout raise / go

'What? Where are you going?' Tony asked. 'But that means … a hell of a lot of money, just to watch two men … each other up.'

Tony's my best friend, but I didn't care. I had been looking forward to … Butcher Jason … Tiger Robinson for months.

'I remember somebody … that he would live to see Jason … world champion,' I said.

'O.K., have a nice time,' Tony said.

Before the fight began, I watched the two boxers … at each other, trying … tough and … each other. Then I heard the gong … .

For a long time I sat and watched the two boxers … round each other as if they were trying … each other. But suddenly I saw Tiger … a left hook and saw his red glove … Jason's chin. The referee stopped the fight … Tiger to his corner. Then he started … . I watched Butcher … on to the ropes. Then, all at once, I noticed his eyes … all funny and his head … forward; a moment later I heard him … to the floor.

All the spectators were on their feet and started … . I heard someone next to me … something I couldn't understand, but it didn't sound nice.

'Get your ass off that floor, you fat slug,' I yelled.

I can't remember … language like that before, ever. Then I felt someone … me on the shoulder, hard. I turned round and saw this big guy … directly behind me.

'You stop … my brother,' he yelled at me.

'I'm sorry, I didn't mean … you,' I said, trying … cool.

But he went on … , getting wilder all the time. Then I saw him … his fists. It was not until I noticed the snake's head tattooed on his right biceps that I really regretted … to the boxing match.

16 **to yell** to shout loudly – 18 **ass** slang word for the part of your body that you sit on – **slug** *Schnecke* – 20 **to tap** to hit quickly and lightly – 22 **to insult s.o.** to annoy s.o. by speaking rudely – 24 **fist** closed hand (as a sign of threat) – 25 **to tattoo** [tə'tu:] to make permanent pictures on the skin – **biceps** ['baɪseps]

'No skill? You try to cut an eye open, left-handed, wearing eight-ounce gloves.'

2 School's over: What now?

GG 101, 103, 107, 116–120; GhE 259, 269–273, 290, 295

Translate into English, using gerunds and infinitives wherever possible.

1 ‚Ich freue mich darauf, endlich Geld zu verdienen.'
2 ‚Nach der Schule will ich Architektur studieren. Ich träume schon davon, mein eigenes Haus zu entwerfen.'
3 ‚Ich habe schon daran gedacht, für ein paar Monate nach Amerika zu gehen und dort zu arbeiten.'
4 ‚Ich möchte ganz gern für eine Reisegesellschaft arbeiten. Aber ich hätte kein Interesse daran, den ganzen Tag im Büro zu sitzen.'
5 ‚Ich finde, man sollte etwas wirklich Lohnendes *(something really worthwhile)* machen, anstatt immer nur ans Geld zu denken.'
6 ‚Meine Eltern wollten schon immer, daß ich im Familienbetrieb mitarbeite. Ich weiß nicht, wie ich nein sagen kann, ohne sie zu enttäuschen. Ich habe Angst, ihnen die Wahrheit zu sagen – aber andererseits hat es keinen Zweck, etwas anzufangen, das mich überhaupt nicht interessiert.'

3 Danger, mountains! GG 101–107, 113, 115–117, 119, 121, 123, 126; GhE 257, 263–265, 274–275, 283, 293

Complete the sentences, using gerunds, participles or infinitives. Choose from the verbs on the left.

be killed set off strand
take think walk walk

Every year there are reports of people … while … in the Scottish mountains. The Scottish hills are not very high, so this often makes tourists … they are harmless. People that are used to … in the Alps, may suddenly find themselves … in fog on much lower hills. Many people fail … appropriate precautions before … .

check climb leave
protect realize take
wear

You can often see people … completely unsuitable clothes. Sometimes visitors try … mountains without … the dangers of the weather. Sandals and T-shirts are not suitable … hikers from sudden rain, fog or even snow in summer. Hikers should remember … the weather forecast and they mustn't forget … a map or a compass and … details of their route.

be be spoilt
believe make make
mark put up seem

The real problem is how … people aware of mountain conditions. 156 information offices warn the country's 13.5 million annual visitors … aware of the dangers. But the Scottish authorities are against … more signposts , and they are also against more clearly … paths because they don't want unspoilt hills … , and they are afraid of even more people … that the hills are more harmless than they really are. Experienced hill walkers are also against … things … easier on the mountains.

4 **to fail to do s.th.** not to do what is expected – **appropriate** correct and suitable – 5 **precaution** an action done to avoid possible danger – 12 **to be aware of** to know of, to realize

4 Pilots win top bravery award for drilling rig rescue

GG 100, 109–110, 118–119, 121, 123, 125–127; GKE 257, 282, 289, 292–296, 300

Complete the newspaper article, using these non-finitive verb forms:

Gerunds:
flying, saving, saving

Infinitives:
to arrive, to escape, go out, to land, to reach, to try

Participles:
being moved, crawling, doing, flying, knowing, landing, relieved, saved, shining, speaking

Four British helicopter pilots have won the world's most famous bravery award for … 51 workers from a North Sea drilling rig during a storm. The pilots repeatedly risked their own lives, … on the rig in 85 mph winds and 25 ft-high waves. Their courage and skill in … the workers just minutes before the rig capsized was recognized yesterday when they were awarded the 1989 Helicopter Heroism Award in Maryland, America.

The two crews were called out on Nov. 8, 1989, when the rig Interocean II broke its tow 65 miles out to sea while … to a new position.

Captain Stuart Gregg and his co-pilot Captain Mike Wood, in their Sikorsky S76, were the first … on the scene. The pilots had great difficulty in … their helicopter in the dense fog and heavy rain. Captain Wood made the first landing, … ten … crewmen to the Sean Papa platform 20 miles away. Then Captain Dale Moon, 42, and his co-pilot Captain Roger Williams managed … on the rig. Ten more men were able … to safety. After two more trips 40 men were aboard the Sean Papa.

Then the pilots saw the rig lights … … that time was running out, Captain Gregg decided … a final landing, with only the helicopter's searchlights … through the dark night. By now the wind was so strong and the deck so slippery that the pilots saw the last 11 men … on hands and knees … the helicopter. Just 15 minutes later Interocean II capsized.

Captain Gregg, … in America, said: 'We were just four guys … a job to the best of our abilities in very difficult conditions. We are happy that all the men could be … .'

Adapted from *The Sunday Express*, April 22, 1990

award prize – **(drilling) rig** platform used to look for oil – 10 **to capsize** to turn over – 16 **tow** [əʊ] the rope etc. by which a boat is pulled

14 Advanced Exercises

1 Help us save the dolphins GG 110, 118–119, 121, 123, 125–127; GhE 257, 288, 292–300

150,000 dolphins killed in tuna nets each year

A FATAL ATTRACTION

For reasons no-one fully understands, **yellowfin tuna** and **dolphins** swim and live together in an area called the Eastern Tropical Pacific. From California to Chile, tuna fishermen set out to take advantage of this association. Easily spotted from helicopters, it is the dolphins who are hunted down in the uncertain hope of catching valuable tuna with them.

Chased for hours by speedboats, the exhausted dolphins are finally surrounded by a mile-long net. Panic-stricken, few, if any, escape.

Dolphin and tuna – the fatal attraction

DROWNED IN THE NETS

Like a giant purse, the net is drawn shut at the bottom and pulled in. In the ensuing confusion, mothers and young are separated, escape routes to the surface are blocked and many dolphins, tangled, terrified and deprived of air, simply drown.

No escape as the net closes in

CRUSHED IN THE WINCHES

Those dolphins 'lucky' enough to survive the 'round-up' are hauled up in the net. Bodyparts ripped away, many animals fall helpless and in agony back to the water. Others end their lives crushed in the winching machinery.

Drowned – the tragic end result

THROWN BACK OVERBOARD – TO SHARKS

The survivors are dumped overboard. Maimed, injured or in shock, many fall victim to the sharks attracted by the carnage taking place.

This slaughter is **totally** unnecessary. Most of the world's tuna is caught **without** hurting dolphins ... **or profits.** It's time for the killing to stop.

HELP US TO END IT

To campaign effectively, we need **your** support. By acting today, you can help stop them butchering entire families of dolphins in the name of profit and greed.

YOU can help us save them by:
- making a donation to our campaign **today.**
- joining the Society if you aren't already a member.
- purchasing our exclusive 'Save the Dolphins' T-shirt.

YOUR support will enable us to:
- inform retailers throughout Europe and persuade them to stock only 'dolphin-friendly' tuna.
- encourage the use of alternative fishing techniques.
- lobby the U.S. Government to restrengthen its Marine Mammal Protection Act and to prosecute offenders.

Disentangling a dying dolphin

TOGETHER WE CAN STOP THE KILLING ...
TOGETHER WE CAN SAVE THE DOLPHINS

Whale and Dolphin Conservation Society

20 WEST LEA ROAD, BATH, AVON BAI, 3RL.
Registered Charity 298656

YES! I WANT TO HELP YOU SAVE THE DOLPHINS

2 **fin** 'wing' of a fish that helps it to swim – 11 **to drown** [aʊ] to die in water because you cannot breathe; to make s.o. drown – 15 **to be tangled** to be caught or trapped – 16 **to crush** to break, to destroy – **winch** machine used to lift heavy objects – 18 **to haul** [ɔ:] to pull – 19 **agony** very great pain – 21 **shark** *Hai* – 22 **to maim** to injure very badly – 23 **carnage** bloody killing and wounding – 30 **greed** excessive desire to have more of s.th. (e.g. food, money) – 32 **donation** gift (of money) – 34 **to purchase** ['pɜ:tʃəs] to buy – 36 **retailer** shopkeeper – 37 **to stock** to keep for sale – 39 **to lobby** to try to influence politicians – 40 **mammal** animal that feeds its young with milk – **to prosecute** to take legal action against – **offender** s.o. who breaks a law

1 *Explain the meaning of these phrases. Your dictionary will help you.*
easily spotted (l. 5) – panic-stricken (l. 9) – the ensuing confusion (l. 13) – deprived of air (l. 15) – bodyparts ripped away (l. 18) – alternative fishing techniques (l. 38)
Example: 'Easily spotted' means that it is easy to see or to find them.

2 a *Explain how the gerund is used in ll. 7, 26, 28-29. (See also Basic Rules, p. 96)*
b *Find two examples of infinitives used to express a purpose or an intention.*
c *What is the grammatical function of these participles?*
'in an area *called* the Eastern Tropical Pacific' (ll. 3-4), 'the sharks *attracted* by the carnage *taking* place' (ll. 23-24).
Replace them by clauses.

3 *The first half of the text is full of past participles* (chased, crushed, thrown, etc.). *Find more examples. What do most of these past participles refer to? What is the effect on the reader of this large number of passive participle forms?*

4 *Look at the bottom part of the leaflet. Then talk about the way other ecological or welfare groups try to help people/animals/the environment and about the way you can help them. (Think of Greenpeace, Robin Wood, The World Wildlife Fund, Unicef, The Red Cross, etc.)*

Greenpeace tries to ... by ... People's support will enable ... to ...

2 Some animals are more equal than others

GG 100, 112, 117–119, 121–123, 126–127; GhE 257, 279–282, 292–295

In George Orwell's political fable Animal Farm, *the animals, after a successful revolution against their human masters, try to establish a democratic government on Animal Farm. The pigs, the cleverest of the animals, take over the leadership and gradually pervert the original ideals of freedom and equality. (Napoleon has become the dictator, Squealer his 'minister for propaganda'; Benjamin is a donkey, and Clover an old mare.)*

to establish to create, to set up – **donkey** [ɒ] *Esel* – **mare** a female horse – 3 **to neigh** [neɪ] to make the loud cry of a horse – 4 **startled** surprised and frightened – **to stop in one's tracks** to stop suddenly – 7 **hind legs** [haɪnd] the legs at the back – 8 **as though** as if – 9 **bulk** fat and shapeless body – 11 **file** line (one behind the other) – 12 **a trifle** [aɪ] a little – 15 **tremendous** enormous – **to bay** to bark – **crow** [əʊ] – **cockerel** young cock – 16 **to cast haughty glances** ['hɔ:tɪ] to look around arrogantly – 17 **to gambol** to run or jump around in a playful way – 18 **whip** *Peitsche* – **trotter** pig's foot –

It was just after the sheep had returned, on a pleasant evening when the animals had finished work and were making their way back to the farm buildings, that the terrified neighing of a horse sounded from the yard. Startled, the animals stopped in their tracks. It was Clover's voice. She neighed again, and all the animals broke into a gallop and rushed into the yard. Then they saw what Clover had seen.

It was a pig walking on his hind legs.

Yes, it was Squealer. A little awkwardly, as though not quite used to supporting his considerable bulk in that position, but with perfect balance, he was strolling across the yard. And a moment later, out from the door of the farmhouse came a long file of pigs, all walking on their hind legs. Some did it better than others, one or two were even a trifle unsteady and looked as though they would have liked the support of a stick, but every one of them made his way right round the yard successfully. And finally there was a tremendous baying of dogs and a shrill crowing from the black cockerel, and out came Napoleon himself, majestically upright, casting haughty glances from side to side, and with his dogs gambolling round him.

He carried a whip in his trotter.

14

19 **to huddle together** to stand close to one another (in fear) – 22 **to wear off** to disappear slowly, to become less strong – 25 **to utter** to say – 26 **to bleat** to make the sound of a sheep – 31 **to nuzzle** to push or rub gently with the nose – 32 **dim** unable to see clearly – 33 **to tug** to pull – **mane** long hair on the neck of a horse – 35 **to gaze** to look for a long time (in surprise) – **tarred** covered by tar *(Teer)* – 36 **to fail** *here:* to become weak – 40 **to consent** [kən'sent] to agree

There was a deadly silence. Amazed, terrified, huddling together, the animals watched the long line of pigs march slowly round the yard. It was as though the world had turned upside-down. Then there came a moment when the first shock had worn off, and when, in spite of everything – in spite of their terror of the dogs, and of the habit, developed through long years, of never complaining, never criticizing, no matter what happened – they might have uttered some word of protest. But just at that moment, as though at a signal, all the sheep burst into a tremendous bleating of – 'Four legs good, two legs *better!* Four legs good, two legs *better!* Four legs good, two legs *better!*' It went on for five minutes without stopping. And by the time the sheep had quieted down, the chance to utter any protest had passed, for the pigs had marched back into the farmhouse.

Benjamin felt a nose nuzzling at his shoulder. He looked round. It was Clover. Her old eyes looked dimmer than ever. Without saying anything, she tugged gently at his mane and led him round to the end of the big barn, where the Seven Commandments were written. For a minute or two they stood gazing at the tarred wall with its white lettering.

'My sight is failing,' she said finally. 'Even when I was young I could not have read what was written there. But it appears to me that the wall looks different. Are the Seven Commandments the same as they used to be, Benjamin?'

For once Benjamin consented to break his rule, and he read out to her what was written on the wall. There was nothing there now except a single Commandment. It ran:

ALL ANIMALS ARE EQUAL
BUT SOME ANIMALS ARE MORE EQUAL THAN OTHERS

From *Animal Farm* by George Orwell

1 *Make lists of the different non-finite constructions used in the text.*
2 a *Look at the past participles in ll. 1-19 and say what the author describes by using them.*
  b *Some of the gerunds in the text are used as nouns and have articles in front of them. What do they describe?*
  c *What is the difference between 'He wasn't* ***used to supporting*** *his considerable bulk' (ll. 8-9) and 'Are the Seven Commandments the same as they* ***used to be?'*** *(l. 38) Translate the sentences.*
  d *Explain the difference between 'the animals* ***watched the long line of pigs march*** *slowly round the yard' (ll. 19-20) and 'Benjamin* ***felt a nose nuzzling*** *at his shoulder' (ll. 31).*
3 *Translate: ll. 14-21 ('And finally … had turned upside-down.')*
4 *Imagine this scene as a film and describe what you can see/watch/hear. Example:*
  At the beginning of the scene we see the animals making their way back to the farmhouse. Then suddenly we hear a horse neigh. *Go on.*
5 *Talk about this scene:*
  a *What role do the pigs seem to play?*
  b *Why do they try to walk on their hind legs?*
  c *What is the animals' reaction to seeing the pigs march on two legs?*
  d *What is the meaning of the whip carried by Napoleon?*
  e *In what way do the sheep seem to influence the other animals' behaviour?*
  f *What is the meaning of the Commandment written on the barn wall?*

3 Traveling through the dark

Traveling through the dark I found a deer
dead on the edge of the Wilson road.
It is usually best to roll them into the canyon:
that road is narrow: to swerve might make more dead.

By glow of the tail-light I stumbled back of the car
and stood by the heap, a doe, a recent killing;
she had stiffened already, almost cold.
I dragged her off; she was large in the belly.

My fingers touching her side brought me the reason –
her side was warm; her fawn lay there waiting,
alive, still, never to be born.
Beside that mountain road I hesitated.

The car aimed ahead its lowering parking lights;
under the hood purred the steady engine.
I stood in the glare of the warm exhaust turning red;
around our group I could hear the wilderness listen.

I thought hard for us all – my only swerving –
then pushed her over the edge into the river.

From *Stories That Could Be True: New And Collected Poems* by William Stafford

4 **to swerve** to turn suddenly to one side – 5 **glow** a soft light – **to stumble** to put one's foot down awkwardly and almost fall – 6 **heap** *here:* a heavy lifeless mass – **doe** female deer – 7 **to stiffen** to become hard – 8 **to drag** to pull along the ground – **belly** lower part of the body – 10 **fawn** very young deer – 13 **lowering** [aʊ] dark and dangerous-looking – 14 **hood** AE part of the car that covers the engine – **to purr** to make a noise like a pleased cat – **steady** [e] moving in a regular and reliable way – 15 **glare** bright light

1 a *Why is it 'usually best to roll' dead animals off the road?*
 b *What does the speaker discover by touching the doe?*
 c *What does 'her fawn lay there waiting' and 'never to be born' mean?*
 d *What does the speaker mean when he says he 'could hear the wilderness listen'?*
 e *What is meant by 'my only swerving'?*

2 a *Look carefully at the description of the deer, and compare it with the description of the car. What contrast do you see?*
 b *The speaker seems to find it difficult to make a decision. What is the dilemma he finds himself in? How does he resolve it?*
 c *What could the title of the poem mean? Think of various possibilities.*

15 Verbs and their Objects

Check-up

1 Tastes differ

Put in the objects with or without to *and choose the best word order.*

Paul: Can you lend *(some money/me)* for this new CD? It's Beethoven's Ninth, conducted by Bernstein. I showed *(it/you)* when we were in here yesterday.
Peter: I can't remember you saying *(anything/me)* about it. Perhaps you showed *(it/Mike)* and not me. Anyway, I owe *(some money/you)* for the theatre tickets last week, so that's O.K.
Paul: Right. We're quits then. This is a really great recording! Perhaps I could lend *(it/you)* some time. I –
Peter: Oh, Paul! You're always trying to teach *(something about music/me)* – I'm fed up with it. Either you're giving *(a lesson on Bach/me)* or trying to sell *(a ticket/me)* for a concert by your third-rate school orchestra. No thanks! I prefer jazz, you know that. I've explained *(it all/you)* hundreds of times.
Paul: O.K., O.K. Sorry. Hand *(that jazz record over there/me)*. Let's listen to it together.

2 At work

Put in the objects in the best order – with or without to *or* for.

1 *Mrs Brown, managing director of 'Pharmaco':* I'll dictate *(the rest of the letter/you)* after lunch, Mrs MacLaren. It'll only take *(a few minutes/us)*. Those people from Johnson and White'll be here in a moment. Make *(some coffee/them)* when they arrive, please, and bring *(a cup of tea/me)* as usual. Perhaps you could get *(a few biscuits/us)*, too.
2 *Sergeant White, police officer:* Ordinary-looking? Now, it would save *(a lot of time/us)* if you could describe *(the woman/us)* in detail, sir. You were quite right to report *(all this/the police)*, of course, but our chances of solving crimes are always greater if people can give *(an exact description of the person in question/us)*. Perhaps if I ask *(a few questions/you)*, your memory may improve. Right then …
3 *Mr Green, Salesperson:* May I suggest *(something/you)*, madam? Buy *(the more expensive model/your husband)*. You won't regret it. Of course, it'll cost *(a few pounds more/you)*, but it'll be well worth it in the long run.

'I'll give you just five seconds to get out of my boots!'

'Pass me the soap, please!'

1 Type *give s.o. sth./give s.th. to s.o.*

Mike *showed* ***the customs officer*** **his passport.**

The basic word order is indirect object + direct object.

We *showed* **our tickets** ***to the woman at the British Airways counter.***
Please *hand* **your boarding-card** ***to the stewardess (not to me).***
What's in this bag? – Presents. I'm *giving* **them** ***to friends.***

The order is reversed and *to* is used when
1 the indirect object is much longer than the direct object
2 the indirect object is stressed
3 the direct object is a personal pronoun (usually *it* or *them).*

Verbs of this type: *bring, give, hand, lend, offer, owe, promise, pass, sell, send, show, teach, tell, write.*

2 Type *explain s.th. to s.o.*

The quizmaster *explained* **the rules of the game** ***to the viewers.***
We didn't see the end of the film, but Stella *described* ***to us*** **all the interesting scenes we'd missed.**

The basic word order is direct object + indirect object.
The word order can be reversed if the direct object is especially stressed, or very long.

Verbs of this type: *announce, describe, dictate, explain, introduce, mention, report, say, suggest.*

Note 1
Type *buy s.o. s.th/buy s.th. for s.o.*
They *bought* ***him*** **a motor-bike** when he was 18/
They bought **a motor bike *for him*** when he was 18.

The word order is either indirect object + direct object, or direct object + indirect object with for.
Verbs of this type: buy, fetch, get, make, order.

Note 2
Type *ask s.o. s.th.*
The bike *cost* ***his parents*** **a lot of money.**

The word order is **always** *indirect object + direct object* (to *and* for *are never used).*
Verbs of this type: ask (a question), cost (time/money), take (time), save (time/money)

Two limericks

There was a señora of Spain,
Who couldn't go out in the rain,
For she'd lent her umbrella
To Queen Isabella,
Who never returned it again.

There was an old man of Calcutta,
Who had an unfortunate stutter,
'Please pass me,' he said,
'The b-b-b-bread,
And the b-b-b-b-b-b-butter.'

'George has passed on his interest in ornithology to the kids.'

ornithology – study of birds

1 Bits and pieces GG 97; GhE 49–50

Use the following bits and pieces to make sentences with two objects.
Example: The children bought themselves ice-creams/bought ice-creams for themselves.

explorers	*announce*	details of journey	*council*
farmer	*describe*	large area of land	*traffic warden*
film director	*hand*	part in the new film	*themselves*
tourist	*buy*	way to the station	*waiting reporters*
demonstrators	*report*	leaflets	*impatient passengers*
loudspeaker	*promise*	news that the flight was delayed	*police*
neighbours	*ask*	burglary	*young film star*
children	*sell*	ice-creams	*crowds in the street*

2 The do-it-yourself cottage GG 97; GhE 49–50

There are a number of other verbs with two objects that are not included in the lists on p. 121.
Here are some common ones that are used in this exercise:

Type 'give'	Type 'explain'	Type 'buy'
leave *(hinterlassen)*	mean	find book

Put in the objects in the most suitable word order – with or without to *or* for.

Not long ago Tom Turner's uncle died and unexpectedly left *(quite a sum of money/him)*. At first Tom did not know what to do with this unexpected legacy. Then one day the idea came to him. Why not buy *(an old cottage/his family)* in the Yorkshire Dales? Holidays in the country had always meant *(a lot/him and his wife)*.

Tom gave *(a lot of thought/the question)* before announcing *(his decision/his family)*, who felt very excited at the idea of renovating the cottage themselves. He also mentioned *(his idea/their friends)*, and some of them offered *(their help and advice/him)*.

Before long Tom had found *(a dream cottage/his family)* – in the little Yorkshire village of Masham. A friend who was an architect drew the plans for the alterations, and the council gave *(planning permission/them)*.

Mr Turner booked *(rooms in the local inn/everybody)*, and the little group of friends travelled to Masham, each of them ready to offer *(as much time as they could/the Turners)*, and promising *(a little holiday/themselves)* at the same time. A friend who was a builder sent *(building materials/Mr Turner and his helpers)*, and local workmen gave *(help/them)* with jobs they could not do themselves.

It took *(a long time/them)* to finish the work – but all in all it had not cost *(very much/the Turners)*. And all in all, it had been a wonderful summer. It was to be the first of many: Mr Turner offered *(free use of the cottage/his friends)* – whenever they felt like a holiday in the Yorkshire Dales.

4 **legacy** ['legəsɪ] money etc. that you receive after s.o. has died

3 At the tourist information centre GG 97; GhE 49–50

Translate these sentences into English, with the help of a dictionary where necessary.

1 Könnten Sie mir bitte ein Hotelzimmer reservieren?
2 Der Weg zum alten Schloß ist ziemlich kompliziert. Leider kann ich's Ihnen nicht gut beschreiben. Am besten geb ich Ihnen einen Stadtplan.
3 Die Stadtrundfahrt ist wirklich ein Erlebnis. Wir empfehlen sie allen unseren Gästen.
4 Ich verstehe nicht ganz, was Sie meinen. Könnten Sie es mir nochmal erklären?
5 Ich kann Ihnen billige Karten für Freitag anbieten. Wenn Sie sie an der Theaterkasse kaufen, kosten sie Sie erheblich mehr.

4 How much to tip? GG 97; GhE 49–50

Esther is one of twelve bright American college girls who have won a free month in New York as a prize in a fashion magazine's writing competition.

When I first arrived at the Amazon, a man in a bellhop's uniform carried my suitcase up in the elevator and unlocked my room for me. Of course I rushed immediately to the window and looked out to see what the view was. After a while I was aware of this bellhop turning on the hot and cold taps in my washbowl and saying 'This is the hot and this is the cold' and switching on the radio and telling me the names of all the New York stations and I began to get uneasy, so I said firmly, 'Thank you for bringing up my suitcase.'

'Thank you thank you thank you. Ha!' he said in a very nasty tone, and before I could wheel round to see what had come over him he was gone, shutting the door behind him with a rude slam.

Later, when I told Doreen about his curious behaviour, she said, 'You ninny, he wanted his tip.' I asked how much I should have given and she said a quarter at least and thirty-five cents if the suitcase was too heavy. Now I could have carried that suitcase to my room perfectly well by myself, only the bellhop seemed so eager to do it that I let him. I thought that sort of service came along with what you paid for your hotel room.

I hate handing over money to people for doing what I could just as easily do myself.

Doreen said ten per cent was what you should tip a person, but I somehow never had the right change and I'd have felt awfully silly giving somebody half a dollar and saying, 'Fifteen cents of this is a tip for you, please give me thirty-five cents back.'

The first time I took a taxi in New York I tipped the driver ten cents. The fare was a dollar, so I thought ten cents was exactly right and gave the driver my dime with a smile. But he only held it in the palm of his hand and stared and stared at it, and when I stepped out of the cab, hoping I had not handed him a Canadian dime by mistake, he started yelling, 'Lady I gotta live like you and everybody else,' in a loud voice which scared me so much I broke into a run …

From *The Bell Jar* by Sylvia Plath

to tip to give a tip *(Trinkgeld)* – 1 **Amazon** hotel in New York – 2 **bellhop** a hotel porter – 17 **ninny** silly person – 22 **eager** keen – 33 **fare** price of the journey – 35 **dime** 10 cent piece – **palm** [pɑːm] inner part of the hand – 37 **cab** taxi – 38 **to yell** to shout

1 *Pick out the examples in the text of verbs with two objects. Which 'type' are they?*

2 *The bellhop at the Amazon Hotel* ***carried Esther's luggage for her.*** *Say what else he* ***did for her/showed her/told her.*** *Then explain why he got so angry.*

3 *Describe the incident with the taxi-driver in a sentence or two, and explain the 'misunderstanding'.*

4 *A good hotel offers all kinds of service to its guests. Think of as many as you can.*
receptionist/porter/waiter (waitress)/ barman (barmaid)/chambermaid/…
order/show/bring/make/get/fetch/ carry/give/reserve/…
early-morning call/meals/taxi/room key/ theatre tickets/bed/menu/drinks/room/ luggage …
Example:
The receptionist will order a taxi for you/order you a taxi if you need one.

5 *What do* ***you*** *think of the problem of 'tipping'? In what situation (if at all) is it 'correct' to give/ leave someone a tip?*

15 Advanced Exercises

Verbs with a direct object and object complement

Type 1: object + object complement with *as*

Not all young people *regard* **further education *as the key to success.***	*Verbs of this type:* acknowledge, choose, look upon, recognize, regard, think of

Type 2: object + object complement without *as*

Tom talked to the careers officer, and *found* **her advice *a great help.***	*Verbs of this type:* appoint, call, crown, declare, elect, find, make, think

Note 1
Practical experience *is regarded* ***as a big advantage.***

The verbs above (Types 1 and 2) are often used in the passive. Then the direct object becomes the subject of the sentence.

Note 2
Many young workers *find* **an eight-hour day *very long.***

The complement is often a noun, but some verbs (e.g. call, declare, find, make, regard, think) *can also be followed by an adjective.*

Note 3
Most people *consider* **a friendly atmosphere *(as) an important factor at work.***

The verb consider *can be used with or without* as.

'I'm going to call it football.'

1 What the British think of the monarchy GG 98; GhE 54, 57

At the beginning of the 1990s, over a thousand British adults were asked for their opinion on the monarchy.

		%
Which statements do you feel fit the royal family?	Bad for Britain's image	2
	Extravagant	16
	Hard-working	51
	Highly respected	57
	Important to Britain	68
	Intelligent	31
Source: *Mori* (published by *The Sunday Times*, 21. 1. 90)	In touch with ordinary people	27
	A family just like any other	19
	Lazy	2
	Important to my life	11

think of
call look upon
recognize find think
regard consider

Talk about the results of the investigation, using the verbs above in the active or the passive.
Examples:
Only 2% of the people interviewed regarded the royal family as bad for Britain's image/as lazy (people).
All in all, the monarchy was considered important to Britain.
Then give your own opinion.

2 Innocent or guilty? GG 98; GhE 54, 57

Use suitable complements (adjectives or nouns) to complete the sentences.

There was a moment of silence, then the judge pronounced the accused man ... Not everyone in the courtroom considered the verdict ... Loud shouts of protest filled the court as some declared the witnesses ..., and others called the judge...

Sitting alone at the back of the courtroom, the man's wife thought the judge's decision ... She had always found her husband ... So the verdict, which she looked upon ..., had naturally made her ...

3 **verdict** (in a court of law) decision whether a prisoner is guilty or not guilty – 5 **witness** (in a court of law) person who appears in court and says what they know about the case

3 Historical facts GG 98; GhE 54, 97

Can you get the facts right? Complete the sentences with suitable complements. Sometimes there will be a number of different possibilities.

1 In June 1953, Elizabeth II was crowned ...
2 Margaret Thatcher was the first woman to be elected ...
3 After the American Civil War, slaves were officially made ..., but not all Americans considered them ...
4 The Declaration of Independence is regarded ...
5 Before women got the vote in Britain in 1918, politics was looked upon ...
6 In the middle of the 19th century, employing children to work in factories was thought of ... It was a long time before child labour was finally made ... in Britain.

4 Melting pot or mixed salad? GG 97–98; GhE 49–50, 57

Teachers in Britain are giving more and more of their attention to the problem of educating multi-cultural school classes. Nationwide, non-whites make up only 4% of the population, but statistics show us a very different picture in many densely populated areas. In Bradford, for example, 25% of the whole population is of Asian origin.

It was in this northern city that a headmaster's methods cost him his job. He had refused to give special treatment to Muslim children. This is how he described his standpoint to the local education authority: 'What's important is integration. I consider a melting pot more realistic than a mixed salad. It's our job to make them British. We've got to teach them the English language, explain English institutions to them, and even offer them lessons in the Christian religion. A multi-cultural policy will never work because it makes the children more aware of their differences.'

The Commission for Racial Equality finds such attitudes very worrying. It regards racism as the major problem facing multi-racial schools. It hopes, however, that as more colleges and universities offer courses in multi-culturalism to teachers, Britain's racial climate will improve. There are simple but practical ways to explain to young people what racism can lead to. In history lessons, for example, teachers could describe to pupils the effects of slavery and oppression before telling them about the growth of the British Empire. They could devote teaching time to Muslim festivals as well as the Christian ones. In school textbooks, children could not only be called Janet and John, but Hanif and Aruna, too.

Adapted from an article in *The Christian Science Monitor*, May 4, 1989

29 **oppression** cruel and unfair treatment

1 *Pick out the verbs with two objects and those with an object complement.*
2 *Use verbs with two objects – or with an object complement – to answer these questions:*
   a *Why did the Bradford headmaster lose his job, and what was his opinion on multi-culturalism?*
   b *What is the attitude of the Commission for Racial Equality?*
   c *In what ways could teachers improve understanding between children of different cultures?*
3 *Translate the second paragraph of the text (ll. 8-19) into German.*
4 *Discuss the headmaster's attitude. Do you consider it racist?*

5 Laurence Olivier: 1907-1989 – virtuosity and daring GG 98; GhE 57

Lord Olivier, regarded not only by English-speaking theatre-lovers as one of the greatest classical stage actors of this century, was an actor of astonishing virtuosity and daring. But he will not only be remembered for his work as an actor. He was also a first-rate movie star, a film director whose Shakespearean adaptations have already become unrivalled screen classics, and a stage director whose productions of contemporary as well as of classical plays were admired by a huge audience. It was his idea to found Britain's National Theatre and later he became its first artistic director.

In 1947 Laurence Olivier, son of an Anglican minister, was knighted and became Sir Laurence Olivier. In 1970 he became a life peer: Lord Olivier. From now on he was a lord of his profession not only in his art, but also in his title.

Although his achievements were many, he was primarily an actor. He played kings, villains, clowns, and popular romantic heroes. In the last ten years of his life he even worked for Hollywood as a highly-paid character actor.

Unforgettable was Olivier's gift for comedy. As the critic James Agate wrote, Lord Olivier was a comedian by instinct and a tragedian by art. Critics often praised him for his honesty as an actor, but Lord Olivier admitted that for him acting was a form of lying. He often smiled to himself when he heard other actors speaking of their need to 'express themselves'. For him acting fulfilled his need to show off.

Adapted form an article by Mel Gussow in *The New York Times*, 12 July, 1989

daring willingness to take risks – 8 **unrivalled** [ʌn'raɪvld] greater or better than any other – 9 **contemporary** [kən'temprərɪ] of the present time, modern – 14 **to knight s.o.** to make s.o. a knight *(Ritter)* – 15 **life peer** member of the nobility whose title cannot be passed on – 19 **villain** ['vɪlən] the main bad character in a play or story – 23 **gift** talent – 27 **to admit** to say, to confess

Adapt the information given in the text to make sentences with object complements.
1 Theatre-lovers have acknowledged Laurence Olivier …
2 His film performances are recognized …, and his Shakespearean adaptations are considered …
3 The National Theatre in London appointed him …
4 In 1970, the Queen made Sir Laurence …
5 In the last years of his life he was often chosen …
6 The critic James Agate considered Olivier …
7 Other critics looked on him …, but Olivier himself said that he actually regarded acting …
8 Other actors might think of their profession …, but Olivier called acting …

Check-up

1 When the railway arrived

Fill in who, which *or* whose. *Say where* that *could be used instead and where the relative pronoun could be left out.*

It was a village … population had little sense of time until the railway arrived. After that, it was not the sun but the trains … villagers noted to keep time. Most people … lived along the line knew the timetables approximately: the train … arrived at 8.19 was called the Eight, the one … left at 11.37 was the Twelve, and so on. Anyone … wanted to catch the train got to the station at least half an hour before the train.

Most of the trains were 'mixed' trains, … carried both passengers and goods. This meant there was usually some shunting to do. If there was no shunting, the train just waited at the station until it was time to leave. On the evening train, a driver … name was Bill Maindy often gave whistling performances from the locomotive. If the owls answered back, Bill stayed even after it was time for the train to leave.

The locomotives … the railway company used were quite unequal to the work, … required trains … had good brakes. Coming down the hill from Bovey, trains often passed the station; and passengers … wanted to get off had to walk back.

Apart from stopping at the stations, drivers stopped at places … were famous for their heather honey, … is still a great favourite round here. Most villagers, … worried little about time anyway, merely shouted loud comments while the guard got out and fixed the hives.

Based on *Small Talk at Wreyland* by Cecil Torr

9 **to shunt** to re-arrange a train – 12 **owl** [aʊl] a large night bird – 14 **unequal to** unsuitable, not good enough for – 16 **Bovey** ['bʌvɪ] small town in Devor – 19 **heather** ['heðə] type of plant *(Heide)* – 21 **guard** man in charge of a train – **hive** a box or basket in which bees live

'I repeat, this is the early morning call you asked for.'

2 Definitions

Use contact clauses with prepositions to make definitions of the following words.

Example:
sleeping bag ▶ A sleeping bag is a bag you can sleep in.

1 washing-machine
2 information desk
3 golf ball
4 bottle opener
5 cycle path
6 tennis net
7 address book
8 non-smoking compartment
9 cricket field
10 teacup

Defining relative clauses
(information necessary for the understanding of the sentence; no commas used)

There aren't many children ***who/that*** **don't like sweets.**
It's unhealthy to eat food ***which/that*** **contains too much salt.**
Weight problems often affect people ***whose*** **alcohol intake is high.**

Non-defining relative clauses
(additional information; commas used)

My sister's children, ***who*** **are six and three,** both eat a lot of sugary foods.
Frozen food is better than canned food, ***which*** **contains fewer vitamins.**
Potatoes, ***whose*** **importance in our diet is now recognized,** are quite easy to grow.

The relative pronoun *who* is used for persons, *which* for things.
In defining relative clauses, *that* is very often used to replace *who* or *which. Whose,* the genitive form (expressing possession, etc.), can be used with persons and things.

Contact clauses
(clauses without relative pronouns)

Is this the coffee *(which/that)* **you brought back from Germany?**
The friends *(who/that)* **I've invited to lunch** are both vegetarians.

The relative pronoun can be left out if it is the object of a defining clause.
'Contact clauses' are especially common in spoken English.

Prepositions in defining relative clauses

A lot of the boxes *(which/that)* **food is packed *in*** could be recycled.
The woman *(who/that)* **we buy our eggs *from*** keeps only about twenty hens.

In defining relative clauses, the preposition usually comes after the verb (+ object).
The relative pronoun is often left out.

Note 1
In non-defining relative clauses, that *cannot be used, and the relative pronoun can never be left out.*

Note 2
The success of home-made bread can depend on the kind of oven ***in which*** **it is baked.**

In formal style, the preposition is usually put before the relative pronoun. (In this case, that *cannot be used.)*

Note 3
Young people under the age of 25 are the customers ***whom*** **fast food restaurants mainly attract.**

Whom *is sometimes used as the object in formal (usually written) English.*

There was once an old sailor my grandfather knew
Who had so many things which he wanted to do
That, whenever he thought it was time to begin,
He couldn't because of the state he was in.
A. A. Milne (1882-1956)

'To me, without whom this book would never have been written.'

1 From wealth to poverty GG 130–135; GhE 308–312

This is the beginning of Beauty and the Beast, *a traditional English fairy tale.*

Once upon a time, in a far-off country, there lived a merchant who had been so lucky in all his undertakings that he was enormously rich. As he had, however, six sons and six daughters, he found that his money was not too much to let them all have everything they fancied, as they were accustomed to do.

But one day a most unexpected misfortune befell them. Their house caught fire and was burnt to the ground, with all the splendid furniture, the books, pictures, gold, silver, and precious goods it contained, and this was only the beginning of their troubles. Their father, who had until this moment prospered in all ways, suddenly lost every ship he had upon the sea, either by dint of pirates, shipwreck, or fire. Then he heard that his clerks in distant countries, whom he trusted entirely, had proved unfaithful; and at last from great wealth he fell into the direst poverty.

All that he had left was a little house in a desolate place at least a hundred leagues from the town in which he had lived, and to this he was forced to retreat with his children, who were in despair at the idea of leading such a different life. They soon found that their former friends showed no intention of offering them any help. So nothing was left for them but to take their departure to the cottage, which stood in the midst of a dark forest.

From *Blue Fairy Book*, collected by Andrew Lang

1 **merchant** trader (doing business with foreign countries) – 3 **not too much** just enough – 4 **to fancy** to like and want to have – 5/6 **to be accustomed to** to be used to – 6 **to befall** to happen to – 10 **to prosper** to be successful – 11 **by dint of** through – 12 **to trust** to believe and depend on – **unfaithful** false – 13 **dire** extreme, terrible – 14 **desolate** ['desələt] lonely – 15 **league** about 3 miles – 16 **to retreat** to draw back, to retire – **despair** the state of having given up hope

1 a *Find the relative clauses in the text. Which are defining, and which non-defining?*
 b *Comment on all the relative pronouns used in the text and replace them with different ones where possible.*
 c *Pick out the contact clauses. Could any of the other relative clauses be rewritten as contact clauses?*

2 *Rephrase the story with the help of relative clauses, using contact clauses where possible:*
At the beginning, the merchant is so rich that he can buy anything …, and his children have every luxury … But one day his luck is changed by a fire … This is not the only unfortunate thing … He also loses the ships … and the people … are unfaithful to him. So he and his family have to leave the house … and move to a little cottage … The friends … are not prepared to help, so there is nothing else …

3 *Use relative clauses to define the following:*
 a undertakings (l.2)
 b misfortune (6)
 c precious goods (8)
 d pirates (11)
 e wealth (13)

4 *Relative clauses are often used to give a short description of something. Think of suitable ones to describe interesting books or stories you have read recently, or good films you have seen.*
Examples:
I saw an old film called 'Midnight Lace' on TV a few days ago. It's about an American woman whose husband is planning to kill her.
I read 'Animal Farm' recently. The story's about some farm animals that organize a revolution and drive out the farmer they have always had to work for.

2 The cure GG 130, 134–135; GhE 308, 310–312

The following text is incomplete. To improve it, and to make the meaning clear, add the additional information given below, in the form of relative clauses. The asterisks (*) will show you where.

The story:

Thomas, the country vet, turned in at the gate of the farm. A tall, thin boy* looked out of a dark building for a moment. He was helping an older man* with a cow*. The boy had his arm over the cow's neck, and his other hand was twisting up the cow's head. His father poured a red mixture* into the cow's mouth.

The man said good day to Thomas*. Thomas asked after the cow. The farmer said it had the hoosh*.

'I've given her a red drink,' added the farmer, and showed Thomas an empty bottle*. The cow showed no immediate bad effects. With a fine, careless confidence Thomas offered to cure the cow at once with his own medicine*. The farmer produced the things* from some dirty bottles on a shelf. They made the mixture, and the boy went to the house. He returned with a teaspoon*. Thomas* was surprised when the cow sank to the ground. The two men* looked from Thomas to the animal with great admiration. But Thomas was afraid the cow might die. He quickly calculated the value of the animal*.

Suddenly the cow got up and coughed energetically several times, and began to eat.

'It always works,' Thomas told the two men*. 'Do it daily for a few days and you'll find it will kill the worms.'

The cow was cured within a short time.

The additional information:

The boy was about 17.
The man was obviously the boy's father.
They were about to treat the cow.
The mixture smelled of aniseed.
Thomas returned the greeting.
The hoosh is a disease caused by long worms in a cow's throat.
The farmer had put the bottle on the shelf beside him.
Thomas's medicine was a mixture of linseed oil and turpentine.
Thomas needed the things for his mixture.
Thomas poured the mixture into the cow's nose with the teaspoon.
Thomas had no idea what the effect would be.
The two men were very pleased with the cow's strong reaction.
Thomas thought the value of the animal was about twenty pounds.
The two men were looking at Thomas as if he were a magician.

11 **confidence** *here:* fearless attitude – 13 **shelf** (wooden) board to put things on – 16 **value** what s.th. is worth – 27 **aniseed** *Anis* – 31 **linseed** *Leinsamen*

3 The body in the library GG 131–133; GhE 309, 311

This is a summary of the beginning of Agatha Christie's famous novel 'The Body in the Library.'

The story starts in Colonel Bantry's house. The house is in the village of Gossington. The Bantrys wake up one morning and find a body lying in their library. It's an unknown blonde girl in a white evening dress. She was killed with a belt from the dress, at some time between ten and midnight.

At once, Mrs Bantry sends for her friend Miss Marple. Miss Marple comes from the village of St Mary Mead. Of course, the police arrive, too, with Inspector Slack in charge. Their first suspect is Basil Blake. The police go to his house. Basil Blake was seen with a mysterious blonde girl the weekend before. But this girl – Dinah Lee – is later found living with Blake. The police discover that the dead girl worked at the Majestic Hotel in Danemouth. So the police talk to Josie Turner. The dead girl (Ruby) worked with her. Ruby had danced an exhibition dance at 10.30 pm and should have danced another at midnight. But she didn't appear at midnight. She was last seen dancing with a young man called Bartlett, at about 11. However, the police are more interested in Colonel Bantry. They talk to him next …

5 **to send for s.o** to ask for s.o. to come – 7 **suspect** ['--] a person you think may be responsible for a crime – 12 **exhibition** *here:* special show (given by professionals)

Answer the questions, using contact clauses with prepositions.
Example:
What role does Gossington play in the story?
▶ It's the village the Bantrys live in.

1 What's special about the library? – It's the room …
2 What's special about the white dress? – It's the dress …
3 Why is the belt important? – It's the thing …
4 What is important about the period ten to midnight? – It's the time …
5 What's interesting about St Mary Mead?
6 Who is Basil Blake?
7 Who is the mysterious blonde girl?
8 What is her relationship with Blake?
9 What is the Majestic in Danemouth?
10 Who is Josie Turner?
11 What is the importance of 10.30 pm?
12 Who is Bartlett?

In which of your answers could you use clauses with where *or* when *instead of contact clauses?*

4 A puzzle
GG 131; GhE 309

ANSWER: THE LAWYER WAS A WOMAN, AND THUS THE SISTER OF THE MAN THAT WENT TO SEA

1 *How long did it take you to get the answer? (Do you think there might be a significant difference between people that get the answer quickly and people that don't?)*
2 *What other jobs would this puzzle 'work' with? Try out a few variations.*

16 Advanced Exercises

More types of relative clauses

The power of the Royal Family today is very limited, ***which* is a good thing.**	The relative pronoun *which* can also refer to a whole sentence. In this case, the relative clause usually expresses a comment.
Henry VIII had six wives, ***two of whom* were beheaded.** His palace of Hampton Court had about 1,000 rooms, ***all of which* were in regular use.** Today thousands of visitors come to see Hampton Court, ***part of which* is open to the public.**	Relative clauses beginning with *... of whom/... of which* refer to part of something or part of a group. They are normally used only in formal English.
10 Downing Street automatically becomes the home of ***whoever* is elected Prime Minister.** Some people criticize ***whatever* the Government plans to do.** There won't be any overnight improvements, ***whichever* party wins the election.**	*Whoever, whatever* and *whichever* are generalizing relative pronouns, meaning 'anyone/anything that...,' 'the person/thing that ...,' 'it doesn't matter who/what/which ...'.

Note

Success in war was ***what* people expected of their king in the Middle Ages.**

What *is used to mean 'the thing that ...'/'something that ...' (German: 'was ...'/'das, was ...').*

1 Records GG 134–136; GhE 310–312, 315

Join the correct pairs of sentences, using relative clauses.

1 The world's first advertised radio programme was in 1906.
2 John Baird sold his first televisions in 1930.
3 In the film *Superman* Marlon Brando appears for nine minutes.
4 The longest film ever made *(The Cure for Insomnia)* lasts 85 hours.
5 The average American child sees 26 000 murders on TV by the age of eighteen.
6 The most successful record is Bing Crosby's version of Irving Berlin's *White Christmas.*
7 Madonna's LP *True Blue* was Number 1 in 28 countries.
8 Agatha Christie's play *The Mousetrap* has been playing in London since 1952.
9 In 1909, *God Save the King* was played 17 times in a row by a band on Rathenau railway station.

a The TV-watching time of an average American child is 32 hours a week.
b Each minute earned him 2 million dollars.
c This was because King Edward VII couldn't get into his uniform quickly enough before leaving the train.
d Handel's Largo was played during the programme.
e Its North American sales between 1942 and 1987 reached 170 million copies.
f The cost of the televisions was 27 pounds each.
g This is more countries than for any other LP.
h This is longer than any other theatre production.
i Its first complete performance was in Chicago in 1987.

Information from the *Guiness Book of Records* 1990

4 **insomnia** sleeplessness

2 Relative clauses: formal and informal style GG 130–137; GhE 308–315

Britain before the Romans

About the year 5000 BC, the waters of what we now call the English Channel and the North Sea joined together, and Britain became an island.

The human population of the new island at that time was a few hundreds, who lived by hunting with the rudely fashioned tools they had laboriously chipped from the softer stones about them. But at the very time that this separation of Britain from the Continent was taking place, a revolution was occurring thousands of miles away in the Near East which was to change for ever the life of man. He was learning not merely to hunt and kill for his food, but to keep the animals who provided it in captivity. He was learning, too, to gather the seeds of the grasses he found he could eat and scatter them about him to grow into the food he desired. He was learning, in short, to be a farmer.

Men with this momentous new knowledge did not cross the still widening waters between Europe and Britain until about 2300 BC. And when they came they had to keep to the chalky and sandy soils where with their clumsy tools they could turn the ground over for their seeds to grow. So the area they settled on was very limited.

These first settlers on the chalk ridges were men to whom the sea was a natural barrier. They crossed it only if they had to, if they needed fresh space in which to live; and they crossed it where it was narrowest. But there were others for whom it held fewer terrors, men living along the coasts of Spain or Britanny. When they crossed, it was where the English Channel was wider. The settlements of these people can be distinguished today by their remarkable burial places, whose roof is a great stone.

It was about the year 900 BC that a large westward movement of races on the European continent, a movement at whose causes we can only guess, produced another invasion of Britain, by a people who are the first to have left this island something more than material remains. These were the Celts, and they spoke a language of which the native tongues of Ireland, Wales and the highlands of Scotland are the direct descendants.

From *A History of England* by J. Thorn, R. Lockyer & D. Smith

6 **rudely fashioned** roughly made – **laborious** [lə'bɔːrɪəs] needing a lot of effort – 7 **to chip** to cut or break off (stone, etc.) – 13 **to keep in captivity** to keep (animals) so that they cannot run away – 14 **seed** part of a plant from which a new one grows – 15 **to scatter** to throw in all directions – 16 **do desire** to want to have – 18 **momentous** [-'--] very important, having a great effect – 21 **chalky** made of chalk, a soft white rock – 22 **clumsy** *here:* not finely made – 25 **ridge** line of high land – 31 **Britanny** region in the north-east of France *(Bretagne)* – 33 **to distinguish** *here:* to recognize – 40 **remains** what is left behind, ruins – 42 **tongue** *here:* language.

A much married man

This is an extract from Somerset Maugham's 'The Round Dozen', a short story in which the narrator meets Mortimer Ellis, a bigamist, who has been in prison for 5 years. He explains that he has had eleven wives, all of whom he left after taking charge of their money …

'There are men who don't like being married. I can't understand them. I like being a married man. It's no difficulty to me to do the little things that women like and that some men can't be bothered with. As I was saying just now, it's attention a woman wants. I never went out of the house without giving my wife a kiss and I never came in without giving her another. And it was very seldom I came in without bringing her some chocolates or a few flowers. I never grudged the expense.'

'After all, it was her money you were spending,' I interposed.

'And what if it was? It's not the money that you've paid for a present that signifies, it's the spirit you give it in. That's what counts with women. No, I'm not one to boast, but I will say this of myself, I am a good husband.'

From *The Round Dozen* by W. Somerset Maugham

bigamist ['bɪgəmɪst] s.o. who has more than one wife (or husband) – 4 **I can't be bothered with it** it's too much trouble for me – 10 **not to grudge** not to mind – 12 **to interpose** to 'break into' the conversation – 14 **to signify** *here:* to be of importance, to matter – 16 **to boast** to show off, to talk 'big'

1 *Make a list of the relative clauses in both texts. In what ways are most of the relative clauses in the second text typical of spoken English? (Look at the choice of relative pronouns and the position of prepositions. Are defining or non-defining clauses used?)*

2 *Pick out the relative clauses in the first text that you think are typical of a more formal (written) style. How could they be expressed more informally, but without changing the meaning?*

3 *Replace these constructions from the first text by relative clauses:*
  a the still widening waters between Europe and Britain (ll. 19-20):
  b space in which to live (27-28)
  c men living along the coasts of Spain and Britanny (30-31)

4 *Add relative clauses with* which *to make comments on these statements.*
  a About 7000 years ago, the North Sea joined the waters of the English Channel.
  b The first people that crossed over to Britain had a certain fear of the sea.
  c Mortimer Ellis considers himself a good husband.

5 *At the time when 'The Round Dozen' was written, the 'ideal' of a 'good husband' and a 'good wife' was rather different from what it seems to be today. Talk about this, using relative clauses where appropriate.*
Examples:
In those days, the husband was generally the one who earned all the money, while the wife was the one …
Most men wanted a wife who …
Women that … were unusual.
Women were expected to do what(ever) …
Housework was a job that …

3 Television: Can it be as bad as they say? GG 130–137; GhE 308–315

Translate into English.

Eins der wenigen Dinge, über die die meisten Leute sich einig sind, ist, daß Jugendliche zuviel fernsehen. Aber was viele übersehen, ist die Tatsache, daß man von bestimmten Sendungen, die im Fernsehen gezeigt werden, eine Menge lernen kann. Verbrechen, Gewalt und Seifenopern *(soap operas)* sind nicht das einzige, was junge Leute sich anschauen.

Vor allem aber für ältere Menschen, von denen sehr viele alleine leben und sich daher einsam fühlen, hat das Fernsehen gute Seiten. Sie betrachten die Familien, die in Fernsehserien erscheinen, beinahe als ihre eigenen Familien – oder als wirklich lebende Personen, über deren Eigenschaften sie sich mit ihren Freunden unterhalten können. Das Fernsehgerät kann auch so etwas wie einen Freund darstellen, auf den man sich immer verlassen kann – was für alleinstehende Leute besonders wichtig ist.

Was auch immer das Fernsehen für Nachteile und Gefahren haben mag, man muß sich darüber im Klaren sein, daß es – genau wie das Telefon oder die Waschmaschine – zum täglichen Leben gehört *(to be a part of)*. Wir können selbst entscheiden, welche Rolle es für uns persönlich spielt.

The Use of Adjectives and Adverbs 17

Check-up

good deep particular
approximate official
near annual popular
incredible large
unfortunate
approximate daily
final
aggressive hard actual
dangerous natural
particular aggressive
exact quick dominant real
surprising unusual aggressive

proper
considerable
incredible recent actual
common basic understandable
general regular

1 Man's best friend?

Adjective or adverb? Decide which form is correct.

It is … known that the British have a … love of pets – … of dogs. The … number of dog-owners in Britain now … stands at over 7 million. These people spend … 300 million pounds … on … makes of tinned food – an … … sum!

But … over half a million stray dogs are wandering the streets, and … 1000 unwanted pet dogs have to be destroyed … by the RSPCA and others. Many people … abandon their dogs because the pet's behaviour has become … and … to control. … this is often the owner's fault. The habit of 'spoiling' pets has … altered the … instincts of dogs, … those of … breeds. A dog which is allowed to do … as it likes, … begins to feel …, and to see itself as the … leader of the family. Not … such dogs soon start to act … … on the street, too.

When treated …, however, dogs can add much to their owners' lives, and even make a … improvement on their health. This may sound …, but a … study shows that having a dog … reduces … everyday illnesses by 50%! Perhaps this is … caused by the … fact that people who buy dogs … take five times more … exercise than they did before.

Adapted from *The Sunday Times*, February 18, 1990

3 **make** *Marke* – 5 **stray** (of pets) homeless – 7 **RSPCA** Royal Society for the Prevention of Cruelty to Animals – **to abandon** to leave (permanently) – 10 **breed** particular type of dog

healthy
disabled handicapped

deaf

handicapped

blind blind
deaf

2 Their problem – our problem?

1 *Complete the sentences with adjectives, followed by prop-words* (person *or* people) *where necessary.*

A … without any disabilities is often unaware of the problems facing the … . It is not unusual for … in wheelchairs to have fewer job opportunities simply because they cannot use public transport to get to work. … are often shut off from society because telephones are not adapted to their needs, and the mentally … are frequently refused jobs because employers wrongly think they are unable to do them. It is easy to forget the difficulties the … have in life, although a … generally receives more sympathy than …, whose problems are less obvious.

2 *Give the English equivalents of …*

a) viele Behinderte; b) die Reichen und die Armen; c) zwei Schlafzimmer: ein kleines und ein großes; d) Jugendliche; e) ein Blinder; f) eine schwarze Katze und zwei weiße; g) der Kleine; h) die billigen Karten, nicht die teuren; i) die Tote; j) die Lebenden und die Toten.

17 Basic Rules and Exercises

Adjectives	Adjectives can be used
Television plays an **important** *role* in our society.	1 **attributively,** i.e. before nouns
	2 **predicatively,** i.e. after verbs expressing
These video tapes *are* **expensive!**	a a state (e.g. *be, seem, remain*)
Don't switch off – this programme *is getting* **interesting** now.	b a changing state (e.g. *get, become*)
There's a film on tonight that *sounds* quite **good.**	c the way something appears to the senses (e.g. *look, feel, sound, taste*)

Adverbs	Adverbs can be used to modify
The play *started* **dramatically.**	1 verbs
The first act was **terribly** *funny.*	2 adjectives
The plot had been thought out **extremely** *well.*	3 adverbs
Luckily, *we managed to get very good seats.*	4 whole sentences

Adjectives with 'prop-words'	
There's something wrong with our *TV set.* We may have to get **a new one.** John always looks through the week's *programmes,* and marks **the interesting ones.**	1 The 'prop-word' *one* is used after adjectives to describe nouns that would otherwise have to be repeated.
	2 Other 'prop-words' (e.g. *man, woman, person, people)* are used after adjectives to describe
The old man next door has his TV on very loud.	a people seen as individuals
Several **disabled people** took part in the film.	b a limited group of people

Adjectives used as nouns	
The deaf are able to enjoy quite a lot of television programmes. TV personalities can seem like real friends to **the old** and **the lonely.**	*The* + adjectives is used to describe people seen as a complete group (e.g. *the deaf, the lonely, the very young)*

'It's not fair. The rich get richer,
the poor get poorer
but the comfortably well-off
just stay comfortably well-off.'

1 Americans and their automobiles GG 37–38, 44, 48–49, 53; GhE 130, 140

The daily chaos on American roads costs the US economy many millions of dollars a year. Naturally, this not only includes the direct costs, such as high gasoline consumption in traffic jams, but also the indirect costs that are inevitably caused, such as lost hours at work and additional pollution.

Like television, the automobile is firmly rooted in modern American life. Over 80% of American workers commute daily to their jobs in private cars, and a large number of American families own two or more cars. The landscape of the United States has been noticeably affected by the automobile; drive-ins have become increasingly common, and stores, restaurants and whole towns are usually planned to accommodate large numbers of cars. Even in a densely populated urban area, a grocery store can look absurdly small in comparison with the huge parking lot designed for its customers.

Recently many Americans have felt extremely critical of the traditional attitude towards the automobile as a symbol of freedom and democracy. Some families have tried living without their cars – at least temporarily. Quite surprisingly, for many people the change was fairly easy – and unexpectedly enjoyable. Although the Americans have adapted terribly slowly to the idea of providing a proper system of public transport, actually there are few places in the States that are absolutely inaccessible to some combination of transport by bus, taxi, train, subway or plane. Some Americans clearly feel that the time will come – possibly in the not very distant future – when the automobile becomes socially and economically obsolete. Others are not so sure …

5 **inevitable** [-'----] unavoidable – 16 **dense** thick – 23 **temporary** ['temprərɪ] lasting for a limited time – 29 **inaccessible** out of reach – 32 **distant** far away – 33 **obsolete** ['ɒbsəli:t] no longer used, out of date

1 *Pick out the adverbs in the text, and say which are used to modify a) verbs, b) adjectives (including participles used as adjectives), c) other adverbs, d) whole sentences.*
2 *Find all the adjectives that are used predicatively, and say what type of verb (according to the Basic Rules) each one follows.*
3 *Name the adjectives 'related' to these nouns: a) chaos (l. 1); b) economy (l. 2); c) symbol (l. 21); d) freedom (l. 21); f) future (l. 32). Then use them to form sentences about cars (or other present-day problems).*
4 *Decide which of the adverbs in lines 19–34 could be left out. Compare the two versions and point out in what way the use of adverbs affects the style and contents.*
5 *Use adjectives or adverbs to complete these sentences suitably.*
   a These days traffic jams are nothing …
   b Drivers who get caught in them can start to feel …
   c Lots of Americans drive their cars to work …
   d The freeways, highways, drive-ins and parking lots in the US have changed the countryside …
   e One day cars may become …, but right now this doesn't seem …

2 The dragon GG 37, 38, 44, 48–49, 53; GhE 130, 147, 152, 154

It was porch-sitting night, so Bob and I moved out to the swing. Bob liked the swing, and sometimes he rocked it so hard that I felt seasick. We could see the city from the porch. At night, the lights made it look beautiful. The oil refineries looked like castles from a children's book. Some even breathed fire, as if dragons were inside.

Bob wasn't looking at the view. Things like that didn't interest him. He was talking about his relatives. He could be so boring. I didn't really hate him. He couldn't help it if he was boring and stupid.

My mother and Bob's mother were friends. That gave Bob a reason to come to see me every night. My mother liked Bob a lot. So I had to sit on the swing getting seasick. I watched the dragon in a refinery breathing fire. Bob was talking about his cousin Jimmy, who played bridge. Bob had a habit of repeating himself. I was glad when he came to the end. 'Do you play bridge, Kay?'

'No,' I said. I tried to make sure we had very little in common.

'How about going to the movies Saturday night?' he asked.

'I'm going to be busy then. Sorry.'

'What are you doing?'

'I have some important poetry to write.'

'You've been busy a lot lately, Kay.'

I almost said, 'Did you ever wonder why?' But I didn't.

Bob sighed. 'I'm worried. It's April, and I haven't heard from a single college.'

'Everything will work out,' I said.

'You can say that because you're smart. College will be a breeze for you. But I want to be a lawyer, and it will be tough.'

'You worry too much.' I felt strange saying this. I felt law school *would* be tough for Bob. But I didn't want to be cruel.

He touched my shoulder. 'You really don't like me, do you, Kay?'

'Bob, that's not a nice thing to say!' Suddenly, I felt guilty.

'But it's true. I'm not as stupid as you think.'

'Have I ever said I didn't like you?' It bothered me that Bob might see through me.

'You didn't have to say it. I know.'

'Bob, you know I think you're a great guy.'

'I'm not a great guy. We both know I'm not. You think I'm stupid because you're smart. You think you're too good for me. I used to be happy here. Now I come because my mother makes me. You think I come here because I love you or something. Well, it isn't that. Not at all.'

I felt wounded. I never thought Bob would see the truth.

'Kay, I'm going and I'm not coming back.'

Suddenly, I was speaking. 'Well, leave then! You are boring and dull. I only sit here because our mothers are friends.'

I expected his eyes to look hurt. But they flashed with excitement. 'I think that is the first time you've ever told me the truth. You're a phony, Kay. And that's worse than being stupid.' He touched my shoulder again, gently. 'I could like you, Kay. I really could. But the truth isn't important to you.'

He smiled. To my horror, my eyes were filling with tears. The orange flame of the refinery blurred.

'Well, I'd better be going,' Bob said. 'I'm going to miss this swing.'

I heard his car drive away. I got up and wiped my eyes on my sleeve. I went inside. My parents were watching television.

'Where did Bob go?' my mother asked.

'He ... he had some poetry to write.'

I stumbled into my room. From my bed, I watched the dragon's orange-and-red flame – until the colors melted and were washed away.

Cynthia Forder wrote this story when she was a senior in high school in Torrance, California. 'The Dragon' received an award in the 1974 Scholastic Writing Awards Contest.

dragon mythical animal breathing fire – 2 **swing** *Schaukel* – 10-11 **he couldn't help it** it wasn't his fault – 34 **a breeze** *here:* easy – 44 **to bother** to worry – 58 **dull** uninteresting – 62 **(a) phony** (someone) pretending to be what he/she is not – 64 **gentle** soft, kind – 67 **to blur** to become unclear – 71 **sleeve** arm of shirt etc – 75 **to stumble** to walk unstedily, almost falling

1 *Fill in suitable adjectives and adverbs to complete this summary of the story:*
Kay found Bob's talk about his relatives ... ..., but she was too ... to say so. She ... didn't want to go to the movies with him, so she ... thought of an excuse, which was so ... that Bob ... saw through it. Bob told her he felt ... about his future, but Kay didn't want to take this remark ..., because she was ... of showing him what she ... thought of him – that he was ..., and that his future ... wouldn't be ... Again, Bob ... realized what she was ... thinking, and he ... decided to tell her the ... truth. It was the first time Bob and Kay had ... been ... with each other, and as Kay discovered to her ... surprise, the truth hurt.

2 *Look at the text carefully and say how Kay feels when a) Bob rocks the swing; b) he talks about his relatives; c) he guesses that she doesn't like him; d) he tells her he only goes there to please his mother; e) he says he is leaving and not coming back; f) she is on her own again.*

3 *What sort of a person do you think Kay is? Think of adjectives that might describe her. And what about Bob? In what way is he different? Then use adverbs to describe how Kay reacts when a) Bob talks about college; b) he says he is not coming back.*

3 The status-climber GG 41; GhE 127

In his book 'The Human Zoo', Desmond Morris takes a look at the society the 'human animal' has created over the centuries. One of the features of this society is the struggle for dominance. The person who is unable to achieve genuine dominance in society often tries to create the impression of higher status ...

The really serious status-climber tends to concentrate on areas where cheap fakes are out of the question. If he can afford a small motor car, he buys a medium-sized one; if he can afford a medium-sized one, he buys a large one; if he can afford a single large one, he buys a second car as a runabout; if large cars become too common, he buys a small, but wildly expensive foreign sports car; if large rear-lights become the fashion, he buys the latest model with even bigger ones, 'to let people behind know he is in front,' as the advertisers so succinctly express it. The one thing he does not do is to buy a row of life-sized, cardboard models of Rolls-Royces and display them outside his garage. There are no fake diamonds in the world of the status-climbing fanatic.

Motor cars are a single example, and an important one because they are so public, but the ardent status-struggler cannot stop here ...

2 **fake** an imitation of the 'real' thing – 8 **succinctly** clearly and in a few words – 10 **to display** to put up for everyone to see – 13 **ardent** full of enthusiasm or 'fire'

From *The Human Zoo* by Desmond Morris

1 *Explain in two or three sentences how a 'status-climber' tries to create the impression of social dominance.*
2 *Use adjectives with prop-words to help complete these ideas.*
   a Fake diamonds are made to look just like ...
   b Our neighbours have got two cars – ... and ...
   c I'd like to buy a computer, but I can't afford ...
   d The black shoes don't fit, but I like ...
   e If you enjoy detective stories, I can recommend ...
   f Which of these jeans do you prefer – ... or ... ?

'That's Marcus in his prime – proud, arrogant and top of the heap, yet tenderness itself with his loved ones. I forget who the man is.'

'Bump the green one, Perkins'.

17 Advanced Exercises

Adjectives used to express abstract ideas

'The Oasis' is the perfect hotel for all lovers of **the exotic** and **the luxurious.**	1 *The* + adjective can be used to express an abstract idea (e.g. *the exotic, the unexpected, the impossible, the obvious).*
The amazing thing *about the voyage* was that none of us got seasick.	2 The 'prop-word' *thing* is used after the adjective if the abstract idea is limited to a certain case.

1 Chain of violence? GG 42–41; GhE 127, 134–135

Fill in the adjectives, with suitable prop-words where necessary.

young — 1 Today it is generally recognized that to hit a child, especially a very … is wrong.
terrible — 2 The … about hitting children is that they are usually powerless to defend themselves.
sensible, similar — 3 If there is a law to protect adults from attack, surely the … would be to insist on a … to protect children.
surprising, small — 4 But the … is that most people who were beaten themselves as … , genuinely believe it did them no harm.
same — 5 Not so surprisingly, these people are generally the … that later in life use violence on their own children.
intelligent — 6 Even … are often blind to the damage that is done in this way.
educated, simple — 7 The … are just as likely to beat their children as … with little schooling.
important, young, proper — 8 The … is not only to protect the … from violence, but also to treat them as … instead of just another part of an adult's 'belongings'.
obvious, impossible — 9 All this may seem like stating the …; but to expect a big change in parents' attitudes would probably be to expect the …

2 Similar adverbs – different meanings GG 46; GhE 144

Choose the correct adverb. Then translate the sentences into German.

fair/fairly
hard/hardly
late/lately
pretty/prettily
right/rightly

1 You've changed so much, I … recognized you!
2 I haven't had much time … – I've been working so … .
3 You did … well in that quiz – you got most of the answers … .
4 John's been sent off the field. – Quite … in my opinion. After all, he really wasn't playing … .
5 It's still … early – but that's good. We don't want to risk arriving … .
6 Those flowers look lovely. You've arranged them so … .

Adjectives and Adverbs: Comparative and Superlative Forms **18**

Check-up

Young people and drugs

Choose between adjectives and adverbs, using the comparative or superlative form.

	Lots of teenagers are offered drugs, but not every offer is accepted. In fact,
many	… people say 'No'. But parents should remember that young people who
likely	are fed up or worried may be … to try drugs than those that are happy at
	home.
difficult	It's … to tell when someone is using drugs occasionally than when they
regular common	are … users. But here are some of the … warning signs that may help you
easy	to recognize the beginning of a problem … . Drugs *may* be the cause if
	your child
aggressive sudden	■ acts …, or changes from one mood to another … than usual,
little	■ begins to show … interest in hobbies, sports – or even food,
few	■ seems to have … contacts with friends than before,
quick often	■ gets tired … – or suffers from sleeplessness …,
bad	■ starts to do … at school.
alarming	The … signs would, of course, be if you noticed money disappearing,
	or unusual tablets, etc. in the house.
soon good important	The … a drug problem is recognized, the … . But even then, the …
	question for parents is how to react. When Helen, 17, broke with her
normal	boyfriend, it seemed the … thing in the world – to her family. But to Helen,
depressing	it was the … thing she had ever experienced. She tried some tranquillizers
good	she found in the family medicine cupboard, and they made her feel … .
late terrible	A few weeks …, her parents discovered this, had the … row with Helen, and
early	locked up the rest of the tablets. This might have worked …, but Helen
	had already gone too far to want to turn back. A schoolfriend offered her
strong	something … (neither of them was quite sure what it was, but they thought
likely late old	it was … to be heroin). … still, Helen took up with a new boyfriend, … than
experienced	herself, and … – in fact, a regular drug user. In the end, Helen's parents got
	to know, and this time they turned to the family doctor for help. She pointed
bad	out that their … mistake had been their over-reaction to the tranquillizer
sensible	incident, when it would have been much … to have dealt with the problem
calm much hard	… and with … understanding. Now, it was far … to help Helen than it would
early	have been … .

Adapted from a leaflet published by the British health service

19 **tranquillizer** ['træŋkwɪlaɪzə] tablet that helps to make you feel calmer and less worried – 21 **row** [raʊ] an angry scene between two or more people – 29 **to deal with** to treat/to handle (a situation)

18 Basic Rules and Exercises

1 Comparative and superlative forms

Adjectives

	1 *-er, -est* with
This road has been made **wider.**	a adjectives of one syllable **(exception:** past participles used as adjectives)
It's **simplest** to park here. There would have been an accident if the road had been **narrower.** Automatic cars are **easier** to drive.	b adjectives of two syllables ending in *-le, -ow, -y*
	2 *more, most* with
That girl at the travel agent's couldn't have been **more helpful.**	a most other adjectives of two syllables
I find flying the **most comfortable** form of travelling.	b all adjectives of three or more syllables

Adverbs

The InterCity leaves **later,** but it travels **faster,** so it gets to London **sooner.**	1 *-er, -est* with adverbs of one syllable
	2 *more, most* with
Would you please walk a bit **more quickly?**	a adverbs formed by adding *-ly*
Do you go into town by bus? – No. I **most often** walk.	b other adverbs of more than one syllable

Note

We had **better** weather in Ireland than in Scotland, but the food was **worse.**
Of all the trips we've had, I enjoyed the hike over the moors **best.**
Some common adjectives and adverbs have irregular comparative and superlative forms:

good/well:	**better, best**	**many:**	**more, most**	**little** (= not much):	**less, least**
bad/badly:	**worse, worst**	**much:**	**more, most**	**little** (= small):	**smaller, smallest**

2 Making comparisons with adjectives and adverbs

I'll take this suitcase. It's **bigger than** the leather bag. Let's go by Underground. The trains run **more regularly than** buses.	■ > □	comparative + *than*
The train fare was**n't as expensive as** I'd expected/ was **less expensive than** I'd expected.	■ < □	*not as … as/less … than*
There may be heavy traffic on the M25, so we'll leave for the airport **as early as** we can.	■ = □	*as … as*

1 Some good, some bad, all different GG 39–40, 47; GhE 136–139, 145-146

In Alan Ayckbourn's short play 'A Talk in the Park' four people are sitting apart from each other on four park benches, when Arthur enters and goes up to Beryl, a young girl on one of the benches. He sits down and tries to start a conversation, but Beryl refuses to be drawn into it. In spite of this, Arthur begins to talk to her about himself …

Arthur: … I'm a very fulfilled person. I have, for example, one of the biggest collections of cigarette cards of anyone alive or dead that I know of. And you don't get that by sitting on your behind all day. But I'll let you into a secret. Do you know what it is that's the most valuable thing there is you can hope to collect? People. I'm a collector of people. I look at them, I observe them, I hear them talk, I listen to their manner of speaking and I think, hallo, here's another one. Different. Different again. Because I'll let you into a secret. They are like fingerprints. They are never quite the same. And I've met a number in my lifetime. Quite a number. Some good, some bad, all different. But the best of them, and I'm saying this to you quite frankly and openly, the best of them are women. They are superior people. They are better people. They are cleaner people. They are kinder-hearted people. If I had a choice, I'd be a woman. Now that makes you laugh, I expect, but it's the truth. When I choose to have a conversation, I can tell you it's with a woman every time. Because a woman is one of nature's listeners. Most men I wouldn't give the time of day to. Now, I expect that shocks you but it's the truth. Trouble is, I don't get to meet as many women as I'd like to. My particular line of work does not bring me into contact with them as much as I would wish. Which is a pity.

From *A Talk in the Park* by Alan Ayckbourn

2 **cigarette card** small card (with a picture of s.o. or s.th. of interest) included in a cigarette packet – 4 **valuable** worth a lot – 5 **to observe** to look at closely – 11 **superior** of a better 'type' or quality – 17 **Trouble is …** The only problem is …

1 *First pick out all examples of comparisons, and of comparative and superlative forms. Say which 'type' (according to the Basic Rules) each belongs to.*
2 *Why does Arthur 'collect' people? What sort of people does he like best, and why?*
3 *Look at Arthur's statements about women, and try to imagine what experiences may have formed his opinion. Use comparatives and superlatives where you can. (Think of his family, people he has known at school/at work, friends, TV personalities he knows or films he has seen.)*
Examples:
Perhaps Arthur's mother was kinder to him/treated him more kindly than his father.
It's possible that he had a brother who didn't play with him as much as his sister.
4 *Even in our 'modern' age, people still have strange ideas about others. Give your opinion on the following statements, using comparative or superlative forms as often as you can.*
a It's more important for a woman to be good-looking than it is for a man.
b Women are better at looking after children than men because they are naturally more patient and understanding.
c All the most famous artists and musicians are men.
d The Germans work harder than other Europeans, but the French are the best cooks.
e Blood is thicker than water. (= Relations are more reliable than friends.)

2 Human aggression GG 39–40, 47; GhE 136–139, 145–146

1 **to dispute** to call into question – 2 **rodents** rats, mice, etc. – **vertebrate** animal with a backbone – 3 **species** ['spi:ʃi:z] *Art* – 5 **repulsive** sickeningly horrible – 8 **confined** limited – 9 **sombre** ['sɒmbə] dark, serious

That man is an aggressive creature will hardly be disputed. With the exception of certain rodents, no other vertebrate habitually destroys members of his own species. No other animal takes positive pleasure in the exercise of cruelty upon another of his own kind. We generally describe the most repulsive examples of man's cruelty as brutal or bestial, implying by these adjectives that such behaviour is characteristic of less highly developed animals than ourselves. In truth, however, the extremes of 'brutal' behaviour are confined to man; and there is no parallel in nature to our savage treatment of each other. The sombre fact is that we are the cruellest and most ruthless species that has ever walked the earth.

From *Human Aggression* by Anthony Storr

1 *Note down the positive, comparative and superlative forms of adjectives and adverbs in the text. Then choose from them to complete this summary sensibly:*
The adjectives '...' and '...' are ... supposed to describe behaviour that is ... of animals, but in fact the ... creatures of this earth do not show such ... behaviour towards each other as we do. Man is the ... and ... creature in the world. This can ... be doubted.
2 *Give opposites of: most repulsive (ll. 4–5); less highly developed (6); cruellest (9).*
3 *Compare the following, using adjectives and adverbs in various forms.*

clean cruel useful fast aggressive dangerous friendly natural frightening

man – animals   horses – cattle
rats – mice   pets – wild animals
cats – dogs   people – robots
primitive weapons – modern weapons

Examples:
Most people find rats more frightening than mice because they are more dangerous.
Rats act more aggressively than mice.

'We've decided that it's healthier to eat a vegetarian.'

1 Buy, buy, buy GG 39–40, 47; GhE 136–139, 145–146

The most powerful, the loudest and the most persistent command in our society is the command to buy, to consume, to make material progress, to 'grow'. The voice of advertising urges us to buy, buy, buy, and it never lets up.

Advertising intended for an audience that can afford what it offers also works (with perhaps even greater effectiveness) on those who cannot afford it; it inflames the desires of the poor without offering them any satisfaction at all. Perhaps the poor are 'better off than they ever were before', but they can hardly be expected to be satisfied after watching television. A continuous display of better living is paraded before them. Rich people know that not every day is filled with sports and glamour; they even know that the person who has everything might not even want all these things. The poor have no way of knowing this: television advertising is far more effective with the unsophisticated. Is there any wonder that we have riots? Television might rightly be called a riot box; it raises a fury of dissatisfaction and mocks those who watch it. But even the well-paid, highly motivated executive, after a demanding day, may feel troubled emotions if he views a TV scene of surfers. The screen tells him to work harder so he can vacation in California. But perhaps he senses, in some almost unconscious way, that the harder he works, the less likely it is that he ever will surf; in fact, real surfers don't work at all …

The one thing that we can be sure of is that the aim of advertising is to create dissatisfaction.

From *The Greening of America* by Charles Reich

1 **persistent** going on without stopping, persuasive – 3 **to urge** to try to persuade – 4 **to let up** to stop – 7 **to inflame** to excite – 8 **better off** richer, in a better position – 10 **display** show – 12 **glamour** ['glæmə] *here:* beauty and social success – 14 **unsophisticated** [ˌ--'----] naturally simple – 15 **riot** outbreak of violence, rebellion – 16 **fury** anger, rage; *here:* violent feeling – **to mock** to make fun of – 17 **executive** [ɪg'zekjʊtɪv] (powerful) person in a business

't is a Newer New, but I'm afraid we're ›ut of stock of the Newest New …'

1 *Use constructions containing comparisons to explain the meaning of:*
   a *to make material progress (ll. 2-3);*
   b *it inflames the desires of the poor (7);*
   c *the poor are 'better off than they ever were before' (8-9)*
   d *not every day is filled with sports and glamour (11-12)*
   e *it raises a fury of dissatisfaction (16).*
2 *What are the reasons why advertising works more effectively on the poor than it does on the rich?*
3 *'The harder he works, the less likely it is that he ever will surf.' (l. 21) Try to explain the logic of the author's argument.*
4 *Do you think people used to feel happier in the days before television and mass advertising? Give examples of how ordinary people's lives and attitudes have changed since then.*
5 *Which do you think affects your own buying habits more strongly – the voice of advertising, or 'peer pressure' (the influence of people of your own age and status)? Explain why.*
6 *Complete the following sentences with your own ideas:*
   a The harder you work, …
   b The more material possessions you have, …
   c The better educated a person is, …
   d The more you know about the tricks used in advertising, …

A savage medieval punishment

2 Were people more aggressive then? GG 39–40, 47; GhE 136–139, 145–146

Complete the text, using positive, comparative or superlative forms of suitable adjectives or adverbs. Sometimes there will be a number of different possibilities.
Example:
In this **modern/civilized/technological/advanced/progressive** age of ours …

In this … age of ours, we tend to think that people living in … centuries were … than people today. In the early Middle Ages, there were no law courts, and people were often … punished by the Sheriff, even for … crimes like stealing firewood or hunting deer. In those … days, a person could be put to death for committing a crime no … than stealing a loaf of bread.

In the 17th century, when there was still no police force in Britain, the streets of London were much … than they are today, and people behaved altogether … than they … do now. The … of all the Londoners were the watermen, who rowed passengers across the Thames. They were so … that they prevented the building of bridges over the Thames, as they feared this would mean … passengers for them – and … money. The 17th century was probably one of the … times in history; … crowds came to watch the … public executions, and it is … to imagine a … sight than the heads of the executed prisoners put up on spikes on London Bridge.

Travelling was … and … than it is today, because of the … condition of the roads, and because of highwaymen. By the 18th century, however, roads had become far …, so coaches were able to travel …, making it … for robbers to attack. But there were still a few highwaymen, the … of them all being Dick Turpin, who was … caught and hanged in 1739. Today, of course, the legal system works … than in those days, there is a … organized police force, and punishments are … . But it is … whether people … behave … towards each other than they used to.

3 Advertising techniques GG 39–40, 47; GhE 136–139, 145–146

Have you ever thought how advertising 'works'? Think of your own experience of advertising techniques, and complete with suitable comparisons.
Example:
Products described by words with pleasant associations, like 'golden' or 'soft' **are most likely to sell well / have a stronger effect on potential buyers.**

1 New 'scientific discoveries' are used in adverts in order to …
2 With the help of photographic tricks, products can …
3 The advertiser repeats the name of the product again and again so that …
4 If the product is recommended by 'experts' such as well-known personalities, …
5 Suggesting that all the 'best' people use a certain product is supposed to make us worry that if we don't use it, …

Check-up

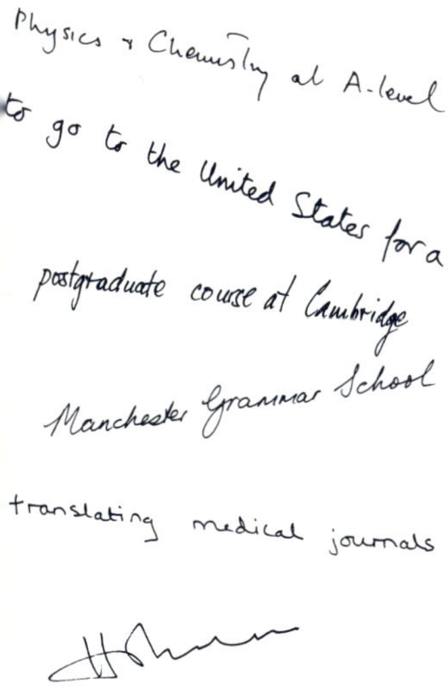

1 Your character in your handwriting?

Put in the adverbs/adverbials in the most suitable position.

1 According to graphologists, your hand is connected with your brain. *(closely)*
2 When you write, it is difficult to hide your personality. *(extremely)*
3 When applying for a job, people are asked to write their application by hand. *(often)*
4 Some couples ask a graphologist if they should get married or not! *(even)*
5 Some American doctors discovered a link between patients' handwriting and their health. *(a few years ago)*
6 Here are some simple signs to look out for. *(quite)*
7 If you are in a hurry *(always)* you forget to dot your 'i's. *(probably)* Or you don't cross your 't's. *(properly)*
8 An energetic person will press the paper. *(hard)*
9 An aggressive person will form his or her letters. *(sharply)*
10 People whose writing leans forward are enthusiastic people. *(usually)*
11 Those whose writing leans backwards could be interpreted as rather cold. *(possibly)*
12 When you write a letter, you sign your name. *(at the bottom)* Can people read it? *(hardly)* If so, it means that you are a self-important person. *(certainly)* Or does it?
13 The 'science' of graphology has its limits. *(obviously)*
14 There are lots of other ways of getting to know people! *(fortunately)*

2 A trip to London

Put the pieces together to form sentences. Think carefully about the word order.

1 we went / last April / for a couple of days / to London
2 at King's Cross Station / we arrived / in the afternoon / at 2 o'clock
3 by Underground / then / to our hotel / we went on
4 the weather / all the time / luckily / was really good
5 to the Tower of London / by boat / on the first afternoon / we went
6 we saw / the next morning / at Buckingham Palace / the Changing of the Guard
7 at the shops / then / in the Oxford Street area / we looked / for a while
8 time / after that / very quickly / began to go / not surprisingly
9 to 'Cats' / that evening / we went / in the West End / at the New London Theatre
10 certainly / the best show / in my life / I've ever seen / it was
11 home / the next day / we had to go / unfortunately / again

19 Basic Rules and Exercises

Adverbs of manner

I *read* **slowly.** I *enjoyed that book* **immensely.**	1 end position: a after the verb if it has no object b after verb + object – for emphasis
He **quickly** *paid* for the newspaper. You*'ll* **easily** *have* time to buy a magazine before the train comes in.	2 mid position (before the main verb), if the adverb is used descriptively **(not** for emphasis)

Adverbs of indefinite time and frequency

Gill **often** *plays* the piano after tea. Brown's *is* **usually** the best place for CDs. I *should* **never** *have bought* that cheap guitar.	1 mid position: a before the main verb, but after the the verb *be* b after the first auxiliary
Sometimes we have the radio on at breakfast time. Have you taken those video tapes back **already?** That was quick!	2 front or end position is possible in some cases (usually for emphasis)

Adverbs and adverbials of definite time and place

We saw 'Julius Caesar' **yesterday.**	1 end position (in most cases)
Today we want to practise those songs again. **Up here** the acoustics are much better.	2 front position (usually for emphasis)

Adverbs and adverbials of comment

Unfortunately, it's impossible to get tickets for 'The Phantom of the Opera'.	1 front position (in most cases)
'Starlight Express' is worth seeing too, **of course.**	2 end position (as an 'after-thought')
You'll **probably** get good seats.	3 mid-position (usual with *probably, certainly,* etc.)

Note

Marion played **beautifully at the concert last night.**
The circus begins **at 3 o'clock on Saturday afternoon.**
When several adverbs are used together at the end of a sentence, the usual word order is MANNER – PLACE – TIME.
The more exact time comes before the more general.

'Once upon a time – well, yesterday, actually ...'

1 Going to college GG 48–55; GhE 142, 147–160

Adverbs are often used to make what you want to say livelier – or more exact. Improve these sentences with the adverbs given, being careful to put them in the most suitable place. Sometimes more than one position is possible.

1 A lot of American students choose to do a four-year college or university program. *(after high school)*
2 A university is different from a college in that it is much bigger. *(usually)*
3 But the word 'college' is used to describe both. *(generally)*
4 A university has an undergraduate college of arts and sciences, a graduate section, and a program for adults. *(normally)*
5 You have to be in the top half of your high school class to have a chance of getting into a college or university. *(nowadays)*
6 The 'Ivy League' colleges (including the universities of Harvard and Yale) are famous. *(extremely)*
7 It is difficult to get a place at one of these. *(not surprisingly)*
8 Most of them are co-educational. *(now)*
9 But they are linked with female colleges of similar status (e.g. Radcliffe and Vassar). *(traditionally)*
10 The guidance counsellor (a member of the high school staff) is trained to advise students about their college career. *(specially)*
11 As there are so many different kinds of college, each student must consider the alternatives. *(carefully)*
12 That is important. *(always)*
13 For a serious-minded person, a college specializing in academics would be the right choice. *(certainly)*
14 But for someone athletic, a college emphasizing sports offers more. *(probably)*
15 Most students work to help finance their studies. *(during the summer vacation)*
16 Some have regular part-time jobs. *(even)*
17 Getting into college isn't difficult. *(terribly)*
18 But quite a number of people flunk out before they finish their studies. *(unfortunately)*

4 **undergraduate** [ˌʌndəˈgrædʒʊət] student (before taking a degree) – **graduate** *here:* research student –
8 **co-educational** for male and female students –
18 **to flunk out** (AE) to fail (an exam)

19 2 Homeless in London GG 48–55; GhE 142, 147–160

Adverbs and adverbials can sometimes be so important to a sentence that the meaning is not complete without them. The following sentences are based on the experiences of homeless people living in London. Add the given adverbs and adverbials in suitable places.

for four years **in a car park** **near the Royal Festival Hall** **so often** **soon** **to London**	*Keith:* My home is a cardboard box. I've been unemployed. I came to look for work. But I discovered London isn't the Utopia it's made out to be.
nearly always **in advance** **in London**	*Barry:* The big trouble is finding a place to live. Landlords demand two months' rent.
only **almost** **an hour** **at one time** **in a restaurant**	But if you're making two or three pounds doing casual work, it's impossible to get that much money together.
at night **at eleven o'clock** **usually** **at the kiosk** **outside Waterloo Station** **even** **for a few minutes** **there** **regularly** **very long**	*Steve:* A tea van comes round. Or if you have 20p, you can get a cup of coffee. And if you have 10p left, you can enjoy the warmth of the station's indoor toilets. But you can't stay. The police check the place.
at the interview **every day** **in clean clothes**	*Bruce:* I look for work. But it's difficult if you aren't dressed.
just **even** **differently** **sometimes**	People treat you when you look scruffy. They pretend they haven't seen you.
from the wind **here** **in the homeless community** **a few days ago**	*Keith:* There's a strong code of ethics. A newcomer made a mistake. He took someone else's piece of cardboard to protect himself.
jokingly **politely** **immediately** **already**	He was told to put it back, and someone said: 'Stealing someone's bed?'
sometimes **really**	*Bruce:* I don't mind feeling hungry, because I know there are other people who are hungry, too.
more **always** **strangely enough**	Whenever I get some money, I end up giving it away to someone who needs it.

Based on an article in *The Guardian,* May 18, 1988

1 **cardbord** strong paper-based material – 4 **to make out** to say (wrongly) – 6 **in advance** (to be paid) before – 8 **casual work** ['kæʒʊəl] work done for short periods, not permanently or regularly – 17 **scruffy** untidy – 19 **code of ethics** accepted 'rules' of behaviour

1 The disastrous growth of world population GG 48–55; GhE 142, 147–162

Translate the text into English. Think carefully about where to put the adverbs/adverbials. These words will be useful:
to triple (l. 3) – disastrous consequences (4-5) – decade (8) – developing countries (10) – to slow down (12) – status (13) – to offer the chance of a proper training (15-16) – to invest in family planning (17-18) – yearly expenditure (used only in the singular) (19) – to double (20)

Die Bevölkerung der Welt vermehrt sich heute schneller als jemals zuvor und könnte sich in den kommenden 100 Jahren sogar verdreifachen. Dies hätte jedoch besonders für die Umwelt katastrophale Folgen.

Nach einem Bericht der Vereinten Nationen, der gestern in London veröffentlicht wurde, wird die Erdbevölkerung im kommenden Jahrzehnt jährlich um *(by)* 90 bis 100 Millionen Menschen wachsen. Die Bevölkerung wächst in den ärmsten Entwicklungsländern leider am schnellsten. Der beste und schnellste Weg, das Bevölkerungswachstum zu verlangsamen, besteht wahrscheinlich darin, den Status der Frauen in diesen Ländern zu verbessern und ihnen in Zukunft den Zugang zu einer ordentlichen Ausbildung zu verschaffen. Selbstverständlich ist es in den Entwicklungsländern besonders wichtig, in Familienplanung zu investieren. Möglicherweise werden die jährlichen Ausgaben hierfür bis zum Ende dieses Jahrhunderts verdoppelt werden müssen.

Adapted from *SÜDWEST PRESSE ULM*, 16. 5. 1990

2 Some positive effects of immigration GG 149; GhE 337.3, 338.3

Attention is constantly being drawn to the problems caused by the immigrants who have arrived in Britain over the past 20 or 30 years. Only rarely do people stop to consider the positive changes they helped to bring about. Back in the 1950s, working people could not do their shopping during the week: no sooner had the factory gates opened in the evening than the traditional British shopkeeper closed his doors. Asian immigrants quickly changed that.

Not only have Asian people improved the trades they have entered, but their hard work is also setting an example to the British. The quality and variety of food in restaurants and shops have also improved greatly during the last few years, thanks to all the foreign foods and cooking methods. Never before has such a wide range of delicious food been available in Britain.

So great have been the problems of assimilation in some areas that British people tend to overlook the superior qualities of many Asian families, whose sense of cohesion and responsibility show up our divorce-ridden society in a very poor light. Not for all the world should the problems some immigrants have created be allowed to let us forget the good influence that others have had.

22 **cohesion** [kəʊ'hi:ʒn] keeping together as a unified whole – 23 **ridden** plagued or polluted by

Inversion as a stylistic device

Never in the history of mankind *has medical science made* more progress than in the last hundred years.
Not only *do doctors understand* more about disease, but they also realize the importance of a healthy diet.

Certain negative or restrictive adverbials (e.g.*never, hardly, no sooner, not only)* can be put at the beginning of a sentence for emphasis. This causes **inversion** (a reversal of the usual word order.)

1 *Pick out all the examples of inversion in the text. Replace them by sentences with normal word order.*
2 *Translate all the sentences containing inversion into German.*

19 3 Different styles GG 48–55; GhĖ 147–160)

First read the texts.

A The discovery of the bodies

Emily Wharton looks after the flowers at St Matthew's Church in Paddington, London. Early one morning, when she goes to the church together with Darren, a 10-year-old boy who sometimes accompanies her, she discovers two dead bodies in the vestry …

And it was then, in that moment, that she felt the first twitch of anxiety. Suddenly she knew that something was dreadfully wrong. Instinctively she called out: 'Darren!'

He turned and looked at her face. And then, immediately, he was back at her side. Gently at first, and then with one sharp movement, she opened the door. Her eyes were dazzled with light. And she saw horror itself.

There were two of them and she knew instantly, and with absolute certainty, that they were dead. The room was a shambles. Their throats had been cut and they lay like butchered animals in a waste of blood. Instinctively she thrust Darren behind her. But she was too late. He, too, had seen …

She pushed him back into the passage, closed the door, and leaned against it, grateful for the support. But neither its strength nor her tightly closed eyes could shut out horror. Brightly lit as on a stage, she saw the bodies still. The images of death she was powerless to shut out swam before her in a swirl of blood.

From *A Taste for Death,* by P. D. James

vestry small room in a church where the priest changes clothes, etc. – 2 **twitch** *here:* sudden feeling – 8 **to dazzle** to blind (with bright light) – 12 **a shambles** in a terrible mess – 13 **a waste** *here:* a large area or sea – 14 **to thrust** to push strongly – 22 **swirl** *here:* a moving sea

B The killers

The door of Henry's lunch-room opened and two men came in. They sat down at the counter.

'What's yours?' George asked them.

'I don't know,' one of the men said. 'I don't know what I want to eat.'

Outside it was getting dark. The street light came on outside the window. The two men at the counter read the menu. From the other end of the counter Nick Adams watched them. He had been talking to George when they came in.

'I'll take ham and eggs,' the man called Al said. He wore a derby hat and a black overcoat buttoned across the chest. His face was small and white and he had tight lips. He wore a silk muffler and gloves.

'Give me bacon and eggs,' said the other man. He was about the same size as Al. Their faces were different, but they were dressed like twins. Both wore overcoats too tight for them. They sat leaning forward, their elbows on the counter.

From *The Killers,* a short story by Ernest Hemingway

12 **derby hat** (AE) *Melone* – 14 **muffler** old-fashioned word for scarf

1 *Compare the use of adjectives and adverbs in the two texts. What do you discover?*
2 *Try to compare P. D. James's style with Hemingway's.*
These adjectives may help you:
atmospheric, clear, complex, concise, descriptive, dry, emotional, impersonal, matter-of-fact, mysterious, personal, simple, straightforward, vivid.
Then say which style impressed you more, and why.
3 *Go through the first part of the Hemingway text again, and say where adverbs/adverbials could have been put in (give examples!). How would these changes affect the style?*

The Definite and the Indefinite Article 20

Check-up

1 Young people and university

Use the definite or indefinite article to fill in the gaps where necessary.

Mary Willams (17, still at school): I plan to go to … university when I leave … school. I'll probably study … English because I love … English literature. At … moment I'm very interested in … poetry of T. S. Eliot. Actually, what I'm looking forward to most is … freedom of … university life. … school I go to is pretty strict – it's … boarding school near York.

Professor Richards (Oxford University): … quite … large number of … candidates who have applied for … place at Oxford this year are from … European Community. More and more students from … Europe, especially … German students, are keen to go to … British university. … most of … foreign students come to Britain because … courses they can take here are shorter – and less crowded – than at … home. All … students I've talked to especially like our traditional system of … close contact with tutors.

John Whitely (19, first-year music student): My father is … clergyman and my mother is … social worker. They always hoped I might study … theology and become … priest – or at least do something to help … society. As … child, when I still used to go to … church regularly, I thought … missionary work mightn't be … such … bad idea. But when I started … secondary school, I began to get interested in … music. That was when … life really got going for me. By … time I was 15, I knew I had to take up … music as … career. So here I am! Luckily my parents have given me … full support. They realize I'm not doing all this as … act of … protest or … rebellion against … upbringing I had.

2 Taken down from the bookshelf

Translate these book titles into English, being careful with your use of definite and indefinite articles.

1 „Krieg und Frieden."
2 „Das tägliche Leben im alten *(ancient)* Rom."
3 „Das Leben Napoleons."
4 „Die chinesische Küche *(cooking)*."
5 „Meine Tochter will Politikerin werden."
6 „Die Geschichte der Vereinigten Staaten."
7 „Die Wunder der Natur."
8 „Als Victoria Königin von England war."
9 „Ein halbes Pfund Reis."
10 „Alle Vögel am Himmel."
11 „Die Schule als Brücke zum Erfolg?"
12 „Er war Engländer."

'If she doesn't make it as a ballet dancer, she wants to be a dentist.'

20 Basic Rules and Exercises

1 The use of the definite article

Without *the*	With *the*
Life is full of ups and downs. **Technology** is an important part of **modern life.** **Cold water** can taste delicious.	Not much is known about **the life of Shakespeare.** **The life we lead today** is very complicated, partly because of **the technology we have developed.** Let's bathe here. **The water** looks so clear.
No article is used before abstract nouns (e.g. *life, society, happiness)* and uncountable nouns (e.g. *water, paper)* when referring to things generally, even if an adjective is used (e.g. *modern life).*	**The definite article is used only** when these nouns are defined more closely (e.g. with an *of*-phrase or a relative clause), or – with uncountable nouns – when a particular case or example is meant.
I missed **school** for two weeks when I was in **hospital.** We sometimes go to **church** by **car.**	That's **the hospital** over there. It's next to **the school.** You can park **the car** behind **the church.**
No article is used before institutions when referring to their function (e.g.*school = lessons),* and before means of transport (with *by).*	**The definite article is used** when referring to a particular institution (usually the building itself) or a particular vehicle.

2 The use of the indefinite article

With *a*	Without *a*
My mother is **a dentist.** Who wants to be **a millionaire?** Judy's grandfather was **a Frenchman.** Her mother is **a Catholic.** She lived in France **as a child.**	I wonder who will be **Prime Minister** next year at this time. John F. Kennedy became **President** (of the USA) when he was only 43. My father was **captain** of the golf club last year.
The indefinite article is used when referring to a person as a member of a certain group (e.g. a profession, nationality, religion), and after *as.*	**No article is used** when referring to functions and titles that can only be given to one person at one particular time.

Note

I'll be ready in **half an** hour.
We've been waiting for **such a** long time!
We were up **half the** night.
All the guests stayed till late.

The article comes ***after*** half, such, all, quite, both, *etc.,* ***not before.***

barber men's hairdresser

'No mate, this is Purgatory. That's Eternity over there.'

purgatory *Fegefeuer* – **eternity** *Ewigkeit*

1 Life-saving GG 9–13; GhE 101–107

Three years ago, a now healthy American five-year-old was pulled from the freezing waters of the Great Salt Lake. She appeared to be dead. She had been in the water for over an hour. She was brought back to life after two hours of first aid.

If the girl had been a Briton, she would probably have died. The problem is that knowledge of basic first aid is very limited in Britain. Help must be given quickly – and persistently. Most children are not given proper training at school, and do not know what to do in an emergency.

Most people who drown do so because they get into difficulties in freezing cold water and the temperature of their body drops. Tony Simcock, an anaesthetist at the Royal Cornwall Hospital in Truro, says: 'When swimmers die from drowning, the real reason for this is hypothermia.' When the temperature of the body drops below 35 degrees, the memory stops working. Below 33 degrees, swimmers become unconscious and drown as the head slips into the water. The average time a victim can survive in water at 5 degrees is an hour.

What can you do if such an emergency arises? First, try to call an expert – maybe a doctor. Second, clear the victim's airway. Then put the body flat on the ground, with the head lower than the rest. Next cover the victim's nose, and breathe into the mouth 15 or 16 times a minute. Massage the heart once a second. Keep the victim warm, to stop hypothermia. Most important, keep going until the expert arrives.

Adapted from an article in *The Independent on Sunday,* July 8, 1990

9 **persistently** without stopping or giving up – 12 **to drown** [aʊ] to die in water – 15 **anaesthetist** [ə'ni:sθətɪst] – 17 **hypothermia** [ˌhaɪpəʊ'θɜ:mɪə] abnormally low body temperature – 18 **memory** the ability to remember – 20 **unconscious** [ʌn'kɒnʃəs] not awake, without the use of the senses

1 *Answer the questions:*
   a *What nationality was the girl found in the Great Salt Lake?*
   b *Where should children learn first aid?*
   c *What is Tony Simcock's job?*
   d *What is the commonest reason for people drowning?*
   e *What happens when your body temperature drops to an abnormal level?*
   f *How quickly should you breathe air into the victim's mouth?*
   g *How often should the heart be massaged?*
   h *Another name for mouth-to-mouth respiration is 'the kiss of life'. Why is it called this?*

2 *Find all the examples of* a/an *and* the *in the text. Where would the use of the article be different in German?*

3 *Translate lines 1-14 ('… drops.'). What further differences do you notice between German and English?*

20 2 An English secret GG 9–13; GhE 100–107

Complete the text, where necessary, with the definite and indefinite article.

... tea is best made in ... brown china teapot. First you warm ... pot with ... hot water, which you throw away after ... moment or two. Then put in ... teaspoonful of ... tea for each person, and ... extra one for luck ('one for ... pot'). Now pour ... boiling water on, and leave ... tea to stand for three to five minutes, before pouring it into ... fine china cups, with or without ... milk and ... sugar. ... hot water is served separately, to make ... tea less strong.

Philip Sidley is ... tea expert. He believes that ... secret of ... good tea lies in ... quality of ... water you use. Jonathan Goodall, who is the manager of ... big firm of ... tea importers, does not think ... type of ... water is ... such ... important aspect. He says ... main thing is to make ... tea immediately after ... water has boiled.

... Queen Elizabeth ... Second would agree with Philip Sidley. Whenever she travels away from ... home, she takes ... special type of ... English spring water with her – for making ... tea.

Although ... coffee is also drunk a lot in England today, ... drinking of ... tea is closely connected with ... certain philosophy of ... life. ... tea-drinking is regarded as ... ceremony, not just as ... way of quenching one's thirst. ... people drink ... tea to forget – if only for ... half ... hour or so – ... worries of ... daily life.

1 **china** *Porzellan* – 19 **spring water** natural mineral water – 25 **to quench** to satisfy (thirst)

A secret of the sea.
Passenger: *'Look here, steward, if this is coffee, I want tea; but if this is tea, then I wish for coffee.'*

Life, liberty, and the pursuit of happiness ...

*'Dear Albert!
Farewell,
I have found love.'*

'We all hear a lot about Women's Liberation these days. Speaking as a Princess ...'

Advanced Exercises

1 Questions about the universe GG 9; GhE 100, 105

We go about our daily lives understanding almost nothing of the world.

We give little thought to the machinery that generates the sunlight that makes life possible, to the gravity that glues us to an Earth that would otherwise send us spinning off into space, or to the atoms of which we are made and on whose stability we fundamentally depend. Except for children (who don't know enough not to ask the important questions), few of us spend much time wondering why nature is the way it is; where the cosmos came from, or whether it was always here; if time will one day flow backward and effects precede causes; or whether there are ultimate limits to what humans can know.

There are even children, and I have met some of them, who want to know what a black hole looks like; what is the smallest piece of matter; why we remember the past and not the future; how it is, if there was chaos early, that there is, apparently, order today; and why there is a universe.

In our society it is still customary for parents and teachers to answer most of these questions with a shrug, or with an appeal to vaguely recalled religious precepts. Some are uncomfortable with issues like these, because they so vividly expose the limitations of human understanding.

But much of philosophy and science has been driven by such inquiries. An increasing number of adults are willing to ask questions of this sort, and occasionally they get some astonishing answers. Equidistant from the atoms and the stars, we are expanding our exploratory horizons to embrace both the very small and the very large.

From Carl Sagan's introduction to *A Brief History of Time* by Stephen Hawking

5 **gravity** *Schwerkraft* – **to glue** to stick – 6 **to spin** to turn round and round fast – 13 **to precede** to come before – 14 **ultimate** final – 18 **matter** substance of which a physical thing is made – 24 **shrug** lifting of the shoulders – **with an appeal to** by calling attention to – **to recall** to remember – 25 **precept** ['pri:sept] rule, principle – **issue** problem, question to be discussed – 26 **to expose** to show up – 29 **inquiry** question – 32 **equidistant** [ˌi:kwɪ'dɪstənt] equally far away – 33 **to expand** to widen – **to embrace** *here:* to include

1 a *Pick out the abstract nouns and uncountable singular nouns from the text. Explain why they are used with or without an article.*
  b *Make a sentence with each of the following nouns, **without** using an article:* machinery; sunlight; gravity (ll. 3-5).

2 *Translate lines 3-15 into German. Note where the article is used differently in German.*

3 *Complete the sentences with suitable nouns, deciding where an article is necessary.*
  a Without … that is given off by the sun, … on our Earth would be impossible.
  b Because of … of …, a ball you throw up into … will inevitably come down again.
  c … is a state in which nothing is ordered; but when we observe … on our planet – … and … of animals and plants, for example – we find everything works according to very definite laws.
  d According to … of relativity, it is impossible for any normal object to travel faster than … of …

There was a young lady named Bright
Whose speed was far faster than light;
She went out one day,
In a relative way,
And returned on the previous night.

2 Agatha Christie

GG 3, 9–14; GKE 73.1, 100–108

Translate the text into English. These words will be useful:
detective story writer (l. 1) – of all time (1-2) – hospital dispenser (7-8) – (detective) novels (10/12) – blackmail (19) – masterpiece (20) – detective fiction (20-21) – to recognize as (21)

Agatha Christie, berühmteste Kriminalautorin aller Zeiten, wurde 1890 in Torquay (Devon) geboren. Sie ging nie zur Schule, denn ihre Eltern ließen sie zu Hause erziehen. Als junge Frau ging sie nach Paris, wo sie Musik studierte mit dem Ziel, Sängerin zu werden. 1914 heiratete sie, und als der erste Weltkrieg ausbrach, arbeitete sie als Krankenhausapothekerin in einem Krankenhaus in Torquay. Ihre genauen Kenntnisse über Gifte, die sie später in ihren Romanen zeigte, stammten aus der Zeit in diesem Krankenhaus.

Während dieser Zeit fing sie an, Detektivromane zu lesen; diese Geschichten machten auf sie einen so großen Eindruck, daß sie beschloß, selbst ihr Glück als Autorin zu versuchen. ‚The Mysterious Affair at Styles', der erste von über 60 Detektivromanen, erschien 1920. ‚The Murder of Roger Ackroyd', ein Roman, der von Mord, Selbstmord und Erpressung handelt, wurde 1926 herausgegeben und wird als Meisterwerk der Kriminalliteratur angesehen.

Agatha Christie, die ‚Königin des Verbrechens', starb 1976. Ihre Bücher leben aber weiter und sind schon in mehr als hundert Sprachen übersetzt worden. Kein Wunder, daß die Namen ‚Hercule Poirot' und ‚Miss Marple' für die meisten Leute heute mindestens so viel bedeuten wie ‚Sherlock Holmes'.

3 When I'm alone

'When I'm alone' – the words tripped off his tongue
As though to be alone were nothing strange.
'When I was young,' he said; *'when I was young ...'*

I thought of age, and loneliness, and change.
I thought how strange we grow when we're alone,
And how unlike the selves that meet, and talk,
And blow the candles out, and say good-night.
Alone ... The word is life endured and known.
It is the stillness where our spirits walk
And all but inmost faith is overthrown.

(Siegfried Sassoon, 1886-1967)

1 *Find the abstract nouns in the poem, and say why the article is or is not used.*
2 *What is this poem by Siegfried Sassoon about? What other abstract themes are often used as the subject of poetry?*

1 **to trip off one's tongue** to be spoken easily – 8 **to endure** to bear, to suffer – 10 **but** *here:* except – **faith** belief, confidence – **to overthrow** to destroy

Check-up

Everbody needs holidays

Complete the text with suitable pronouns or determiners.

all any
each every
everyone
everyone
few none some

A … goes on holiday. Kings, presidents and dictators – … of them is too grand to take a holiday somewhere. For the … very famous and mighty it is a way of demonstrating their common humanity, of showing that they, like … else, need … time off work. There is only one exception to … this: Her Majesty the Queen does not take … holidays. Rather, she resides, at set times … year, at … of her various homes – Sandringham in the winter, Balmoral in the summer.

a few all
anyone both
each most
no

B … people now think of holidays as necessary. An increase in the number of paid holidays … year is one of the fundamental demands of trade unions everywhere. … who doubted the need of holidays would be regarded as not quite right in the head. … the progressive movements in the 20th century have put holidays for the workers at the centre of their agenda. Even Hitler and Mussolini were … eager to show that in their regimes holidays were no longer the preserve of … upper class people. … politician would have a chance of being elected today if he wanted to reduce people's holidays.

a few a little all
everyone
little many
most some
something

C The modern idea of a holiday came into existence in the Twenties with the German invention of sunbathing. Instead of carrying on with their normal social life, mixing with their friends in … especially delightful or healthy place, … people now thought of a holiday as … completely opposed to their usual everyday life and work. The modern holiday depends on the idea that for … people work is of … interest because it is often boring and mechanical, so that what … needs is … relaxation from the daily routine. The best holiday is one which helps us … to forget about our normal lives for … weeks.

all all
many many
nothing
nothing
some some
something

D What is most completely different from working is doing absolutely … in … perfectly natural surroundings. For … people the purest expression of this idea is to lie on … beach, sunbathing. Sunbathing is one of the strangest of … human inventions. On the one hand it is an example of perfect sloth – of doing … at all. On the other, it is a passive way of doing … . It is a nonsensical and primitive idea, and contrary to … medical evidence. But it has somehow become an article of faith for … millions.

Adapted from *The Sunday Telegraph,* August 12, 1990

9 **trade union** organization of workers – 12 **agenda** [ə'dʒendə] *here:* political programme – 14 **preserve** [prɪ'zɜ:v] privilege – 18 **delightful** very pleasant – 19 **opposed to** completely different from – 28 **sloth** [sləʊθ] laziness – 30 **contrary to** ['---] opposed to – **evidence** knowledge of facts – 31 **faith** belief

some

My uncle usually gives me **some** *money* for my birthday.
Could I have **some** *10p coins* for the phone, please?

Some and its compounds *(someone, somebody, something)* are used in affirmative statements. In questions *some* is used when the speaker expects a positive reply. (These questions are in fact offers or requests.)

any

I'm afraid there aren't **any** *postcards* for less than 50p.
I haven't got **any** *small change.* Have you got **any?**

Any and its compounds *(anyone, anybody, anything)* are used in negative statements. In genuine questions (when either *yes* or *no* is expected as an answer) *any* is used.

no* and *none

Most people have **no** *idea* how to invest their money.
How much *money* did you save last month? – **None.**
None *of my friends* have started earning yet.

No (kein) can only be used before a noun.
None can be used to avoid repeating the noun.
It is also used before an *of*-phrase.
(The compounds of *no* are *no one, nobody* and *nothing.)*

'No one likes to give anyone anything for nothing. Couldn't you at least stand up?'

much, a little **(= some),** ***little*** **(= not much)**

Have you had **much** *experience* with computers?
Of course, it takes **a little** *time* to adjust to a new job. *(ein bißchen/einige Zeit)*
At the moment John shows very **little** *interest* in his work. *(sehr wenig Interesse)*

Much, a little and *little* are used with uncountable singular nouns.

many, a few **(= some),** ***few*** **(= not many)**

Mrs Russell has worked with us for **many** *years.*
We've only had the new machine for **a few** *months. (seit ein paar Monaten)*
I'm afraid we have only very **few** *jobs* to offer at the moment. *(sehr wenige offene Stellen)*

Many, a few and *few* are used with countable plural nouns.

Note

I have**n't** got **much** money left.
– Well, you've spent rather **a lot** (of money) on unnecessary things.

Much *is mainly used in questions and negative statements.*
In affirmative statements a lot of, lots of *and* plenty of *are preferred.*

'You do ask some tricky questions.'

every, each and *any* for German *jeder*

I play golf **every** *week.*	*Every* can only be used before a noun (German: *jede(r/s) ohne Ausnahme).*
Each *hole /* **Each** *of the holes* on our course is different in some way.	*Each* can be used before a noun or an *of*-phrase.
These *golf balls* aren't very expensive. They're only £1.80 **each.**	It can also be used alone to refer to something already mentioned. *Each* describes persons or things seen individually *(jede(r/s) einzelne).*
Any *time* you feel like a game just give me a ring.	*Any* can mean 'practically every', 'it doesn't matter which' *(jeder(r/s) x-beliebige).*

Note

Everybody enjoys playing on our course. *(jeder ohne Ausnahme)* **Anyone** can learn how to play. No matter how old they are. *(jeder x-beliebige)*	*The compounds of* every *and* any (everyone, anything, *etc.) are used similarly.*

all and *all the*

I think **all** *golfers* are fanatics.	*All* without the article means 'everyone/everything in general'.
All the *players* that I know have got golf on the brain.	*All* with the article means 'everyone/everything from a limited number or amount'.

both, neither, either

Both *my parents/My parents* **both** used to play.	*Both* means 'one and the other'.
Neither *(of them)* was very good, but they enjoyed a round on a Sunday afternoon.	*Neither* means 'not one and not the other'.
Shall I use a 6 or 7 iron from here? – I think **either** would do.	*Either* means 'one or the other, it doesn't matter which'.

Note

Can you see **the two** men on the 16th green? They **both** look pretty hopeless. *(Sie … beide)*	Both *is never used after* the. *For German* die beiden/die zwei, the two *must be used.*

'Everybody has an off day occasionally, Bill!'

'OK, everyone's gone – you can pick it up now.'

21 1 Famous words GG 23–29; GhE 114–121, 124–126

For this exercise, you may sometimes need to refer to the Basic Rules (p. 160–161)

1 For many are called, but few are chosen.
(Holy Bible, St.Matthew)

Who do you think are the 'many' and the 'few'? Who calls and chooses them?

2 Some have too much, yet still do crave;
I little have, and seek no more.
They are but poor, though much they have,
And I am rich with little store.
(Sir Edward Dyer, c. 1504–1607)

Add suitable nouns to some, much *and* little. *Try to explain the meaning of the verse.*

3 It is the common wonder of all men
how among so many million faces,
there should be none alike.
(Sir Thomas Browne, 1605–1682)

Replace all men, *which sounds old-fashioned today, by a suitable pronoun. Why is* none *used?*

4 A little knowledge is a dangerous thing.
(Alexander Pope, 1688–1744)

What is the difference between the use of little *here and in No. 2? Why should 'a little knowledge' be dangerous?*

5 You can fool all the people some of the time,
and some of the people all the time,
but you cannot fool all the people all of the time.
(Abraham Lincoln, 1809–1865)

What is the difference between all men *(No. 3) and* all the people? *Try to explain what Lincoln could have meant.*

6 Animals are such agreeable friends – they ask no questions, they pass no criticisms.
(George Eliot [Mary Ann Cross], 1819–1880)

Rephrase this saying, using any *instead of* no.

7 When everyone is somebody,
Then no one's anybody.
(Sir William Schwenck Gilbert, 1836–1911)

Explain the meaning of this quotation.

8 Anybody can make history. Only a great man can write it.
(Oscar Wilde, 1854–1900)

Why did Oscar Wilde use anybody *rather than* everybody?

9 Everybody talks about the weather, but nobody does anything about it.
(Mark Twain, 1835–1910)

Try to express the second part of the sentence in the passive voice. Translate the saying into German.

10 A little of what you fancy does you good.
(Marie Lloyd, 1870–1922)

Express the meaning of this saying in a negative way; use too much.

11 Never in the field of human conflict was
so much owed by so many to so few.
(Winston Churchill, 1874–1965)

Winston Churchill spoke these words after 'The Battle of Britain' in 1940. Can you explain who the 'few' were that did 'so much'? And who were the 'many'?

12 We shall bear any burden, support any friend, oppose any foe to assure the survival and success of liberty.
(John F. Kennedy, 1917–1963)

How is any *used in this quotation? Translate Kennedy's words into German.*

2 **to crave** to want very strongly – **to seek** to look for – **store** *here:* wealth, goods – 10 **to fancy** to like, to want to have – 12 **to bear** to accept bravely – **foe** opponent, enemy – **to assure** to make certain

2 Born again GG 23–25. 28; GhE 114–115, 120–121, 124

In America there are many different religious beliefs and religious groups. For some of these denominations and sects it is important to have a very personal relationship towards God or Jesus. Here a 'Jesus Freak' talks about an emotional crisis in his life. This sort of deep religious experience is often described as being born again.

Complete the text with any, every, no, some *or their compounds.*

denomination religious group that is part of a larger religious group but has slightly different ideas – 1 **to bum s.o. out** *(slang)* to get on s.o.'s nerves – 4 **zero** *here:* at the lowest possible level – 5 **misery** great unhappiness – 6 **evil** bad – 7 **hassle** confusion – 9 **to take over** to take control – 11 **to churn** to turn round and round

The people I came into contact with … day were bumming me out so much I wanted to scream. … cared about … … had … meaning for their lives and it scared me because I was the same way. One day I was home in my room. I had … to do, didn't want to see … … was zero. I was just waiting for … to bring me a key and unlock me out of my misery. – I walked over to my window and looked up into the sky and thought 'Why are people so evil? Why am I so burnt out? Why is there always a hassle in my head? Why do I hate?' – I wondered why I was even in the world in the first place. I didn't have … answers. I just wanted Jesus to take over. – I said 'Jesus, forgive me. I don't know what to say to you. I don't know …, but I know you're listening. I'm just tired of hassling in my head.' After that, my head stopped churning, and I felt calm for the first time. I had a smile on my face. I never used to smile much, but from that day on I've had a smile on my face and my mind's been calm! Before, I couldn't talk to people, but now I can talk to … – old ladies, kids, … .

From *Truth,* the Jesus People's newspaper

3 Rangers – few spectators and little enthusiasm GG 23–24, 26–27; GhE 115–119

Replace (a) little *and* (a) few *by equivalent expressions.*

Example: There seems to be **little** hope … ▶ There does**n't** seem to be **much** hope …/There seems to be **hardly any** hope …

1 There seems to be little hope of Rangers finishing at the top of the league this season.
2 So far they have won fewer home games than in previous seasons.
3 A few of their players have been injured for a long time.
4 The club has a few good players, but so far they have scored very few goals.
5 Few spectators are keen on their defensive tactics.
6 Few towns have such an attractive stadium, but very few people want to spend money on second-rate football.
7 The club must have a little money left from selling Alan Bates, but so far the management has given little thought to investing in new players.
8 Little has been done to improve the situation.
9 Now there are only a few matches left to play.
10 Peter Thomson, the ever-optimistic coach, says, 'All that is needed now is a little patience.'

The facts of life

There is a true story about four people named **Everybody, Somebody, Anybody** and **Nobody:**
There was an important job to be done, and Everybody was sure Somebody would do it. Anybody could have done it, but Nobody did it. Somebody got angry, because it was Everybody's job. Everybody thought Anybody could do it, but Nobody realized that Everybody was too lazy to do it. It ended up with Everybody blaming Somebody because Nobody had done what Anybody could easily have done.

21 Advanced Exercises

1 The Story-Teller GG 23–30; GhE 110–126

In Saki's short story 'The Story-Teller' a 'bachelor' is travelling in the same compartment as three little girls and their aunt. After the aunt has told her nieces a very conventional and boring story, the girls ask the bachelor to tell them another story.

'Tell us a story,' demanded the bigger of the small girls.

'Once upon the time,' began the bachelor, 'there was a little girl called Bertha, who was extraordinarily good. She did all that she was told, she was always thoughtful, she kept her clothes clean, learned her lessons perfectly, and was polite in her manners.'

'Was she pretty?' asked the bigger of the small girls.

'Not as pretty as any of you, but she was horribly good'.

There was a wave of reaction in favour of the story; the word horrible in connection with goodness was a novelty that commended itself.

'She was so good that she won several medals for goodness, which she always wore, pinned on to her dress. There was a medal for obedience, another medal for punctuality, and a third for good behaviour. They were large metal medals and they clinked against one another as she walked. No other child in the town where she lived had as many as three medals, so everybody knew that she must be an extra good child.'

'Horribly good,' quoted Cyril.

'Everybody talked about her goodness and the Prince of the country got to hear about it, and he said that as she was so very good she might be allowed once a week to walk in his park. It was a beautiful park, and no children were ever allowed in it, so it was a great honour for Bertha to be allowed to go there.'

'Were there any sheep in the park?' demanded Cyril.

'No, there were no sheep.'

'Why weren't there any sheep?'

'There were no sheep in the park because the Prince's mother had once had a dream that her son would either be killed by a sheep or else by a clock falling on him. For that reason the Prince never kept a sheep in the park or a clock in his palace. But there were lots of little pigs running all over the place.

Bertha was rather sorry to find that there were no flowers in the park. She had promised her aunts, with tears in her eyes, that she would not pick any of the kind Prince's flowers, and she had meant to keep her promise, so of course it made her feel silly to find that there were no flowers to pick.'

'Why weren't there any flowers?'

'Because the pigs had eaten them all. The gardeners had told the Prince that you couldn't have pigs and flowers, so he decided to have pigs and no flowers.'

There was a murmur of approval at the excellence of the Prince's decision; so many people would have decided the other way.

'There were lots of other delightful things in the park. There were ponds with gold and blue and green fish in them, and trees with beautiful parrots that said clever things at a moment's notice, and humming birds that hummed all the popular tunes of the day. Bertha walked up and down and enjoyed herself immensely. Just then an enormous wolf came prowling into the park to see if it could catch a fat little pig for its supper. The first thing that it saw was Bertha; her pinafore was so spotlessly white and clean that it could be seen from a great distance. Bertha saw the wolf and saw that it was stealing towards her, and she began to wish that she had never been allowed to come into the park. She ran as hard as she could and the wolf came after her. She managed to reach a shrubbery of myrtle bushes and she hid herself in one of the thickest of the bushes. The wolf came sniffing among the branches; however, the scent of the myrtle was so strong that he could not sniff out where Bertha was hiding, and the bushes were so thick that he might have hunted about in them for a long time without catching sight of her, so he thought he might as well go off and catch a little pig instead. Bertha was trembling very much at having the wolf prowling and sniffing so near her, and as she trembled the medal for obedience clinked against the medals for good conduct and punctuality. The wolf was just moving away when he heard the sound of the medals clinking and stopped to listen; they clinked again in a bush quite near him. He dashed into the bush, and dragged Bertha out and devoured her to the last morsel. All that was left of her were her shoes, bits of clothing, and the three medals for goodness.'

'Were any of the little pigs killed?'

'No, they all escaped.'

'The story began badly,' said the smaller of the small girls, 'but it had a beautiful ending.'

From *The Story-Teller* by Saki (abridged)

bachelor an unmarried man – 7 **manners** behaviour – 12 **in favour of** in support of; for – 14 **novelty** s.th. new, unusual and interesting – **to commend** to say that s.th. is good; to praise – 17 **obedience** willingness to do what you are told – 18 **punctuality** being on time – 53 **approval** agreement; admiration – 56 **delightful** very pleasant – 59 **at a moment's notice** any time you like – 60 **humming bird** very small bird whose wings beat very fast and make a humming noise – **tune** melody – 63 **to prowl** [aʊ] move quietly, trying not to be noticed – 65 **pinafore** [ˈpɪnəfɔː] *Schürze* – **spotless** perfectly clean – 68 **to steal** to move secretly – 71 **shrubbery** lots of bushes planted together in a group – **myrtle** *Myrte* – 73 **to sniff** to draw air into the nose trying to discover a smell – 74 **scent** pleasant smell – 83 **conduct** [ˈ--] behaviour – 86 **to dash** to run quickly – 87 **to drag** to pull roughly – **to devour** [dɪˈvaʊə] to eat quickly and hungrily – 88 **morsel** very small piece of food

1 *Complete the sentences about 'The Story-Teller' with suitable indefinite pronouns or determiners.*
  a At the beginning … of the three girls seems to be very interested in the story.
  b … people would use the word 'horrible' in connection with goodness.
  c But … the girls thought that this made the story interesting.
  d Bertha always wore … her three medals.
  e … of them was for a different thing.
  f There wasn't … else that had as … as three medals.
  g So far the Prince hadn't allowed … children to walk in his park
  h The Prince and his mother were … afraid of sheep.
  i … of them wanted … sheep or clocks around.
  j As there were … flowers in the park, Bertha was – of course – unable to pick … .
  k Only very … people would normally prefer pigs to flowers in a park.
  l When the wolf had finished, there was … left of Bertha apart from … bits of clothing, … her shoes and … the three medals. But luckily, … of the pigs were killed.

2 *Look at the following lines of the text again.*
  l. 4 *Explain the difference between* a **little** girl *and* Bertha showed **little** interest in the pigs.
  l. 5 *Replace* all *by another pronoun.*
  l. 10 *Express the phrase* not as pretty as **any** of you *by an affirmative statement.*
  l. 15 *Replace* several *by a different determiner.*
  l. 21 *Why is* many *and not* much *used here?*
  l. 25 *Replace* everybody *by an expression with* all.
  ll.34-36, ll. 42-48 *What is the stylistic difference between* no *and* any? *(Notice who uses* no *and who uses* any.)
  l. 56 *What would the opposite of* lots of *be here?*

2 Life's too short for doing dishes

GG 23–29; GhE 114–121, 124–125

Translate this advert into English.

alles = everything
alle (Leute) = everybody

Alle wissen, daß das Leben kurz ist. Aber nur sehr wenige Menschen machen sich klar, wie viel dieser kurzen Zeit wir vergeuden. Nehmen wir einmal an, Sie verbringen etwa 20 Minuten, um nach jeder Mahlzeit abzuwaschen. Das heißt, daß all die Menschen, die abwaschen müssen, jeden Tag etwa eine Stunde am Spülbecken *(kitchen sink)* stehen. Das sind 7 Stunden jede Woche, über zwei Wochen jedes Jahr. Und so vergeuden manche Menschen zwei Jahre ihres Lebens – es sei denn *(unless)* sie kaufen sich eine Spülmaschine.
Niemand wäscht besonders gern ab; jeder, der schon einmal nach dem Weihnachtsessen in der Küche gestanden ist, weiß, daß das wenig Spaß macht. Wir haben Spülmaschinen in allen Größen, passend für jede Küche. Unsere Maschinen reinigen praktisch alles, ganz egal wie schmutzig Ihr Geschirr ist.

22 Reflexive and Reciprocal Pronouns

Check-up

1 What's the problem?

Put in the correct verb forms from the list below, deciding where reflexive pronouns are necessary.

apologize, behave, change, cut, defend, feel (2x), hurt, lie down, move (2x), quarrel, relax, tell, wonder, worry

sich streiten sich überlegen
sich entschuldigen
sich fühlen

1 'Jane and I … again last night. Now I … what to do to put things right.' – 'Why not ring up and …? That would probably make you both … much better.'

sich schneiden
sich Sorgen machen sich verletzen
sich hinlegen
sich entspannen

2 'What's all that blood?' – 'Oh, I've … with the breadknife. Don't …, I haven't … badly.'
– 'You look a bit pale, though. Perhaps you should … for a few moments and …!'

sich bewegen
sich verteidigen
sich sagen sich verhalten
sich bewegen
sich fühlen sich ändern

3 'John keeps criticising me for … too slowly on the tennis court.' – 'How do you generally react?' – 'By …, of course.' – 'Well, don't. Another time, just quietly … not to … that way. Then say to John, "You're right, I *do* … slowly." You'll … less aggressive that way – and maybe John will … after a while.'

2 Help each other – don't just think of yourselves!

Use reflexive or reciprocal pronouns to complete these sentences.

Examples:
– Cooperative people are people that help **each other/ one another.**
– Selfish people usually think only of **themselves.**

1 In an ideal society, people wouldn't try to take unfair advantage of ….
2 Modest people do not make a habit of praising ….
3 When their eggs are hatched, most parent birds help … to look after the young ones until they are old enough to feed ….
4 At Christmas time we all give … presents; but most of us buy the sort of presents we would choose for …. (No wonder so many things have to be taken back to the shops after Christmas and changed!)
5 Quite a lot of people talk to … when they're alone.
6 Good friends can always depend on ….

2 **modest** *bescheiden*

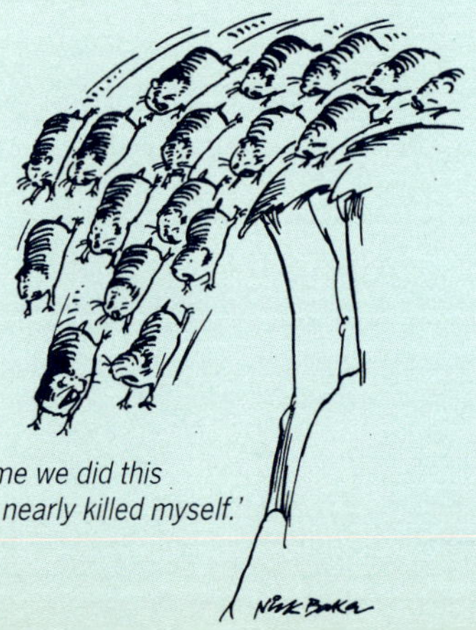

'Last time we did this I damn nearly killed myself.'

Reflexive pronouns

Marion fell down the stairs yesterday.
Luckily she **didn't hurt *herself.***

By the time John was five, he had learnt to **wash** and **dress *(himself)*** without help.

1 A reflexive pronoun is used if the object of a sentence is the same person or thing as the subject.

2 After some verbs, the reflexive pronoun can be left out, e.g. *wash (o.s.), dress (o.s.), hide (o.s.), prepare (o.s.).*

Verbs that are not reflexive in English

Sally **lies down** for an hour or so after lunch if she **feels** tired.

Many verbs, unlike their German equivalents, are **not** reflexive in English.

Some common examples:

to apologize	*sich entschuldigen*
to change	*sich (ver)ändern*
to hurry	*sich beeilen*
to feel	*sich fühlen*
to move	*sich bewegen*
to open	*sich öffnen*
to quarrel	*sich streiten*
to remember	*sich erinnern*
to sit down	*sich setzen*
to wonder	*sich fragen, sich überlegen*

Reciprocal pronouns

Judy and Tim often fight – but they **like *each other*** a lot really.

The reciprocal pronoun *each other/one another* is used to express an exchange between persons or things.

Compare:

The children **bought *themselves*** big ice-creams.
= Each child bought one for himself/herself.

Tom and Susie **bought *each other*** presents.
= Each bought a present for the other.

'Bad news, Partridge – the computers can sell themselves now.'

A limerick

A young schizophrenic named Struther,
When told of the death of his mother,
Said, 'Yes, it's too bad,
But I can't feel too sad.
After all, I still have each other.'

1 Self-esteem GG 21; GhE 86–87

'A Woman in Your Own Right,' by Anne Dickson, was written to help women to live more assertively. In this excerpt, the author sums up the basic qualities of 'Selma,' the 'ideal' of an assertive woman.

self-esteem good opinion of oneself – **assertive** positive and sure of oneself – 1 **to acknowledge** to realize and accept – 2 **to value** to know the worth of – 6 **self-reproach** finding fault with oneself – 8 **to cling** to hold on tightly – **desperate** ['desprət] *verzweifelt* – **familiar** well-known

Selma accepts herself as she *is,* which means acknowledging her strengths and weaknesses. The more she values herself and feels strong in herself, the more she can allow herself to look at those parts of herself which she does not like very much but can accept. The more she accepts herself with her limitations, the more she is open to listening to other people's criticism and learning from it, without sinking into self-reproach. The more open she feels, the more she is free to be herself. She can take the risk of changing without clinging desperately to the known and familiar.

If she experiences rejection, she is not demolished: her self-esteem is anchored within herself and this helps her to survive hurt and disappointment.

From *A Woman in Your Own Right* by Anne Dickson

1 *What is wrong? Correct the following statements, according to the ideas you have understood from the text.*
   a The assertive woman must correct all her own faults before she can accept herself fully.
   b The more you learn to value yourself, the more you feel free to criticize other people.
   c Changing is too big a risk; women should keep to the limited roles they know if they want to be really themselves.

2 *Translate the first paragraph of the text into German. Note which verbs are reflexive only in German.*

3 *The following words and expressions with* self *are very common in English. Explain what they mean. (You may need a dictionary for some of them.)*
   Example: Self-esteem is a good opinion of oneself./If you have *self-esteem,* it means that you feel good about yourself.
   a self-centred; b self-control; c self-defence; d self-help book; e self-pity; f self-portrait; g self-service restaurant;
   Do you know any other examples?

2 The tale of Hansel and Gretel GG 21–22; GhE 86–88

Translate the sentences into English. These words will be useful:
to comfort (l. 4) – to lose one's way (4) – gingerbread house (4-5) – witch (6) – to lock up (6) – oven (8) – to hug (8)

Erinnerst du dich noch an das Märchen von Hänsel und Gretel? Die Eltern sind arm und entschließen sich dazu, die Kinder in den Wald zu führen und dort zu verlassen. Als die Kinder merken, daß sie allein sind, versuchen sie sich erst zu trösten. Aber sie verirren sich im Wald. Als sie an das Knusperhäuschen kommen, freuen sie sich. Die Tür öffnet sich aber, und eine alte Hexe kommt heraus. Die Hexe sperrt Hänsel in einen Käfig ein, und Gretel überlegt sich, wie sie sich und ihren Bruder retten kann. Als Gretel die Hexe in den heißen Backofen gestoßen hat und Hänsel befreit hat, umarmen sich die beiden Kinder. Im Hexenhaus befindet sich eine Kiste mit Goldmünzen. Die Kinder nehmen sich den Schatz und machen sich glücklich auf den Nachhauseweg.

1 Ernest and the two girls GG 21–22; GKE 86–88

Ernest is a lonely, middle-aged man, who has never got over the shellshock he suffered during the First World War. One morning, when he is sitting by himself in a café, two sisters, the elder girl about 12 years old, come in and sit down at his table, each with a cup of tea. As he listens to their conversation, his feeling of loneliness deepens …

The two girls sat before him wholly engrossed in themselves, still debating whether they should buy a cake, or whether they should ride home on a bus.

'But it'll be cold,' reasoned the elder, 'walking home.'

'No, it won't,' the other said, but with no conviction in her words. The sound of their voices told him how lonely he was, each word feeding him with so much more loneliness that he felt utterly unhappy and empty.

Time went slowly: the minute-hand of the clock seemed as if it were nailed immovably at one angle. The two girls looked at each other and did not notice him: he withdrew into himself and felt the emptiness of the world and wondered how he would spend all the days that seemed to stretch vacantly, like goods on a broken-down conveyor belt, before him. He tried to remember things that had happened and felt panic when he discovered a thirty-year vacuum. All he could see behind was a grey mist and all he could see before him was the same unpredictable fog that would hide nothing. He wanted to walk out of the café and find some activity so that he would henceforth be able to mark off the passage of his empty days, but he had no will to move. He heard someone crying so shook himself free of such thoughts and saw the younger girl with hands to her eyes, weeping. 'What's the matter?' he asked tenderly, leaning across the table.

The elder girl replied for her, saying sternly:

'Nothing. She's acting daft.'

'But she must be crying for some reason. What is it?' Ernest persisted quietly, bending closer still towards her. 'Tell me what's wrong.' Then he remembered something. The girls' conversation came to him through an intricate process of recollection. 'I'll get you something to eat,' he ventured. 'Can I?'

She unscrewed clenched fingers from her eyes and looked up, while the elder girl glared at him resentfully and said: 'We don't want anything. We're going now.'

'No, don't go,' he cried. 'You just sit down and see what I'm going to get for you.' He stood up and walked to the counter, leaving them whispering to each other.

He came back with a plate of pastries and two cups of tea, which he set before the girls, who looked on in silence. The younger was smiling now. Her round eager eyes were fascinated, yet followed each movement of his hands with some apprehension. Though still hostile the elder girl was gradually subdued by the confidently working actions of his hands, by caressing words and the kindness that showed in his face. He was wholly absorbed in doing good and, at the same time, fighting the feeling of loneliness that he still remembered, but only as a nightmare is remembered.

The two children fell under his spell, began to eat cakes and sip the tea. They glanced at each other, and then at Ernest as he sat before them smoking a cigarette. The café was still almost empty, and the few people eating were so absorbed in themselves, or were in so much of a hurry to eat their food and get out that they took little notice of the small company in the corner. Now that the atmosphere between himself and the two girls had grown more friendly, Ernest began to talk to them …

From *Uncle Ernest* by Alan Sillitoe

shellshock mental disorder caused by shells *(Granaten)* going off – 1 **engrossed in** totally concentrating on – 5 **conviction** firm belief – 10 **to withdraw** to retire or go back – 12 **vacant** ['veɪkənt] empty – **conveyor belt** moving band of an assembly line – 14 **mist** fog – 17 **henceforth** from now on – 19 **to weep** to cry – 20 **tender** gentle, soft – 21 **stern** strict – 22 **daft** informal word for 'silly' – 23 **to persist** to keep on *(here:* asking) – 26 **intricate** complex – **recollection** remembering – **to venture** to dare (to say) – 28 **clenched** tightly closed – 29 **to glare at** to look at angrily – **resentful** angry and bitter – 34 **pastry** ['peɪstrɪ] kind of cake – 36 **eager** enthusiastic – 37 **apprehension** fear and doubt – **hostile** unfriendly – 38 **to subdue** [səb'dju:] to quieten and soften – **confident** sure, self-assured – **caressing** [-'--] *here:* kind and caring – 41 **nightmare** bad dream – 42 **spell** magical influence

1 *Use reflexive or reciprocal pronouns in your answers to these questions:*
 a *Why don't the two girls notice Ernest at first?*
 b *How does Ernest react when he hears one of them crying?*
 c *How do the girls behave when Ernest gets up to fetch them something to eat?*
 d *Why does nobody else notice what is going on at their table?*

2 *Look closely at lines 8-20, and find the equivalents of: a) sich erinnern; b) sich bewegen; c) sich anschauen; d) sich beugen, e) sich ereignen; f) sich fragen; g) sich erstrecken, h) sich zurückziehen; i) sich losreißen.*

3 *Note the author's use of reflexive and reciprocal pronouns. In what way do they help to underline the difference between Ernest's situation and that of the two girls?*

2 What a face can tell you GG 21-22; GhE 86-88

Famous four: Beethoven and the Princess of Wales are left-faced, while Einstein and Burton fall in the right camp

Translate into English. These words will be useful:
to be like (2) – to have in common (2) – muscle (7) – side of the face (7) – eyebrow (7) – characteristics (8) – to be linked with (8) – gifted/talented (10) – to confirm (a theory) (12) – to be worthwhile (16) – from a completely new angle (18) – athlete (21) – understanding of movement (22) – to compete against (25)

Schauen Sie sich die Bilder von Beethoven und der Princessin von Wales genau an. Ähneln sie sich? Wohl kaum, aber eines haben sie gemeinsam: beide sind 'left-faced'.

Nach einer neuen Theorie, die der amerikanische Professor Karl Smith nach 15 Jahren Forschung der Öffentlichkeit vorgestellt hat, ist jeder von uns entweder 'left-faced' oder 'right-faced'. Bei 'left-facers' entwickeln sich die Muskeln in der linken Gesichtshälfte stärker, und die linke Augenbraue liegt meistens höher. Diese Merkmale verbinden sich mit der Fähigkeit, die rechte ('musikalische') Seite des Gehirns besonders intensiv zu benutzen. Smith hat entdeckt, daß beinahe alle musikalisch begabten Menschen tatsächlich 'left-facers' sind. Dies läßt sich durch Fotos und Porträts von bekannten Musikern bestätigen.

Aber nur etwa 10–15% der Bevölkerung sind 'left-facers'. Deshalb rät Smith allen Eltern, die sich überlegen, ob sie teure Musikstunden für ihr Kind bezahlen sollen: 'Sehen Sie sich Ihr Kind erst kritisch an, um festzustellen, ob sich der Unterricht lohnen wird.' Durch diesen einfachen 'Test' können also Familienmitglieder und Freunde, die sich seit Jahren kennen, sich nun von einer ganz anderen Seite kennenlernen!

Die vielen 'right-facers' unter uns sollten sich jedoch nicht beunruhigen. Denn Smith hat herausgefunden, daß fast alle führenden Politiker, Mathematiker, Schauspieler und Athleten 'right-faced' sind. Besonders Tänzer und Athleten verlassen sich auf ein hoch entwickeltes Bewegungsgefühl, das 'right-facers' durch intensives Nutzen der linken Gehirnseite bekommen. Kein Wunder, daß alle Athleten, die bei den Olympischen Spielen in Seoul gegeneinander antraten, 'right-facers' waren.

Testen Sie sich! Schauen Sie sich im Spiegel an! Welcher Gruppe gehören Sie an?

Based on an article in *The Sunday Times,* 28 January, 1990

Key to the Check-up Exercises

1 Present Tense – Simple and Progressive (p. 9)

1 *comes – takes – goes – is watching – are sitting – am just watching – starts – come – always find – don't mind – don't think – qualify – like – don't mean – feel – often remember – forget – love – are playing – persuade – don't need – are catching – is getting – fall – look – don't influence – go – only buy – are wearing – is coming*

2 *comes – walks – is barking – says – is just making – always does – comes – know – never bites – says – know – know – does* the dog *know*

2 Past Tense – Simple and Progressive (p. 16)

had – lived (was living, if considered temporary) – *used – enjoyed – was returning – drove – saw – was – was – knew – were coming – increased – was driving – tried – lost – twisted – turned – seemed – was spreading – was driving – took – reached – expected – saw – was – was/were burning – looked – went – asked – told – did* you *see – asked – seemed – said – nodded – burnt/burned – thought – said – noticed – was looking – explained – happened*

3 Present Perfect – Simple and Progressive (p. 22)

1 1 *has started – has become – has been – have had to – have consisted – has collected – has been done – has been working – have been going/have gone – have talked – has been acting – has come*
2 *has been sitting – has been neglecting – has stopped – has not been – have heard – have mentioned – has not shown – has stopped*
3 *have never liked – has been – have been trying – have thought – has worked – have been meeting – have reacted – has been blaming*

2 1 *She has been waiting for 20 minutes.*
2 *They have eaten their hamburgers.*
3 *He has lost his ticket/money/purse/…*
4 *It has been standing there/at the platform for 15 minutes/a quarter of an hour.*
5 *She has not bought anything/any other magazine.*
6 *They have been there for quite a while/for some time/for a long time.*

4 Past Tense and Present Perfect Contrasted (p. 28)

1 1 *When did the Normans conquer England? – They conquered England in 1066.*
2 *Since when has the present British government been in power?*
3 *How many times has Britain been invaded since the Norman conquest? (– It has never been invaded since then.)*
4 *Where did the potato plant come from originally? – It came from America.*
5 *Where did the Summer Olympics take place in 1972? – They took place in Munich.*
6 *How long has the present British monarch been on the throne?*
7 *Who first climbed Mount Everest? – Sir Edmund Hillary and Tenzing Norkay first climbed Mount Everest in 1953.*
8 *In which century did the USA become independent of Britain? – It became independent in the 18th century.*
9 *Which American president was shot in 1963? – President John F. Kennedy was shot in 1963.*
10 *How many people have landed on the moon so far?*
11 *In what year did the first German win the men's singles championship at Wimbledon? – The first German (Boris Becker) won the men's singles championship at Wimbledon in 1985.*
12 *What city has been chosen for the next Summer Olympics?*

2 1 *have been waiting – did* you *get – have been standing – have got – didn't* you *leave – rang – was putting – kept – didn't get – arranged*
2 *have* you *read – gave – started – haven't finished – have liked – have* you *got – have* you *started – met – said – have been collecting – have been – came – was bathing*

5 Forms of the Future (p. 36)

1 *will be – am going to stay on – will have* (spontaneous decision) / *are going to have* (plan made before)
are going to book – will be – will mean
are going to sail – will be – are going to take
will come/is going to come – will probably *be*
am going to spend – is going to show – will come

2 *are going – Are* you *going – will be – are setting off – leaves – change – arrive – starts – will show – will* you *do – isn't – will be – will have – will reach – will be – go – is spending*

6 Sequence of Tenses (p. 44)

1 1 *came – had parked;* 2 *discovered – had closed;* 3 *leave – will have – will arrive;* 4 *looked – wouldn't get;* 5 *have had – serve;* 6 *got – was*

2 1 *… from the school will be on the mat with all the other letters that came while they were away.*
2 *No, all through the holiday she has been trying to forget all about it.*
3 *She'll take the envelope up to her room, then she'll lock the door and read the results on her own.*
4 *(She knows that) her parents are expecting her to do well, but (she also knows that) her Biology teacher wasn't very impressed with her efforts before the exams.*

5 *(The worst thing is that) (she knows that) she didn't do as much revision as some of her friends.*
6 *If her marks aren't good enough she won't get into University – which has always been her dream.*

7 Conditional Sentences (p. 52)

1 *looks – will go – were/was – would look – won't be able – go – didn't go – would do – didn't complain – would feel – give – will work*
had left – wouldn't have got – would have been able – hadn't spent – wouldn't have got – had listened – hadn't forgotten – wouldn't have needed – wouldn't have wasted – stops – will have

2 1 …, *they would have been able to slow down in time.*
2 … wouldn't have *been so difficult if the road hadn't been icy.*
3 If the lorry *hadn't broken down shortly before, one of the lanes wouldn't have been blocked.*
4 … if *drivers took enough notice of weather conditions.*
5 … if *people don't learn to be more responsible behind the wheel.*

8 Reported Speech (p. 60)

'Well, Mrs Beale told me to *sit down,* and then she asked me why *I had applied for this kind of work,* and so I told her *(that) I liked the idea of helping other people,* and *(that) I thought I'd enjoy the work.* Then she asked *whether/if I had ever worked with elderly people before,* and of course I said *(that) I hadn't,* but that *I didn't think I'd have any problems.* She also wanted to know *where I live/lived,* and asked *whether/if I would be able to start work at 7.30 most mornings.* I told her *(that) I'd easily be able to manage it by then,* as *I live/lived quite near.* Then she asked me *whether/if I could cook,* so I said *(that) I often helped to get meals ready at home,* but that *I hadn't often cooked a whole meal by myself.* She told me *not to worry* about that, and explained that *I wouldn't have to cook whole meals without help,* but that *she did need/she needed someone with a bit of experience in the kitchen.* She also told me *(that) I would have to do jobs like vacuum-cleaning, washing, setting tables and so on.*
… 'Well, Mrs Beale said *(that) a young man was coming to see her in the afternoon,* so *naturally she couldn't make a decision until she'd talked to him, too.* She told me *to ring up tomorrow morning* to find out.

9 The Passive Voice (p. 68)

1 … *The plan for the new road had been agreed to by the county council* two years ago.
… but now *the council has been informed (by the Department of Transport)* that *the project cannot be financed* until the late 1990s.
'The by-pass is needed now,' … . *'The existing road through the village is used by an enormous number of cars* on their way to the East Coast. *People living on Botesdale High Street are badly affected by the constant noise of traffic.* Over the past six years *nine people have been killed or seriously injured by lorries driving at high speed. Botesdale is no longer considered a safe place for children,* who are especially at risk; not surprisingly, *property is being sold here at an alarming rate. Our village community must be saved* before it is too late.'
At the end of the meeting, *a course of action was decided on. People were asked* to sign a petition, *which will be sent to the Department of Transport* before the end of the month.

2 *were attacked – was/had been started – was/had been shattered – had been done/was done – were beaten* and *kicked – was not required – were helped – was/had been done – have been arrested – will be heard – are* still *being carried out – are asked*

10 Modal Auxiliaries (p. 77)

1 1 It *may not* be so sunny … – I *can't* find … – You *can* use mine. – But we *can't* take them. He *won't* let … – That *will* be his … – … swimming *can* be … – You *may* be right.
2 We *must* have walked … – We *needn't* go … – We *mustn't* swim … – it *may* be because of … – There *must* be some reason – *May* I borrow … – you *mustn't* wade out … – You *needn't* worry …

2 we all *had to* wear … – We *weren't allowed to* wear shorts … – we *weren't* even *allowed* to be seen … – *were able to* afford a car … – I *wasn't* often *allowed to* drive it … – ought not *to be allowed to* drive at all … – You *didn't have to* take a driving test … – you *were allowed to* drive off … – people that *weren't able to* control … – it was quite usual to *be able to* park … – *were able/allowed* to go to university … – I automatically *had to* give up … – if they *had to* do that …

11 The Infinitive (p. 86)

1 *to arrive – to be* late – *to be delivered – to get* cold – *to arrive – to be* on time – *to help – sit – to have – to deliver – to be informed – stop – to turn – ring – to come – to let* the childen *stay – to say – to come – to run – to know – to collect – to stay – to come – to be invited/to have been invited*

2 1 … *the only sailor to explore* …
2 … *the first explorer to think* that west was *the direction to take/(to be taken).*
3 … *believed the earth to be round.*
4 … it was *impossible for any ship to (be able to) make* …
5 … *decided to travel* west and *expected to get* to India …
6 … A lot of money was needed *(for him) (to be able) to buy and equip* the ships …
7 … *the distance to be covered.*
8 … they *had hoped to find land* … *told him to turn back.*
9 He *promised to give up* the search …
10 … *was overjoyed to have reached* the 'East Indies'.

12 Gerunds (p. 95)

1
1 … if you stopped *smoking* altogether.
2 … avoid *eating* …
3 … keen on *eating* … look forward *to having* a drink …
4 … How *about having/eating* muesli … instead *of eating/having* …
5 … Have you ever thought *of losing* weight? How *about taking* some exercise?
6 But I can't stand *running* round a track or *swimming* …
7 … in danger *of having* a heart attack.
8 … I'll give up *going* to work … get used *to using/riding* my old bike … difficulty *(in) sleeping/falling asleep.*
9 What *about going* for a nice walk …
10 And carry on *taking* those red pills …

2
1 … *has no/doesn't have any difficulty (in) remembering people's names.*
2 … *doesn't worry about/is not afraid of speaking in public.*
3 … *looks forward to becoming a government minister after the next elections.*
4 … *is (very) good at shaking hands and kissing babies/hand-shaking and baby-kissing.*
5 … *avoids disagreeing with her or his party bosses.*
6 … *enjoys being seen together with famous film stars, athletes etc.*
7 … *never gets/doesn't get tired of praising her or his party's achievements.*
8 … *is not afraid of answering/doesn't worry about having to answer awkward questions.*
9 … *is (very) good at acting.*

13 Participles (p. 103)

1
1 A *barking* dog never bites.
2 A penny *saved* is a penny *earned.*
3 A *rolling* stone gathers no moss.
4 Let *sleeping* dogs lie.
5 Once *bitten,* twice shy.
6 First come, first *served.*
7 First impressions are the most *lasting.*
8 There's many a good tune *played* on an old fiddle.
9 A trouble *shared* is a trouble *halved.*
10 *United* we stand, *divided* we fall.
11 If you want a thing *done* well, do it yourself.
12 Well *begun* is half *done.*

2
2 *After having (had)/Having had his supper, he sat down on the sofa and switched on the TV.*
3 *On the screen he could see two men getting into a car.*
4 *With heavy eyes he watched them driving slowly away.*
5 *The man driving the car looked very much like Franco Costellini.*
6 *Finnegan leaned back on the sofa, closing his eyes./Leaning back …, Finnegan closed his eyes.*
7 *His beer stood on the table next to him untouched.*
8 *He heard some soft voices talking about something he couldn't quite make out.*
9 *There was this third man standing in front of the bank waiting for someone or something.*
10 *Never having seen him before, Finnegan tried to concentrate on the other two. …*
11 *Suddenly he found himself in some dark room, lying on a bed./Suddenly he found himself lying on a bed in some dark room.*
12 *He lay there covered with some sort of blanket.*
13 *Not knowing where he was, he felt frightend.*
14 *Then he heard someone opening a door somewhere.*
15 *When he tried to get up he noticed someone standing in front of him. …*
16 *Jumping up in panic, he screamed for help./He jumped up in panic, screaming for help …*

14 Non-finite Verb Forms: Mixed Exercises (p. 112)

1 *speeding – motoring – to drive – to take – driving – doing – travelling – to give – stopped – complaining – going – operating – roar – come – to be – pass – to take – driving – motoring – to stop thinking – being caught – having to do – need – hear – think* of *handing in – to drive*

2
1 a stop *complaining* b stop *to get*
2 a remember *to send* b remember *seeing*
3 a forget *to shut* b forget *climbing*
4 a try *to get* b try *going*
5 a mean *getting up* b mean *to go*
6 a regret *to inform* b regret *buying*

15 Verbs and their Objects (p. 120)

1 Can you lend *me some money* … I showed *it to you/(you it)* …
… saying *anything to me* … Perhaps you showed *it to Mike* … I owe *you some money* …
… Perhaps I could lend *it to you/(you it)* …
… to teach *me something about music* … Either you're giving *me a lesson on Bach* or trying to sell *me a ticket* … I've explained *it all to you* …
… Hand *me that jazz record over there* …

2
1 I'll dictate *the rest of the letter to you* … It'll only take *us a few minutes* … Make *them some coffee/(some coffee for them)* … and bring *me a cup of tea/bring a cup of tea for me* … get *us a few biscuits/(get a few biscuits for us).*
2 … it would save *us a lot of time* if you could describe *the woman to us* … to report *all this to the police* … can give *us an exact description of the person in question* … if I ask *you a few questions* …
3 May I suggest *something to you* … Buy *your husband the more expensive model/the more expensive model for your husband…* it'll cost *you a few pounds more* …

16 Relative Clauses (p. 127)

1 ... a village *whose* population ... – the trains *(which/that)* villagers noted ... – Most people *who/that* lived ... – the train *which/that* arrived ... – the one *which/that* left ... – Anyone *who/that* wanted ... – 'mixed' trains, *which* carried ... – a driver *whose* name ... – The locomotives *(which/that)* the railway company used ... – the work, *which* required trains *which/that* had ... – passengers *who/that* wanted ... – places *which/that* were famous for their heather honey, *which* is ... – Most villagers, *who* worried little about ...

2
1 *A washing machine is a machine you (can) wash clothes in.*
2 *... a desk you (can) get/ask for information at.*
3 *... a ball you (can) play golf with.*
4 *... a thing you (can) open bottles with.*
5 *... a path you (can) cycle on.*
6 *... a net you (can) play tennis over/hit the tennis ball over.*
7 *... a book you (can) write (people's) addresses in.*
8 *... a compartment you mustn't/aren't allowed to smoke in.*
9 *... a field you (can) play cricket on/in.*
10 *... a cup you (can) drink tea out of/drink tea from.*

17 The Use of Adjectives and Adverbs (p. 135)

1 *well – deep – particularly – approximate – officially – nearly – annually – popular – incredibly large – unfortunately – approximately – daily – finally – aggressive – hard – Actually – dangerously – natural – particularly – aggressive – exactly – quickly – dominant – real – surprisingly – unusually aggressively – properly – considerable – incredible – recent – actually – common – basically – understandable – generally – regular*

2
1 A *healthy person* – the *disabled* – for *handicapped people* – *Deaf people* – the mentally *handicapped* – the *blind* – a *blind person* – *deaf people*
2 a) *many/a lot of handicapped people;* b) *the rich and the poor;* c) *two bedrooms: a small one and a large/big one;* d) *young people;* e) *a blind man/person;* f) *a black cat and two white ones;* g) *the little one/boy;* h) *the cheap tickets, not the expensive ones;* i) *the dead woman/girl;* j) *the living and the dead*

18 Adjectives and Adverbs: Comparative and Superlative Forms (p. 141)

most – more likely/(likelier) – more difficult – more regular – most common/(commonest) – more easily – more aggressively – more suddenly – less – fewer – more quickly – more often – worse – most alarming – sooner – better – most important – most normal – most depressing – better – later – most terrible – earlier – stronger – most likely/(likeliest) – Later – older – more experienced – worst – more sensible – more calmly – more – harder – earlier

19 The Position of Adverbs and Adverbials (p. 147)

1
1 ..., your hand is *closely* connected ...
2 ..., it is *extremely* difficult ...
3 ..., people are *often* asked ...
4 Some couples *even* ask a graphologist ...
5 *A few years ago* some American doctors discovered .../Some American doctors discovered ... and their health *a few years ago.*
6 Here are some *quite* simple signs ...
7 If you are *always* in a hurry, you *probably* forget to dot your 'i's. Or you don't cross your 't's *properly.*
8 ... will press the paper *hard.*
9 ... will form his or her letters *sharply.*
10 ... are *usually* enthusiastic people.
11 ...could *possibly* be interpreted as ...
12 ... you sign your name *at the bottom.* Can people *hardly* read it? If so, it *certainly* means ...
13 ... graphology *obviously* has its limits.
14 *Fortunately* there are ...

2
1 *Last April we went to London for a couple of days./We went to London for a couple of days last April.*
2 *We arrived at King's Cross Station at 2 o'clock in the afternoon.*
3 *Then we went on to our hotel by Underground.*
4 *Luckily the weather was really good all the time.*
5 *On the first afternoon we went to the Tower of London by boat./We went to the Tower of London by boat on the first afternoon.*
6 *The next morning we saw the Changing of the Guard at Buckingham Palace./We saw ... the next morning.*
7 *Then we looked at the shops in the Oxford Street area for a while.*
8 *Not surprisingly time began to go very quickly after that.*
9 *That evening we went to 'Cats' at the New London Theatre in the West End./We went ... that evening.*
10 *It was certainly the best show I've ever seen in my life.*
11 *Unfortunately we had to go home again the next day.*

20 The Definite and the Indefinite Article (p. 153)

1 I plan to go to *university* when I leave *school.* I'll probably study *English* because I love *English literature.* At *the moment* I'm very interested in *the poetry* of T.S. Eliot. Actually, what I'm looking forward to is *the freedom* of *university life. The school* I go to is pretty strict – it's *a boarding school* near York. *Quite a large number* of *(the) candidates* who have applied for *a place* at Oxford this year are from *the European Community.* More and more students from *Europe,* especially *German students,* are keen to go to *a British university. Most* of *the foreign students* come to Britain because *the courses* they can take here are shorter – and less crowded – than at *home.* All *the students* I've talked to especially like our traditional system of *close contact* with tutors.

My father is *a clergyman* and my mother is *a social worker.* They always hoped I might study *theology* and become *a priest* – or at least do something to help *society.* As *a child,* when I still used to go to *church* regularly, I thought *missionary work* mightn't be *such a bad idea.* But when I started *secondary school,* I began to get interested in *music.* That was when *life* really got going for me. By *the time* I was 15, I knew I had to take up *music* as *a career.* So here I am! Luckily, my parents have given me *full support.* They realize I'm not doing all this as *an act* of *protest* or *rebellion* against *the upbringing* I had.

2 1 *'War and Peace'*
2 *'Daily Life in Ancient Rome'*
3 *'The Life of Napoleon'*
4 *'Chinese Cooking'*
5 *'My Daughter Wants to Become/to Be a Politician'*
6 *'The History of the United States'*
7 *'The Wonders of Nature'*
8 *'When Victoria Was Queen of England'*
9 *'Half a Pound of Rice'*
10 *'All the Birds in the Sky'*
11 *'School as a Bridge to Success?'*
12 *'He was an Englishman'/'He Was English'*

21 Indefinite Pronouns and Determiners (p. 159)

A *Everyone* goes on holiday. Kings, presidents and dictators – *none* of them is too grand … For the *few* very famous and mighty it is a way … of showing that they, like *everyone* else need *some* time off work. There is only one exception to *all* this: Her Majesty the Queen does not take *any* holidays. Rather, she resides, at set times *every* year, at *each* of her various homes …

B *Most* people now think of holidays as necessary. An increase in the number of paid holidays *each* year is one of the fundamental demands of trade unions everywhere. *Anyone* who doubted the need of holidays would be regarded as not quite right in the head. *All* the progressive movements in the 20th century have put holidays for the workers at the centre of their agenda. Even Hitler and Mussolini were *both* eager to show that in their regimes holidays were no longer the preserve of *a few* upper class people. *No* politician would have a chance of being elected today if he wanted to reduce people's holidays.

C … Instead of carrying on with their normal social life, mixing with their friends in *some* especially delightful or healthy place, *many/most* people now thought of a holiday as *something* comletely opposed to their usual everyday life and work. The modern holiday depends on the idea that for *most/many* people work is of *little* interest because it is often boring and mechanical, so that what *everyone* needs is *a little* relaxation from the daily routine. The best holiday is one which helps us *all* to forget about our normal lives for *a few* weeks.

D What is most completely different from working is doing absolutely *nothing* in *some* perfectly natural surroundings. For *many* people the purest expression of this idea is to lie on *some* beach, sunbathing. Sunbathing is one of the strangest of *all* human inventions. On the one hand it is an example of perfect sloth – of doing *nothing* at all. On the other hand it is a passive way of doing *something.* It is a nonsensical and primitive idea, and contrary to *all* medical evidence. But it has somehow become an article of faith for *many* millions.

22 Reflexive and Reciprocal Pronouns (p. 166)

1 1 *quarrelled – wonder/am wondering – apologize – feel*
2 *cut myself – worry – hurt myself – lie down – relax*
3 *moving – defending myself – tell yourself – behave – move – feel – change*

2 1 *each other/one another;* 2 *themselves;* 3 *each other/one another – themselves;* 4 *each other/one another – ourselves;* 5 *themselves;* 6 *each other/one another*

Acknowledgements

The editors wish to thank all authors, publishers and literary agencies who have given permission to use copyright material.
Every effort has been made to trace owners of copyright material, but in some cases this has not proved possible and repeated enquiries have remained without an answer. The publishers would be glad to hear from any further copyright owners of material reproduced in this book.

12: Adapted from an article by Carolyne St John-Brooks, © Times Newspapers Ltd. 1989
13: Reprinted by permission of Chatto and Windus Ltd., © Ann Tyler
14: Reprinted by permission of SÜDWEST PRESSE, Ulm
15: Adapted from an article by Richard Palmer, © Times Newspapers Ltd. 1989
16: Reprinted by permission of the Hamlyn Publishing Group Ltd.
18: Reprinted by permission of Methuen Children's Books
19: © 1955 by Verlag Kiepenheuer & Witsch, Köln
21: From *The Children of the Night* by Edward Arlington Robinson (New York: Charles Scribner's Sons, 1897)
24: Adapted from an article by Michael Durham, © Times Newspapers Ltd. 1989
25-26: Reprinted by permission of Harper Collins Publishers (New York), © 1945
30: Adapted from an article by Ian Birrell and Richard Palmer, © Times Newspapers Ltd. 1989
31: © *The Guardian*
32: © Methuen, London
39-40: Copyright © 1963 by Charles Webb. Used by permission of the New American Library, a division of Penguin Books USA Inc.
42: Published by Vision Books, London
45.1: Reprinted by permission of Thomas and Hudson Ltd.
45.2: Copyright © The Estate of Daphne du Maurier. Reprinted by permission of Curtis Brown on behalf of the Estate
48: Reprinted by permission of Weiden and Nicolson
50/51: © The Sunday Telegraph Ltd.
57: Reprinted from *World & Press*, August 1988
58: Published by Penguin. First published in the USA, © 1956
62: Copyright 1954 by Roald Dahl. Reprinted from *Kiss, Kiss* by Roald Dahl by permission of Alfred A. Knopf Inc.
64: First published 1953 by Hamish Hamilton
66: Published by Michael Joseph Ltd., © 1960 by Stan Barstow
67: Reprinted by permission of William Heinemann Ltd.
71: Reproduced with the permission of the Controller of Her Britannic Majesty's Stationery Office
72: Reprinted by permission of Collins, London
74-75: Copyright © Nina Bawden 1983. Reproduced by permission of Curtis Brown Group Ltd., London
79: Published by Century Hutchinson Ltd. 1989. Reprinted by permission of the Random Century Group
83: Reprinted by permission of *The Sunday Correspondent*
88: Reproduced by permission of the Leonard Cheshire Foundation
92: Reprinted by permission of John Murray (Publishers) Ltd.
93: Reprinted by permission of Mockingbird Books Inc.
96: Reprinted by permission of USIS, Bonn
98: Reprinted by permission of Victor Gollancz Ltd.
98-99: Reprinted by permission of *The Daily Express*
100-101: © Times Newspapers Ltd. 1988
101-102: Reprinted by permission of Laura Huxley and Chatto & Windus
106: Reprinted from *Room and the Top*, published by Eyre & Spottiswoode, by permission of David Higham Associates Ltd. London
107: Adapted from an article by Dylis Powell, © Times Newspapers Ltd. 1989
108: © Stephen Pile. Reprinted by permission of Martin Secker & Warburg Ltd.
109: Reprinted by permission of Jonathan Cape Ltd., London
110-111: Reprinted by permission of Faber and Faber Ltd., London, from *Collected Poems 1902-1962* by T. S. Eliot
112: Reprinted by permission of the *Daily Mail*
115: Reprinted by permission of *The Sunday Express*
116: Reprinted by permission of the Whale and Dolphin Conservation Society
117-118: Reprinted by permission of The Estate of the late Sonia Brownell Orwell and Martin Secker & Warburg Ltd.
118: Copyright 1966; reprinted by permission
122-123: Copyright © 1972 by Sylvia Plath. Reprinted by permission of Harper Collins Publishers
124: Adapted from an article by Richard Burgess and Jan Moores, © Times Newspapers Ltd. 1990
125: Adapted from an article by Maria Balinska. Reprinted by permission of the author
126: Copyright © 1989 by The New York Times Company. Reprinted by permission
128: Reprinted from *Now we are Six* by A. A. Milne by permission of Methuen Children's Books
133/1: Reprinted by permission of A & C Black (Publishers) Ltd.
133/2: Reprinted by permission of William Heinemann Ltd.
135: Adapted from an article by Richard Caseby, © Times Newspapers Ltd. 1990
138: © 1974 by Scholastic Magazines Inc. Reprinted by permission of Scholastic Inc.
139: Reprinted by permission of Jonathan Cape
143: Reprinted by permission of Methuen Drama
144: Copyright © Anthony Storr 1968. Reprinted by permission of Penguin Books Ltd.
145: Reprinted by permission of Charles A. Reich
151: Reprinted by permission of Associated Press, GmbH, Frankfurt
152.1: Reprinted by permission of Faber and Faber Ltd.
152.2: Copyright © 1927: all rights outside U.S., Hemingway Foreign Rights Trust
155: Adapted from an article by Penny Chorlton. Reprinted by permission of *The Independent*
157: Reprinted by permission of the author
158: Reprinted by permission of George Sassoon
159: © The Sunday Telegraph Ltd.
168: Reprinted by permission of Quartet Books Ltd., Namara Group
169: © Alan Sillitoe 1959, 1987

Picture Credits

Every effort has been made to trace copyright owners of cartoons, but in some cases this has not proved possible and repeated enquiries have remained without an answer. The publishers would be glad to hear from any further copyright owners of cartoons reproduced in this book.

Bavaria: 94 (After Image), 137, 149
The British Library: 146
Allan Cash: 125, 151
The Christian Science Monitor: 128 (Martin, © 1987 TCSPS)
The Daily Mirror (reprinted by permission of Mirror Group Newspapers Ltd.): 97.1, 127
Deutsches Institut für Filmkunde: 126
dpa: 170.2
FOCUS: 170.4 (Douglas Kirkland, CONTACT Press Images)
Rolf Günther, Gerlingen: 38
Hutchinson Library: 31.2
Christa Janik, Leinfelden-Echterdingen: 11, 16, 55, 92, 107, 119, 130
Peter Knight, Knight Features, London: 29, 131 (Reproduced by permission of United Feature Syndicate, Inc.)
Marine Mammal Fund, San Francisco: 116
Methuen, London: 18.1, 89.2 (Norman Thelwell)
The Museum of London: 105
The New Yorker Magazine: 64
Penguin Books: 31.1 (Copyright © Nigel Calder, 1970), 156.2 (Cartoon by André François)
Punch: 9, 10, 14.1, 18.2, 19, 23, 27, 35, 37, 43.1, 46, 49, 54, 56, 59, 63, 68, 69, 73.1, 74, 80, 82, 87, 89.1, 91, 95.1, 96, 97.2, 103, 104, 112, 114, 120, 121, 124, 134, 136, 139.1, 144, 145, 148, 153, 154, 155, 156.1+3, 160, 161.2, 166, 167
Fritz Spiegl (ed.), *A Small Book of Grave Humour,* Pan Books, London: 76
Studio X/gamma: 25, 70 (Eric Sander Liaison)
The Sunday Telegraph: 161.1 (© The Sunday Telegraph Ltd.)
Times Newspapers Ltd.: 24, 30, 60 (© The Times, London), 100
Transglobe: 158, 170.1+3
United Media International Syndication: 17 (*Peanuts,* Charles M. Schulz, © 1950, 1952 United Feature Syndicate Inc.), 53 (© 1983 United Feature Syndicate, Inc.), 73.2, 159 (*Peanuts,* Charles M. Schulz, © 1952, 1958 United Feature Syndicate, Inc.)
USIS, Bonn: 90
Warner Bros.: 41
World & Press (Eilers und Schünemann Verlag): 81